9/20

CLEARER, CLOSER, BETTER

CLEARER, CLOSER, BETTER

How Successful People See the World

Emily Balcetis

BALLANTINE BOOKS

NEW YORK

Published in the United States by Ballantine Books, an imprint of
Random House, a division of Penguin Random House LLC, New York.

BALLANTINE and the HOUSE colophon are registered trademarks of
Penguin Random House LLC.

Image p. 95: Reprinted by permission of Springer Nature: Fisher, G. H.
"Ambiguity of Form: Old and New." *Perception & Psychophysics* (1968)
4: 189–192. https://doi.org/10.3758/BF03210466, © Psychonomic Journals 1968.

Image p. 177: Albert Einstein–Marilyn Monroe hybrid image by Aude Oliva and
Philippe G. Schyns, from *The Oxford Compendium of Visual Illusions,*
edited by Arthur G. Shapiro and Dejan Todorović,
copyright © 2017 by Arthur Shapiro and Dejan Todorović.
Reproduced with permission of the Licensor through PLSclear.

Library of Congress Cataloging-in-Publication Data
Names: Balcetis, Emily, author.
Title: Clearer, closer, better: how successful people see the world /
Emily Balcetis, PhD.
Description: First edition. | New York: Ballantine Books, [2020] |
Includes bibliographical references and index.
Identifiers: LCCN 2019038080 (print) | LCCN 2019038081 (ebook) |
ISBN 9781524796464 (hardcover) | ISBN 9781524796471 (ebook)
Subjects: LCSH: Goal (Psychology) | Visual perception. | Achievement motivation. |
Successful people—Psychology.
Classification: LCC BF505.G6 B35 2020 (print) | LCC BF505.G6 (ebook) |
DDC 153.8—dc23
LC record available at https://lccn.loc.gov/2019038080
LC ebook record available at https://lccn.loc.gov/2019038081

Printed in the United States of America on acid-free paper

randomhousebooks.com

2 4 6 8 9 7 5 3 1

First Edition

Book design by Andrea Lau

To Pete and Mattie, obviously

Contents

CONTENTS

Introduction

On a crisp Saturday morning one spring, in a borough of Berlin called Mitte, I sat alone at a bistro munching away on a carrot-beet scone in between sips of a cappuccino. Or at least I thought. I could read the German menu only slightly better than I could name the street on which I was renting an apartment for the month. Despite brunching solo—an endeavor considered so gauche back home that *The New York Times* had once decreed it shouldn't be done—I was having a marvelous time.

I was flipping through a copy of *New York* magazine and came upon an article about paint. While that might sound as enticing as watching it dry, the article was fascinating. You see, the author of the article focused his reporting on black. New Yorkers love it, I've learned, having lived in the city for about ten years, not only because of its ability to contrast starkly against any exposed sun-deprived skin but also because of its ability to mask the grime that the streets kick up onto you as you walk to work. However, the author was interested by a particular variant of black paint because it wasn't quite paint at all.

In the "Antenna" wing of the Science Museum in London, the

author explained, there sat a bronze bust of the BBC personality Marty Jopson. It was about six inches tall and an accurate enough likeness, especially in how light bounced off the dimples, the bushy eyebrows, and the handlebar mustache. Jopson was a props designer, inventor, and math hobbyist. He presented his scientific work on television for a while. On his show he asked, from behind safety goggles, whether an opera singer was capable of shattering a crystal wineglass with one powerful note. (She was.) With the help of the townspeople of Ashford, England, who lived on Butterside Road, he tested whether falling toast always landed buttered side down. (It mostly did.) Though the Marty Jopson bust was an unusual choice of subject matter, all in all there was nothing particularly remarkable about it.

Except for the nearly identical bust that sat beside it. When the two sculptures were viewed side by side, the second bust seemed to be only a silhouette, as if someone had taken a scalpel and cut a hole in space the exact shape and size of Jopson's head. You couldn't see the dimples or the mustache. There were no shadows. There were no contours. Had you been allowed to touch this bust, you would have felt all the texture of the face, the wrinkles on the forehead, and the hair on the chin. But to the viewer, all such detail seemed to have disappeared into a void. Or a black hole.

This second bust, like the first, was made of bronze, but it was cloaked with something special: Vantablack—the blackest black ever created.

Vantablack isn't actually a pigment. It is a substance that is grown by scientists directly on the metal surfaces it is intended to cover, and it has virtually no mass at all. Vantablack is a densely packed collection of ultra-thin carbon nanotubes, like the material that makes up the bodies of Formula One racing cars and the Enzo Ferrari. It is as dark as it is because it absorbs 99.965 percent of light that hits it straight-on. For comparison, the blackness of asphalt consumes only about 88 percent. For us to see something, we need light to hit an object *and* to bounce back. Otherwise, we're not going to see much of anything at all.

Vantablack has been used to coat the outsides of stealth jets. It has lined the insides of telescopes. And, just a few months before I read that article, scientists from Berlin Space Technologies—which was just a few train stops away from where I was sitting—had applied it to a microsatellite bound for outer space.

Recently, the famous British artist Sir Anish Kapoor had been granted exclusive rights to use one version of the product in his work, which includes the bust in the Science Museum. Kapoor explained that Vantablack is "blacker than anything you can imagine. So black you almost can't see it . . . Imagine a space that's so dark that as you walk in you lose all sense of where you are, what you are, and especially all sense of time."

He's hardly exaggerating. When we look at the bust, we lose all sense of dimensionality. What we see is not what's really there. It's an illusion. A trick of the eye.

For Kapoor, the gap between reality and perception was the key to transforming an otherwise unremarkable sculpture into a groundbreaking work of great artistic intrigue. What we actually see makes all the difference. Even—or especially—when what we see diverges from what's really there.

This book is about that "especially."

We think we see the world the way it actually is. We think that when we look at ourselves in the mirror, we see our face the same way others do. We believe that when we peer down the street in front of us, we know what we'll pass by on our journey. We are certain that when we scan the food on our plate, we see what it is we'll be eating. But none of this is always true. Instead, our visual experiences are often misrepresentations. We form an imperfect impression and our eager mind fills in the gaps, putting in place the missing pieces. We do this with the things we see even when they aren't shrouded in Vantablack. And, interestingly, this can happen without our awareness, both in everyday circumstances and when we're making some of the most important decisions of our lives.

Based on the research I and my colleagues have conducted, I

believe that we can take advantage of the fact that we do not see the world perfectly, accurately, or completely—as long as we know when and why it happens. By learning more about how our eyes work in conjunction with our brain, we can direct our perceptual experiences to help us see the world in ways that will help us overcome some of the biggest challenges we face when working toward our most important goals.

I'm a social psychologist and scientist at New York University, and I have been conducting research on perception and motivation for more than fifteen years. I've worked with some of the most accomplished scholars and amassed my own talented team. Together, we have conducted investigations, analyzed the data from experiments we've designed, and reviewed new reports emerging from labs all around the world on how people best pursue their goals, and what stands in their way.

Through this work, I have noted commonalities among the problems that people face when they set out on a personal quest to master some ambition. I have encountered these problems too. Just as having a medical degree doesn't protect a doctor from getting the sniffles, having a PhD in motivation science doesn't inoculate me from the challenges of meeting my own goals. But I happen to be uniquely positioned to know the scientific data on the problems that arise along the way, and what the solutions to these problems might be. As a result, I have discovered strategies that work to overcome the difficulties that challenge the likelihood of our own success. I've learned what works—and what doesn't—for myself and thousands of others who have been involved in my research.

What's interesting is that our discoveries align with the methods used by successful entrepreneurs, athletes, artists, and celebrities. Ample scientific data underscores the effectiveness of approaches that these incredible individuals take to surmounting some of their biggest obstacles. And their habits, routines, and practices, my research finds, can be distilled into four general strategies with far-reaching application.

In the chapters that follow, I explain how knowing when to **narrow our focus of attention** helps us to exercise more effectively, save more for retirement sooner, and find more time in our day to do what we really want to. Understanding how to **materialize** a goal, our steps, or our efforts improves the way we track our progress. Becoming aware of the power of **framing** can improve our ability to read others' emotions, negotiate better deals, improve the relationships we have with other people, and overcome a fear of public speaking. And **a wide bracket** reduces the allure of temptations, the appeal of multitasking, and the inclination to push on when changing course might be best.

We can think of these strategies as four different tools in a toolbox we select from when working on a self-improvement project. Consider them your hammer, screwdriver, wrench, and pliers—pretty basic implements, but useful for almost every job. Sometimes the goals we set require us to use multiple strategies, just as any home repair may require more than one tool. Sometimes what we've set our sights on can be accomplished with one plan but not another, so having options for how to get the job done can be beneficial—just as a fully stocked toolbox offers us the possibility of trading in a screwdriver for a wrench when the first choice isn't right.

Interestingly, these four strategies share one feature: they are all about harnessing the power of our eyes. Challenging ourselves to quite literally *look differently* can help us better our odds of succeeding at things that don't seem related to vision at all. I recently set my sights on learning to play one particular song on the drums. (I had my own reasons for wanting to do this, which I'll get to shortly.) I found that using the strategies I study in my professional life helped me persevere despite the difficulties I knew I'd experience in learning to lay down a beat—as well as those I hadn't even anticipated.

In telling you about my own use of these concepts, I hope that you, too, will be able to look at the world—and what you hope to accomplish in it—in new, creative, and better ways. By investigating the what, why, when, and how of these strategies, I have learned that we can teach ourselves to truly see life from a different perspective. We can take control of our own perception. We can direct our eyes to see in ways that promote good fortune, and to avoid seeing in ways that don't. If we take advantage of our visual experiences, we might see our way to happier, healthier, and more productive lives every day.

Indeed, it is my hope that when you've finished reading this book, you'll be able to envision new paths forward and different perspectives. It's not only about winning gold medals and making more money, though I'll cover those things too. With more insight into your perceptual experience, you'll obtain a better understanding of your life's objectives, how far you've come, how far you have to go, and how you can get there more quickly. You'll also have a better handle on why other people may earnestly believe they've seen something you don't see, and you'll understand how that impacts the ways in which you pursue success. Once you understand when and how vision is biased, you can learn to use those biases in your favor, and to counteract them when necessary.

There is no one right way to see the world, and this book will respect that. Instead, the work I share with you aspires to offer suggestions for improving how you confront challenges by building up the cache of resources at your disposal. I'll give you a set of powerful and largely untapped perceptual tactics you can use to create and sustain views of yourself, others, and your environments that will help you see the possibilities in what you *can't* see now. To do this, I'll draw from research that sits at the intersection of social psychology and visual perception. My work, and that of others I draw from, taps into the neurobiological nature of the human visual system, which is itself a kind of interdepartmental collaboration between the eyes and the brain. When we understand the scientific basis for how we perceive the world around us, the path to most goals becomes clearer, success looks closer, and the process feels better.

CLEARER, CLOSER, BETTER

Seeing a New Way Forward

One summer, my research team asked more than 1,400 men and women from sixteen countries which one of their five senses they would least like to lose. Which would be the most difficult to live without if it were taken away? Regardless of where they were from, their age, or their gender, seven out of every ten people said that losing their sense of sight would be the worst. The majority thought that they couldn't live without vision. But actually, they could.

Let's take a step back and make sure we're on the same page with some of the fundamentals of vision science. We experience the sense of sight because of the connection our eyes have with our brains. We pick up on the brightness of the sun or register the hue of the sky with our eyes, but we only really experience *seeing* once our brains translate those sensations into something meaningful. Consider the following example. Linseed oil, mineral salts, bristle brushes, linen, and wood are products in their own right, but only when Claude Monet combined them in the right proportions and manner were we able to see the water lilies he painted outside his home in Giverny.

Alvaro Pascual-Leone is a neurologist at Harvard Medical

School, and he's famous for discovering what happens in our brains when we lose our sense of sight. He found that the visual cortex—the part of the brain at the back of our head that specializes in making sense of the signals the eyes send it—is incredibly quick to retool when something changes in how our eyes operate. He invited people with normal vision to experience life without sight for five days. The volunteers wore blindfolds. These weren't the kind you get in your travel kit when you fly internationally. They were high-tech and lined with photographic paper that would react to light exposure, so the researchers would know that none of the volunteers had seen the light of day (or bulb) since putting them on.

Pascual-Leone and his colleagues used the five days of blindness as an opportunity to teach basic Braille. The volunteers learned that the Braille alphabet is derived from bumps that protrude in various places on a two-by-three grid. The letter *A* feels like a dot popping up in the upper left corner of this grid. *B* feels like *A* but with the addition of the left-side dot in the middle row. The volunteers trained their index finger to feel the differences in where the bumps were and how many appeared at once. By the end of the five days, they weren't reading Shakespeare with their fingertips, but they had the basic alphabet down.

Each day, the researchers also invited the volunteers to lie down in an fMRI machine that would make a movie of what happened in their brains when they read Braille. On the first day, their brains were most active in the somatosensory cortex, the part of the brain responsible for what we touch and feel; their visual cortex did nothing in response to feeling the Braille letters. But by the end of the five days of having no sight, this pattern had reversed: the somatosensory cortex responded less, and the visual cortex responded more, when the volunteers felt the Braille letters. In other words, the work their fingers were doing was now registering in the part of the brain that for its whole life had been responsible for actual seeing. In less than one week, the visual cortex adapted and repurposed itself to reflect what happens in the brains of truly blind people who are proficient in reading Braille—the visual centers in the brain registered what their fingers were "seeing."

When Pascual-Leone blindfolded his volunteers, he was in a sense reinventing the process of perception. The brains of his volunteers still wanted to see, but they couldn't do it with their eyes. He was changing their medium, but they were still artists. When the brushes are gone or can't do the trick, an artist finds a new way to apply paint. Jackson Pollock dripped it from cans. Gerhard Richter crafted a squeegee to scrape across canvas. When Pascual-Leone usurped his volunteers' sense of sight, they found a new way to see.

The amazing adaptability of vision that Pascual-Leone discovered through his volunteers' experience is an example of neuroplasticity, and it's a trick for which the visual cortex has gotten quite famous in the brain-science world. But there are more reasons to appreciate our sense of sight than its chameleon nature. Consider its strength. If we found ourselves in a place that was really dark and clear, without haze in the air, we could see a candle flickering thirty miles away with the naked eye. When we look into the night sky, we can easily see the International Space Station 250 miles up, or all the way to Saturn—about a billion miles off—if we know where to look.

And our eyes are speedy. They transfer data at the rate of about 8.75 megabits per second. That's about three times the speed of the average Internet connection in the United States. We can recognize what's in front of us faster than the speed of sound. And, though the taste of salt is starkly different from that of sugar, it takes our brain twice as long to register the difference in flavor than to distinguish the face of someone we like from that of someone we don't. Indeed, scientists have discovered that it only takes $1/76$ of a second to know we're looking at the face of a friend, the car of our dreams, or the roses in our wedding bouquet.

What we see with our eyes feels real, accurate, and honest—so much so that it can be scary. In 1896, audiences saw moving images for the first time in history. French aficionados watched a short film called "L'arrivée d'un train en gare de La Ciotat" in a Paris cinema.

The fifty-second black-and-white movie featured a train heading directly toward the viewer on its way into a coastal station. Though the audience sat in their seats and the film was a silent one, the image of the steam locomotive barreling closer was rumored to have led audience members to jump from their seats in terror.

We favor and intuitively trust our visual experiences, often over everything else. We believe that what we see is an accurate and complete representation of the world around us. But that's not always the case. Take the example of the line drawing of an animal below. Give yourself about one second, but not more than that, to take a look. What is it? What's your first impression?

Most people see the head of a horse or donkey. That's what I see too. But look again, now for perhaps a bit longer. With this second glance, or from a changed perspective, you might see something quite different. A seal, perhaps? It's possible that you saw the marine animal to begin with and then with my mention of the horse you looked back and tried to figure out if there was a typo in the text.

I have shown this image to hundreds of people, most recently to an auditorium in New York City's Rubin Museum of Art full of patrons attending a lecture on the science and art of deception. I opened the conversation with this image, projected on a screen for one second. Then I polled the crowd, asking "Who saw the farm animal?" About 80 percent of arms shot up. At the same time, the remaining 20 percent started whispering, and the sound grew quickly to a din. I heard one older woman near the front, vintage eyeglasses pressed up hard against her eyes: "What is she talking about?!"

The group grew restless. The horse-seers turned in their seats, staring at the seal-seers, who swore there was no horse there. The seal-seers were audibly riled, certain that I, along with what must be the baited and staged audience, was pranking them. Everyone was certain that what they had seen was an artistic depiction, sure, but very obviously of whichever animal they themselves had seen first.

We have a blind faith in our visual experiences that we don't hold for nearly any other source of information or inspiration. Though our reliance on and trust of our visual sense may occasionally lead us astray—as it did with my unsuspecting museum audience and with the Parisian audience unaccustomed to the sight of a train on the silver screen—visual perception is powerful.

All of this, combined, positions our eyes to be one of our greatest allies in the battle against ourselves as we work toward meeting our goals. Our eyes play a role in overcoming the mental hang-ups that plague our attempts to stay committed, the physical challenges that slow progress, and the constraints of reality that place a heavy burden on even getting started in the first place. When we tell ourselves we can't do something, it might just be that we are seeing something as more challenging than it really is. When we say that what we're up against is the impossible, it might not appear that way to someone else—and it doesn't have to look that way to us. Just as the bespectacled woman in the front row of the museum auditorium eventually understood that the drawing could be of both a horse and a seal, any of us can teach ourselves to see the world differently if we understand how to take control of perception. Our eyes are incredible tools for shaping our experience. With them, we can quite literally see a new way forward.

Setting My Sights

In high school, I played saxophone in a band that covered punk, ska, and funk tunes. We spent loads of time together driving around with the stereo cranked, listening to bands that featured horn lines and whatever songs gave solos to the sax, trumpet, or trombone. Think Chicago meets whatever was hot in the late '90s. When we heard on the radio that our favorite band from Los Angeles was coming to a nearby festival, we bought our tickets that day. Weeks later, when we realized that Goldfinger would be there without their horn section, what we'd spent on the tickets seemed like a tremendous waste. Goldfinger needed their saxophone, trumpet, and trombone, we adamantly thought. A show without that part of the group just wouldn't sound the same—so much so that our trumpet player decided we should tell the band.

In our parentally subsidized rehearsal space, on beanbag chairs in the basement, we crafted the email message jointly. In it, we professed our utter disappointment in the half-act that the festival had booked, but also offered up our services. We knew the licks for "King for a Day." We made our own for "Here in Your Bedroom." Did they want us to play with them at the show?

Goldfinger's lead singer, John Feldmann, emailed back. "Sure."

Elated, we redoubled our commitment to the basement practice sessions, chose outfits that in hindsight are some of our most unfortunate decisions in this whole story, printed out the email from Feldmann, packed up our horns, and headed off to the show.

After some pleading with security to let us backstage—they were dubious that our dot-matrix-printed email, now smeared from sweaty palms holding it all day, was legitimate—we met up with Feldmann in his trailer. He had more tattoos on his arms than I had seen on all of my friends combined to date. And as monumental a moment in my life as that was, the conversation was equally banal. He asked us about school. How old we were. How long we'd been playing music. He offered us only water, even though we'd seen enough of VH1's *Behind the Music* to be disappointed in this form of hospitality. We practiced a few licks with him strumming his un-plugged guitar. Then it was go-time, and that genteel disposition was replaced with something else entirely. Every other word was something I can't bring myself to put into print. But before the Frankenstein-like transition happened, Feldmann offered the three of us advice: "If you don't have something to play, sing—because we can't." Then we all took to the stage.

There was incredible energy and power. The sound coming from behind us through the speakers drowned out the roaring crowd of fifteen thousand in front. The mosh pit was in full force at our feet. Bodies, sweat, and dust flying everywhere. It was gross, yes, but electric.

I'd love to say that this was the start of a lifelong career in enter-tainment. That I spent the next decade living the jet-set lifestyle with bags under my eyes from too many nights spent sleeping on tour-bus couches. I wish I could say you might search my name on the Internet and find an article with the colon title "Where Are They Now?" But you can't. Because that was the peak of my rock stardom.

At this point in my life, I'm very much okay with the insight that I'm not going to ever become a rock star. The only way I'll appear on the cover of *Rolling Stone* is if I leave a copy of it on the dashboard of my car under a photograph of my face on a hot summer afternoon and the two melt together. I'm too scared to get even one tattoo. I don't want my hair to be pink (though I tried that briefly in high school). And I couldn't stomach the drugs and alcohol anyway. I'm at a different place in life now, and the door to real rock fame has closed for me.

But one Saturday about a year ago, I kicked it back open just a bit. I decided to become a drummer. The challenge I posed for my-self was to learn enough that I could lay down a beat for one song and sound sufficiently amazing. Just one song. Just sufficiently amaz-ing. I never wanted to be a lead singer, but I did want to have some shtick in my back pocket that was cooler than my current hobbies.

Learning one song on drums, but *really* learning how to wail on it, was going to be my magnum opus.

For a number of reasons, this was a dumb idea, or at least an unlikely quest, and I knew it from the beginning. For starters, I lived with my infant son, Mattie, and my husband, Pete, in a one-bedroom apartment in Manhattan that's smaller than most people's garage. We couldn't spare the square footage to set up a proper drum kit. Any extra space was currently housing our reserve diaper supply. We didn't know if the neighbors had earplugs, and since you don't knock on other people's apartment doors here, we couldn't figure out how to warn them that they would likely need some. This was a goal doomed to fail. Or get us evicted.

And then there was my drumming IQ. Woodwind adventures in my youth notwithstanding, I didn't know the difference between a tom-tom (it's a drum) and a tam-tam (and that's a Chinese gong). I didn't realize that you step on the pedal to make the hi-hat quiet down, or that when a drummer referred to the "bell," they probably meant the dome at the center of a cymbal and weren't asking for more of the kind that hangs around a cow's neck in Switzerland. Oh, and it's a "throne," not a seat.

I'm also not particularly coordinated. I can't rub my belly and pat my head at the same time. I fell off the balance beam more than I stayed on it when I tried gymnastics. I wasn't invited to play the second season of basketball in fourth grade because I tripped over my own feet, fell into my teammate, and knocked us both out of bounds when she had the ball. My inadequacy with a pair of drumsticks would be the obvious and first of many places where this plan would fail.

So why decide to learn drums? My reasoning is as old as motherhood itself.

When I started this adventure, Mattie was four months old and the moments of quiet and calm in my life were short-lived and only sporadically found. On most days, the ratio of time spent grooming Mattie versus myself was easily five to one. For a wash, he required the bathroom to first be transformed into a steam room, his towel pre-warmed in the kitchen oven we no longer had time to use for cooking. I couldn't remember a time since he'd joined our club when my own elusive showers lasted longer than six minutes. Likewise, what I would accomplish in a day was now dictated by my mini-me, who couldn't care less about yearly performance appraisals or eating meals at a table. I did most of my work while sitting at a 45-degree angle, which through trial and error I computed as the balance point where I could both see my laptop's screen and hold sleeping Mattie on my chest without him sliding off onto the floor as I typed around him.

I fully realize that there's nothing new or different about my struggle relative to the challenges every other parent before me has faced. It's just that now I was experiencing them firsthand. My problem: The slice of life's pie that was cut just for me was ever-shrinking. My solution: Set a goal that was just for myself. This exercise in taking time for a personal challenge—learning to play the drums— would be a fun, new, and strange journey for me and my brain.

To be honest, this goal was also a little bit about our son. Mattie hadn't seen the close of two seasons yet, but Pete and I both wanted to instill a love of music in him as soon as possible, or at least before the end of the critical period for rhythmic development, after which he might always be that guy who clapped when everyone else's hands were silent between beats. I had just read a study conducted by a group of Canadian psychologists who found that six-month-old infants could learn some fundamentals of music. But interestingly, parental involvement was key to their success. By a flip of the coin, researchers asked some parents to sing lullabies and nursery rhymes to their babies once a week for an hour in class and to listen to recordings of the songs at home. The researchers asked other families to play games, make art as a family, and read books while music played in the background. All the parents in the study cared equally about their children's education and were actively engaged in enriching their daily experiences. The only difference was that the first group of babies heard their parents singing along to the music while the second group heard only the recordings in the background.

Around the time the kids turned one year of age, the researchers tested their musical skills. They selected eight measures from a piece of music that none of the kids had heard before—a sonatina by Thomas Attwood—and altered every other note in the melody by just a half-step. This was a slight change, but one that had a big impact on how the piece sounded. The transformed snippet seemed dissonant, and a bit off from the type of harmonic structure that appears most often in music written by Bach or Mozart, or in common lullabies—the type of music all the children had been listening to.

The researchers found that the children paid more attention to the music their parents were making as compared to the altered sonatina. But this single difference meant many things. First off, the kids whose parents were involved in their musical training at six months of age could tell the difference between these two different types of harmony. That kids can develop a musical ear so early in life is pretty remarkable, I came to believe. When I turned on the stereo at home, it seemed to me that Mattie thought John Coltrane's 1965 recording of "My Favorite Things" live in Belgium with McCoy Tyner, Jimmy Garrison, and Elvin Jones was no more fascinating than the synthesized rendition of Rossini's finale to the *William Tell* Overture that played from the plastic star hanging from his jungle gym when he kicked it. We had work to do.

Even more impressive in the study, though, was what type of music the kids preferred. Both groups of kids chose to listen to music for the same amount of time overall. They liked music to the same degree. But those who had heard their parents sing lullabies to them had begun to develop an understanding of harmonic texture and refine their acoustic style. They knew what they liked, and they liked what was most similar to what they had learned with their parents. On the other hand, the kids who played games with their parents while listening to music in the background couldn't tell the difference between the tonal and dissonant harmonies.

I have taught psychology at universitites for about fifteen years, and I knew from the research my colleagues were doing that having some understanding of music, even as a little kid, has implications for development beyond the recording studio. German scientists found that small children who created and danced around to music with other kids and adults were more helpful to other kids later on, compared to those who played games with others but without any musical accompaniment. In fact, only four out of twenty-four children in the latter group helped a friend fix a broken toy. But thirteen of twenty-four children who'd made music as a part of their playtime activities helped their buddy. The researchers explained that making music in a group requires the musicians, regardless of their age, to remain aware of others. Musicians coordinate with other people, sharing emotional experiences and patterns of movement, and creating sounds that require synchronization. Across evolution, music helped us bond in groups. When we practice making music, we are also practicing good social skills.

Deciding to fill the precious moments while Mattie slept with my own musical training—more noise, chaos, and inevitable frustration—may seem like a pretty self-defeating idea. But I reasoned that building music into my day would give my brain something to mull over rather than the over-under on when Mattie would bellow for his next meal. I could now crank the stereo, cue up Blue Öyster Cult rather than "Baa, Baa, Black Sheep," and call it studying. And with the research I read and used as my justification, I could also claim to be teaching Mattie some valuable life lessons. This was a goal that I knew would be difficult to meet, but it was my brass ring and I wanted to grab it.

Of course, this period in my life wouldn't be the first time I struggled to meet a goal that posed a great challenge, and I wouldn't be the first person who did so. Every December, Marist College polls about a thousand adults, representing a broad swath of America, asking whether they are planning to set a New Year's resolution. Each year, the numbers are the same. About half of the respondents say they are. But when asked if they held to the commitment they made the previous year, about one in three says they did not. Setting the goal isn't enough to see it through. Personally, I know this quite well. I, too, have vowed on the first of the year to learn more about how to invest for retirement but eventually let that educational pursuit fall by the wayside. I've renewed gym memberships that come with bills that end up being monthly reminders of my own inactivity. I've tried an arsenal of strategies to help me make the right choices—giving myself pep talks on achieving fiscal health, writing myself reminders to buy a new gym-locker padlock—but they didn't seem to bring my wallet or my waistline any closer to where I wanted either of them to be.

These same issues plagued my early attempts to improve my groove. For my first practice session, I sat on the floor next to Mattie and we knocked around on an upside-down metal bowl with a silicone bottom, using a starter-sized whisk as a drumstick. I was treating the bowl as my practice pad. Mattie was using it as a chew toy. Neither of us did much to keep a beat. I was far from mimicking Dave Grohl or Buddy Rich or even Animal from the Muppets.

When that first practice session (a generous description for what it actually was) came to an end, it was clear that my interest in this endeavor wasn't going to sustain itself. I wasn't good. I didn't like listening to the sounds I made. And it would take a while before either of those things would change. Even before I really got started, I found my own interest in this project waning, just as it had every time someone tried to talk to me about balancing risk in my financial portfolio, the intricacies of insurance coverage when I rented a car, or sports in general. If I was going to stick with this drum thing, I would have to get creative about how I kept myself committed.

Like so many other people do, I tried to remind myself of my goal, and why it was important. I had friends stopping by to meet

Mattie for the first time. When they asked what was going on, I desperately wanted to have something to report on other than the size of the onesies Mattie was now wearing, or his preference to sleep in a position that resembled a cactus. I reminded myself that music was food for the soul and the brain, and looked for evidence of the benefits of personal time for new mothers. I would like to say that I spent those middle-of-the-night hours when Mattie needed a milk-hit gazing lovingly at my guzzling, snuggly baby. But I didn't. Usually I was holding him with one hand and using the other to pull up synopses of scientific reports on my phone. (It was the only thing that kept me from falling over dead asleep onto him.) I thought that the data would strengthen my resolve to keep up the practicing when it sounded just as grating as construction workers tearing up a road, and felt as uncoordinated as a baby emu learning to walk. But the process of searching out the published investigations—especially when I'd rather have been sleeping—and then evaluating the quality of the scholarship, understanding its implications, and translating them into a message I could use to remember why it was important to let both of us whale away on the kitchen products was intensive. It cost me time, energy, and mental bandwidth that I honestly couldn't afford to spare. And every day when I needed a reminder about why we were subjecting our ears to this, it wasn't sustainable.

Why not?

Because these strategies, the ones we use most often in pursuit of our goals, are exhausting.

The go-to tactics for maintaining motivation that occurred to me, and that most readily come to mind for others, can't meet the demands of the job. In my case, the personal reminders and self-encouragement would likely prove as successful as grabbing a pool noodle when you're standing on the upper deck of a sinking ship. The titanic undertaking of learning the drums would require something better.

And that's true for challenges well beyond just the musical one I faced. When dieting, denying ourselves the cheesecake for dessert requires that we regularly defeat the pull of temptation. When balancing a budget, following through on making a monthly contribution to a health savings account does not feel as gratifying as spending that same money on a cappuccino at the corner coffee shop on the way to work each morning. Doing the unfamiliar thing, the demanding thing that will help us reach our goals, requires in-the-moment mastery. Repeating the mantra "I think I can, I think I can, I think I can . . ." gets old fast. And when we try to rid our minds of temptations and vices, our efforts backfire.

Female dieters in search of solutions tried out this effortful approach. Following the direction of experimenters, they worked to avoid thinking about eating chocolate. Another group was told to indulge their imaginations and savor the illusory sensations of eating chocolate in their minds. While you might think that imagining the taste and feel of that silky sweetness would whet dieters' appetites for the delicious treat, it didn't. Those who actively tried to stop their thoughts from wandering toward the delicacy ate eight or nine pieces later in the study, when offered the chance to sample Cadbury Shots and Galaxy Minstrels. Compare this to how much was eaten by the dieters who had thought intensely about how chocolate smelled, tasted, and melted away in their mouths. These dieters ate, on average, only five or six pieces. As with the first group of dieters, the strategies we generally use to approach the goals that matter most are the wrong ones. They aren't making our tough jobs any easier, because they deplete our limited reserves of energy, time, and interest.

This matters because, in many cases, our mental states have a bigger impact than our physical ones on our ability to persevere past obstacles. We don't realize it, but when we assess our own stamina and take stock of our strength and pep, our judgments affect our performance even more than the actual energy our bodies have available to do the job. If we think we've worked hard and believe we have drained our mental energies, we aren't as effective later on. That's regardless of whether we're actually beat or well rested.

To evaluate the importance of self-assessments relative to the physical states of our bodies, students from Indiana University agreed to do some pretty boring but depleting things. Everyone started the study by crossing out every letter *e* that appeared in a page of text. Boring, I agree, but simple enough to do, which is why it didn't take too much out of individuals who were asked to cross out *e*'s on the next page as the second part of the study. However, it was precisely because of how easy the task was that when the rules changed for another group of participants, it took a lot more out of them than it had the first time around. This group, for their second task, was also told to cross out every *e* in the text—except when another vowel followed the *e* in the same word (as in "read") or when a vowel was one letter removed from the *e* in either direction (as in "vowel"). It's tiring just trying to figure out what these new rules were.

The experimenters didn't leave it at that, though. They made up false claims about the effects of colored paper on human energy levels. They told participants that the source of their physical state might originate from the color of paper in front of them. Regardless of whether they did the easy or the taxing assignment, half were told that yellow paper exhausts people's attention and ability to think carefully. The others were told that yellow paper energizes, replenishes attention, and encourages careful thought. Then the researchers measured everyone's concentration and perseverance in a final test of analytical thinking.

Though they were just a ruse, the claims about the impact of paper color had real power. The people who were told that the yellow paper contributed to exhaustion gave up faster and made more mistakes when trying to solve anagrams. They were much slower to recognize that a pattern they were searching for had appeared. And they were unable to distinguish between poorly written and well-supported arguments they read later on.

It didn't matter whether they had just completed something challenging or finished a pretty easy job; their belief about whether they had more or no more to give affected how well they performed on the next activity. Personal assessments of the availability of mental resources, independent of the actual energy they had, impacted their performance. Interestingly, they weren't less motivated. The goal was still important to them, even when they felt like they had just exerted a great deal of effort (even if they hadn't really), but their ability to succeed at the goal was impaired. Their mental state mattered more than their physical one.

So, when we think about taking on some of our biggest challenges and approaching them using strategies that we *think* will help but that really require a lot of effort, we're likely to fail. It's not that we don't care. It's not that we aren't trying hard enough. We're using the wrong tools for the job.

Searching for a Strategy

In my middle-of-the-night search for techniques that would better assist me with meeting tough challenges, I found the backstory of Dale Chihuly, an American glassblower and sculpture revolutionary. His brilliantly ribbed figures of shells and braided bulbous grasses defy the laws of balance. His *Rotunda Chandelier* hangs in the lobby of the Victoria and Albert Museum in London. President Bill Clinton presented Chihuly's work to Queen Elizabeth II and French president François Mitterrand. Robin Williams bought his work. Elton John, Mick Jagger, and Bill Gates did too. More than twelve million visitors have seen his art in ninety-seven exhibitions in seven countries over the past decade alone. His popularity has grown every year since 1976, when contemporary art curator Henry Geldzahler first acquired three Chihuly glass baskets for New York's Metropolitan Museum of Art.

That's the same year that Chihuly flew through a windshield in a head-on car accident on a rainy night in England. Glass ravaged his face with gashes that required 256 stiches to repair. It blinded his left eye, leaving him unable to perceive visual depth. Three years later, he dislocated his right shoulder in a bodysurfing accident. After that, he couldn't hold the weight of the blowpipe when it became piled with molten glass.

But these shattering experiences marked the start of his sharp change in direction. Chihuly had to redesign his approach to art and adapt his technique to accommodate his ability to see with only one eye. As he explained, "I think it's probably made me see things differently." Precisely. His artistic acclaim and entrepreneurial success came only after he took a step back and saw his work from a different perspective.

And that's what needs to happen with our goals. We need to find a new way to approach them. We need a different tack when trying to meet them. We need to see our approach differently.

I started with no plan or manifest for the course of my musical journey. But I headed off, nonetheless, first to uncover the capacities and liabilities of my mind, my will, and my resolve. I took Chihuly's comment perhaps more literally than he intended it, and focused on my eyes. I wanted to *see* a new way to success.

2

Finding the Right Kind of Challenge

If I was really going to become a drummer, I had to pick my first song. I asked Pete for help. He's actually been playing drums for forty years on the same set he built up by saving money from the corner-store job he had as a teenager. Tunes he spent months mastering in high school came back to him decades later after working through them only a few times. When we stopped by a musical instrument showroom on a trip to visit my sister up in Canada, Pete sat down at a floor model and cranked out some of Neil Peart's lines in "La Villa Strangiato," which brought a ruddy-faced salesman running over in awe. Pete's good. Really good. So asking him to help me get started seemed like a natural choice.

He suggested I take a week to choose what I wanted to learn. He advised listening to it on a loop in order to nail down what I heard in the drum part (rather than just practicing singing the lyrics like I was readying myself to jump in as a backup singer—a position I'd be equally unlikely to rock). I'd been bingeing on U2 lately and chose "Bullet the Blue Sky" off the *Joshua Tree* album. Seemed pretty repetitive. Kind of like Ravel's "Boléro." I put that tune on repeat and let it sink in. After a week, I reported back that I was ready. Not a good choice, he advised. Surprised, I asked why. He said the beauty of that song is how complex it actually is, and the sheer number of subskills a drummer has to master and coordinate. Specifically, sticking the sixteenth-note snare drum pickup into the fourth beat requires you to move off the hi-hat, whack the snare, and get back on the hi-hat fast. Even harder, you have a fourth of a beat to get your left stick off the snare and up to the hi-hat; and another fourth of a beat to slide back down to the snare. And you do it over and over and over again. Sticking it each time. That makes it tough. Way, way too tough for a first-time performer. He wasn't wrong.

I conceded, and realized that I had just committed one of the fatal flaws in goal pursuit. I'd set my sights too high, and tried to take on too much right out of the gate.

This is all too common an error. Aspiring home chefs, among other hobbyists, do this all the time. Want to try cooking? Don't start with a Baked Alaska. A high-quality rendition of the dessert requires that you first churn your own ice cream, then craft a chiffon cake that weighs as little as a box of paperclips, and select French, Italian, or Swiss meringue, whichever better suits your nationalistic palate. The assembly could go all wrong for any number of reasons. What starts as essentially a rectangular piece of two-dimensional sheet cake must transform into a three-dimensional sphere surrounding the ice cream. The confection is topped off with piped meringue resembling a 1950s synchronized swimmer's cap covered in flowers. Toss the whole thing into a 500-degree oven, and when it's set, douse it in flaming liquor. Without the frozen ice cream melting.

The first song I set my sights on playing was my Baked Alaska.

Pete gave me another band to check out. The Outfield. They were an English rock band based in London. Their top single was "Your Love." It reached No. 6 on the Billboard Hot 100 in 1986, and barely survived beyond the '80s, which is an aspect of the song's history that resonated with me personally. (The middle-school years were rough.) It had a basic rock beat, and the drummer didn't do anything for the first sixty-five seconds of the song anyway. Even though it was pretty straightforward, coordinating all my limbs in space repeatedly was definitely going to pose a challenge for me. A challenge that I'd feel pretty proud of myself for if I mastered, but one that didn't require I take on the impossible for my first song. I thought I'd give it a go—despite Pete's warning that this would defy my aspirations of finding something cool to brag about. The song was re-released over thirty years after its debut—six months into my musical studies of it—as a jingle for dryer sheets. But being cool has rarely been a priority of mine. Case in point: In marching band, I wore one of those hats with a giant feather plume sticking out of the top. For eight years. By choice. This was the song for me.

What Pete seemed to understand intuitively about how to foster success was what researchers know to be true: the best-laid goals are the ones that are set at just the right level. They can't be too hard, or people give up before they've even really started. Set a goal that requires a number of incremental milestones to be passed along the way, or a very rapid rate of progress, and the pursuit of that goal will exhaust us. Set a goal that's too easy to achieve, and we sit back on our laurels unmotivated to move forward, because the future rewards just don't seem that great. Goals set at levels that are moderately challenging but not impossible are the ones that inspire. Just as people can't complete a marathon sustaining a sprinter's pace but won't win a footrace by walking, setting goals is about balancing between taking on too much and not trying for enough.

To wit: Companies that set goals at just the right level—far from easy, but seeming almost too high to meet—have the potential for fostering innovation at record rates. For instance, 3M holds as a company expectation that 25 percent of each year's revenue will come from products that did not exist five years ago. It produces more than 55,000 products each year that span the spectrum from adhesives for sticking stuff together to abrasives for rubbing it off. It also creates medical products like wireless stethoscopes to see inside people's bodies, and health-care software to process the numbers faster than humanly possible. 3M's goal for the creative pursuit of new designs is a lofty one, but by all reports it has designed a corporate culture that allows the company to meet it. It expects its creative innovation teams to give 15 percent of their time to the free exploration of ideas of their own choosing, which may or may not turn into anything lucrative. The research and development departments present posters at internal science fairs to showcase projects still in development, awaiting potential collaborators' involvement. In the five years since 3M's launch of this initiative, net sales attributed to products that weren't on the books five years earlier have topped 30 percent every year.

The song Pete suggested and that I elected for my percussive debut followed 3M's principle for goal setting.

And when I tried the same goal-setting approach early on in my lessons, the benefits were palpable. My first attempts to coordinate all four of my limbs while playing "Your Love" were far from graceful or effective. I chose to set my sights on something more manageable. I focused first on the snare and the bass drum, leaving out the hi-hat and ride cymbal. My right arm lay in wait at my side, presumably at the ready to deaden the incoming sound by covering one ear at a time. Tapping my right foot on the bass drum pedal on each of the four beats of the measure and whacking the snare with my left hand on the second and fourth, I am embarrassed to say, required that I take the song down to about half the speed of the recording. But this was where I started and stayed; it was a relatively small but manageable goal.

After executing the snare and bass drum pattern became less of a fluke and more the result of intention, I switched up the parts. My right arm reached across my body to *chink-chink* on the closed hi-hat. My right foot was squarely positioned on the bass drum pedal; I tried *tap-tapping* on the hi-hat at twice the rate of my foot. None of these combinations would rock music make, but breaking down the goal of achieving star status into manageable subgoals—beginning with grooving on the backbeat, half the sounds at a time—was something I could and did achieve.

Focusing on the Goal

After my relative success at laying down a rudimentary beat for "Your Love," I would encounter other challenges along the way. It turns out that successful goal pursuit is more difficult when you are spread too thin or find your attention drawn to too many things (especially when those things might be too intensive to pursue at the time). We are not always as efficient as we think, and when we try to take on multiple tasks, we're usually not generating a product that reflects our best abilities. Marcel Just, a neuroscience researcher at Carnegie Mellon University, sought to quantify this concept. He set up drivers in a virtual-reality simulator and asked them to navigate the road while occasionally focusing on what someone else was saying. Drivers were 50 percent more likely to run their car off the road when they tuned in to the conversation than when they drove uninterrupted. The issue, it turned out, had to do with changes in neural functioning. The parietal lobe is an area of the brain responsible for handling information about our bodies and the environments around us. When drivers multitasked, their parietal lobes showed an average reduction in activity of 37 percent compared to when drivers were focused just on the road. In other words, their brains were acting as if they too were spread too thin to do the job well. Our best work requires us to focus on the target of our aspirations, and to ignore objects, events, experiences, and people on the periphery.

Toward this end, I found some inspiration in someone who might initially seem like a pretty lusterless character. When he was in the fourth grade in the early 1800s, in an area we now know as Slovakia, a boy named Joseph Petzval seemed destined to become a shoemaker; this was the profession his parents had chosen for him.

Maybe one reason for this choice was that he wasn't a traditionally strong student. Math, in particular, didn't click for Petzval, and he was going to have to repeat his last year of studies in the subject. But that summer he decided on his own to read the rather sophisticated-sounding *Analytic Paper on the Elements of Mathematics,* and a transformation occurred.

A year later, Petzval went on, not to an apprenticeship in shoes, but instead to attend a lyceum in preparation for university study at the Institutum Geometricum, in engineering. The same year he earned his degree, Petzval started a graduate program and was appointed chair of the physics department. He worked as an urban engineer in Buda, applying his studies of mathematics, mechanics, and practical geometry to flood abatement, dam construction, and sewer issues for the city. After receiving his PhD, he was invited to join the professoriate, as a mathematician, at the University of Vienna. He lectured there, some say arriving to class each day on the back of a black Arabian horse. He rented an abandoned Piarist monastery north of the city at Kahlenberg Mountain, overlooking the Danube River. And it was here, in the ruins of this religious center, that he changed the course of photography forever.

Within the stone walls of his monastery, Petzval built his own glass-sharpening workshop and crafted the lenses that would revolutionize how people create photographs. Before Petzval, the most commonly used technique for capturing personal portraits was the daguerreotype. Daguerreotypes were those hauntingly shadowy and often blurred images of stoically posed figures. They were very difficult to make because they required the subject to remain still for thirty minutes or so, while the copper plate onto which the image was being etched was exposed to light.

In 1840, Petzval crafted a lens and an aperture that could allow more light into the camera, quickly, so that people didn't have to sit still nearly as long. But it's what happened in the background of Petzval's photographs that still fascinates photographers today. Though the subject in the foreground is sharply in focus, whatever is situated behind is softly and lusciously pixelated. The backdrop is blurred and seems to swirl like a whirlpool. The effect is mysterious and alluring, so much so that the lens, now 180 years old, recently saw a resurgence in interest with a Kickstarter campaign to finance its remanufacturing, exactly to Petzval's original specifications, for the commercial market.

Petzval had invented a way to shoot with what photographers call open aperture, where the foreground is in focus while all that serves as the backdrop is blurred. The effect highlights the subject at the expense of any surroundings that might otherwise distract from it. Petzval's nineteenth-century optical breakthrough serves as the basis for the best-designed portrait lenses today—and the visual effect it produces is the basis for one of the most inspiring strategies to motivate our goal pursuit: narrow focus.

Narrowing the Focus of Our Visual Attention

It was an early spring blizzard that had led New Yorkers to batten down their hatches. The city's streets were sprayed in a thick white snow that few people dared to disrupt. Despite the weather, I headed out for what ended up being an "only in New York" kind of adventure. I had been invited to speak about visual attention and optical illusions to an eclectic group of individuals. They drank bee-pollen-spotted vodka cocktails and noshed on beet focaccia while I talked science. There were more Academy Award winners floating around the room than I had handbags in my closet. Business cards came wrapped in bespoke paper you could plant in the ground and watch bloom. I am pretty sure the guests had flown in from every continent but Antarctica.

I arrived early to set up but had loads of time to kill before any of my responsibilities kicked in. I started up a conversation with a guy, Jeff Provenzano, who I thought was assigned to be my tech assistant. I was wrong. He is a professional skydiver. He is heavily sponsored to put on a leotard that makes him resemble a flying squirrel and jump off cliffs in Norway. He has strapped on parachutes and has fallen, intentionally, off the Princess Tower in Dubai, the second-tallest residential building in the world. He has been launched out of the back of a cargo plane at 10,000 feet while sitting on a couch playing video games. Once, Provenzano jumped out of a plane and, swooping in on a lake in Texas at a hundred miles an hour, landed on the back seat of a moving Jet Ski driven by a guy he'd met only the day before. He was challenged by a Ford F-150 off-road truck called the VelociRaptor 475 in an episode of the television show *Top Gear*. They raced for five miles, the truck crossing the Arizona desert horizontally versus Provenzano falling headfirst vertically. Provenzano won.

As we waited for the event to start, he took out his cell phone. The screen was cracked, which, with a career like his, comes with the territory, I suspect.

We started sharing stories about our jobs. As the list of his achievements above can attest, his were far more interesting. But there was one story in particular that piqued my curiosity, speaking directly to the power of perspective and the value of narrow focus.

Provenzano and his skydiving teammates Luke Aikins and Jon Devore were challenged to jump out of a plane at 25,000 feet and land in a net—without a parachute. Their first reaction was to pass on the chance to widow their wives and semi-orphan their children, but then they changed their minds and decided to give it a try. Aikins would be the designated jumper.

The trio amassed a team: the stunt coordinator for the last *Iron Man* movie; lighting designers who created bulbs for airport runways; a GPS systems engineer; a costume designer of sorts, who could make a flight suit that minimized drag but still allowed room for the spine protector and neck brace needed for landing; and NASA engineers used to computing the force-of-impact of things that hit the earth, like meteors or, in this case, humans.

Together, they designed and built a 100-by-100-foot net that weighed six hundred pounds. They suspended it from cranes. At three tension points, a portion of the suspended net could be released at precisely the right moment before Aikins's impact, to soften the blow. Release too soon, and the net would have too much give. Release too late, and the net would be too stiff. Nick Brandon, an expert stuntman who specialized in timing systems, controlled the release buttons manually with guidance from two team members calculating fall-rate information and an experienced skydiver acting as a spotter, watching the smoke flying off Aikins's heels.

The net was also attached to air pistons to create what was billed as a gentle braking system, though I wonder how gentle the stop could be when scientists calculated that Aikins would experience 2.4 g's of force in his fall, just under what astronauts experience during rocket launches.

Aikins planned to jump with a bailout oxygen bottle that prevents hypoxia, the condition of cognitive confusion, ringing in the ears, color blindness, and blue lips that arises from insufficient oxygen at extreme heights, like at high camp on Everest, cruising altitudes for airplanes, or the place in the sky from which he was going to jump. Aikins's cousin planned to jump simultaneously, meeting Aikins in midair to take away the bottle when they hit an altitude where he could get enough oxygen from breathing the air itself.

Provenzano and his teammates planned to wear live-streaming cameras so that the event could be televised from 25,000 feet up through the full descent. There would be witnesses. Lots of witnesses.

But what fascinated me most was how Aikins was going to find and land on that net. The job seemed harder than finding a needle in a haystack. (At least you get to be on the ground for that chore, and the only thing you might die from is boredom.) The team purchased eight precision approach path indicators—fancy lightbulbs usually used to guide airplanes into position to land on runways. For this jump, the lights would guide Aikins to the center of the net they hoped would catch him. Each lightbulb emitted red and white high-intensity beams alongside one another, a combination that created a single beam that should be easy to detect even from a few miles up. The team placed indicator lights outside the net, forming two concentric circles like the double and triple rings surrounding the bull's-eye on a dartboard. Aikins's goal was to position himself over the center of the net. When he moved off the net, the light would look red. When he moved back over the center of the net, the light would appear white again. Aikins knew that as he was falling—or as they say, flying—he needed to stay inside that white light. The challenge (as if there weren't enough already) was that in practice runs even when it might *feel* like they were falling straight down, GPS tracking systems had shown they could be moving by as much as twenty miles per hour horizontally. I told Provenzano that if I was jumping to what would inevitably be my death, I didn't think I'd be keeping track of colors and what they mean. Provenzano said it wasn't hard. "White, you're all right, but red and you're dead."

As dodgy a career path as this seemed to me, Provenzano and the team did not intend to toss Aikins out of a plane without a trial run, or two, or two hundred. They chucked a weighted dummy out a few times and jumped with backup parachutes to practice. Each test run was meant to push the equipment and the team to find their limits.

On their first trial run, they realized that the lighting system they'd designed wasn't doing the job. The lights were misplaced. One set of lights marked the edges of the 100-foot-wide net. The second ring circumscribed it, 250 feet out from the center. Even though these rings were close enough that you could block them out of view with your thumb on an outstretched arm for most of the trip down from the plane, Provenzano told me that on that test jump, he and Aikins didn't see the second ring. All of the beams of lights were pointed straight up. They were strong enough to cut through the atmosphere, and the pilot could see them before they jumped. But once Provenzano and Aikins stepped off, they were so focused on the four lights surrounding the bull's-eye that the other lights making up the outer ring had essentially disappeared. The skydivers did not see anything outside their narrow field of view, upon which they were intensely focused.

So the team made an adjustment. They shrank the diameter of both the inner and outer rings to 30 percent and 40 percent, respectively, of their original sizes. The window of white light was much smaller now. But unlike before, it illuminated the only space on which Aikins needed to, and in fact did, focus his attention.

So how did it all end up? On July 30, 2016, 25,000 feet above the ground, Aikins moved to the Cessna's door, clutching his bailout oxygen bottle. He stuck his head outside and looked down. He couldn't see the net, but he stepped out anyway. He flew through the sky. Monitors registered Aikins's heart rate at 148 beats per minute. He was more relaxed and composed than I am when mimicking hip-hop moves in Zumba class. He was gliding through the air, searching for the white lights. Once he locked on to them, he stayed in the white for the rest of the trip down. When he was three hundred feet from the net, Aikins barrel-rolled onto his back so that the net could cradle his body as it bent him at the waist. Two minutes and nine seconds after he'd left the plane, he hit the net. Aikins screamed on impact—not from pain, but from the overwhelming sense of relief and pride in having accomplished something that had seemed impossible.

Though the Arizona desert is vast and wide, Aikins's visual focus was narrow and sharp, much like Joseph Petzval's camera lens. The view he could have had from so far above the earth might have been wide and vast, with layers of mountains off to the side and the streams and roads snaking around the landscape. But as he fell from the heavens, he didn't see any of that. Once he locked on to the position of the net, all else that surrounded it was a blur. And that was key for this job.

Narrow Focus Among the Athletic Elites

Joan Benoit Samuelson kept her shoes no more than two feet off the ground, a far cry from the 25,000 that marked Luke Aikins's story, but in so doing she accomplished what literally no other woman had done. She was the first-ever women's Olympic marathon champion, trouncing the competition in the 1984 Summer Olympics in Los Angeles, the year the women's marathon was introduced to the games. Samuelson had taken up long-distance running in high school to help her recover from a broken leg she'd suffered in a skiing accident. As a college student, she entered the 1979 Boston Marathon as a relative unknown. She won the race, knocking eight minutes off the competition record—a time she beat four years later, when she improved by more than twelve minutes and set a new world record.

How did she do it?

Though Samuelson never met Petzval or Aikins, her technique for conquering the challenges in her field echoes the engineered designs of the camera lens and bull's-eye lighting system. She looks at the world around her with a narrow focus.

When she runs, Samuelson scans the runners ahead of her. She picks one—a runner in pink shorts, say—and passes her. She then identifies a new mark, and passes that one too. She takes a goal that seems far off—26.22 miles, to be exact; a goal that sure sounds impossible for most of us to hit—and breaks it down, essentially unpacking it, into manageable parts. Samuelson establishes goals that are challenging but possible to achieve, inspiring without being crushing; goals that push her to move faster without exhausting her. Samuelson does this for the last quarter of a marathon, until she reaches the finish line. She trains her eyes to focus on each new subgoal, which motivates her to move faster despite the fatigue that nearly everyone experiences at some point. And in doing that, the larger goal, which once appeared remote, becomes tangible and in view.

Samuelson's accomplishments set her apart from the pack, quite literally, but her technique is actually shared by other accomplished runners, as I discovered one cold night in January while sitting on the floor of a Brooklyn YMCA.

Once a week, an elite team of runners called Zenith Velocity trains on an orange rubber track a quarter of the normal size at this YMCA. Members are well decorated. One is the fastest man out of Nigeria. Another is the third-quickest Trinidadian, who trained alongside Usain "Lightning" Bolt, the fastest human in history. And a third, Lalonde Gordon, is a double Olympic bronze medalist and the first Tobagonian to medal at any Olympic Games.

Before they found their way to their blocks that night, these elite runners each spent some time talking to me about how they look at the path ahead.

I described what "focused attention" means to the scientists who study it. I asked what the runners looked at when they were running. Did they focus their eyes and their attention on a mark, like the finish line or the end of a straightaway?

I also asked if they used an expansive style of attention. Did they turn their heads to see the bend ahead or the people on their left and right? Did they move their eyes around so they could see everything off to the sides?

Though tracking the competition is tempting, they admitted, every one of these Zenith Velocity elites said they used something similar to Samuelson's visual technique. They all said they used narrow focus more than anything else, or were certain it would work better than the alternative for beating the pack.

What We See Is the Problem

Tabling the fact that these athletes never worry about the imminence of swimsuit season, there are many facets of their daily experience that differ from mine, and from those of other people who don't find themselves among the athletic elite. One big difference is clearly how they look at the space around them: they don't seem to pay it much regard. But they also seem to hold a different perspective on what constitutes a challenge. Research, in fact, confirms that the physical state of our bodies literally changes how we perceive exercise. Across the board, evidence suggests that people who are tired and burdened by extra pounds see walkable or runnable distances as being longer than do people who weigh less and have more energy. The same is true when we look at staircases we might climb, or hills we might hike up. When it's harder to get up and around, we visually experience our environments as posing greater challenges.

In one University of Virginia study, sixty experienced runners who routinely jogged three miles or more at least three times a week agreed to answer questions both before and after they went out for a jog. They knew they would go on a run, taking any route they liked, as long as they started at the foot of one particular hill and ended at the foot of another. Before they started and when they ended, the runners estimated the slope of each of these hills by moving the swinging arm on a protractor to match the incline they saw before them.

Despite the fact that all were fit runners, the participants reported that the hills appeared markedly steeper when they were tired. In fact, it looked up to an additional 50 percent steeper when the runners were tired compared to when they weren't.

In my own lab, I've found that it doesn't take a miles-long jog to make the world look like a more taxing place to get around in. We measured the circumference of people's waists and hips as an indication of overall fitness. Then we asked our participants to estimate the distance between themselves and a finish line to which they would carry weights. They did this by indicating the location of the finish line on a mostly blank map; it showed only the outline of the room we were in, and a marker representing their starting position. Their job was to indicate on the map where they thought the finish line was.

Although the participants didn't know it, their waist-to-hip ratio was a reliable predictor of where they placed the finish line. People who were less physically fit indicated that the finish line was farther away from them than did those who were more fit. The same perceptual exaggerations that happen when people are tired appear for people who are struggling to manage their weight on a daily basis. The exercise looked more daunting to people likely to find it a struggle to complete.

Learning to See an Easier Exercise

This led me to ask: If perception is part of the problem of exercise, could perception be part of the solution? My research team and I designed an intervention that trained people to look at their surroundings differently, as a technique for helping them exercise better and more easily. We set out to teach people to look at the corner store they are walking to, or the playground they are racing toward with their child, in the same way that Zenith Velocity runners and other world-class athletes look at the finish line. We hoped this would improve the quality of exercise even when a person isn't suited up for competition.

Two of my students, Shana Cole and Matt Riccio, started by asking people working out in a community gym if they wanted to test their exercise ability. We explained that we would put weighted cuffs on their ankles that would add 15 percent to their body weight. They would walk as quickly as they could to a finish line—a moderately challenging, but not impossible, exercise.

Before the groups set out, we gave them separate coaching on where to focus their attention. One group was told to keep their eyes on the prize, like Samuelson and the Zenith Velocity runners. They were to imagine their eyes as a spotlight, shining just on their goal, the finish line, and to avoid looking around. The other group could look around at the walls, the basketball hoop to the side, or the other gym patrons as they naturally would.

Before they started the exercise, the participants each estimated how far away the finish line appeared to be. They gauged the distance in a few different ways, but regardless, we found that the group told to keep their eyes on the prize estimated that the finish line was 30 percent closer than the group who looked around naturally. A narrow focus made the exercise look easier.

But did it improve performance? To test this question, the exercisers walked as quickly as they could to the finish line and then reported how much effort it required. The narrow-focus group said that it required 17 percent less effort than the other group did. This result wasn't just subjective. We also timed how long each person took to complete the brisk walk. The narrow focus got the walkers to the finish line 23 percent faster than the other group. I can put that increase into perspective. Let's say you're a man and you're considering running the Berlin Marathon. A 23 percent increase in speed would mean that you've gone from a respectable time of 2 hours and 45 minutes to being only 5 minutes off the fastest time ever run on a record-eligible course. Kenya's Eliud Kipchoge ran the Berlin Marathon in under 2 hours and 2 minutes in 2018.

Narrow focus is a literal directive for how to look at the surrounding world, changing both how we see the workout we are about to tackle and how good we are at completing it. But the reason behind the effectiveness of this visual strategy lies inside our own minds. People who keep their eyes on the prize experience more effective workouts because the proximity they perceive directly changes their own confidence in themselves. When a goal looks closer rather than impossibly far away, our mindset inspires us to double down on the pursuit of challenge.

Seeing Our Savings Successor

Narrow focus can also improve our fiscal health, pushing us (at least mentally) to the retirement finish line faster.

By the time we reach retirement age, most of us feel like we don't have enough money to live the life we hoped to have. More than 60 percent of Americans surveyed by the Federal Reserve in 2017 don't think or are unsure if their retirement savings are on track. Our feelings aren't wrong. In that same survey, the Federal Reserve found that a quarter of working adults reported having no retirement funds saved or invested in any form. It's not that everyone without retirement savings accounts is just independently wealthy. In fact, an analysis released in 2019 by the Employee Benefit Research Institute found that over 40 percent of American households in which the official head is between their mid-thirties and mid-sixties are projected to run short of money in retirement. This fact hits unmarried individuals harder than others. Single men in the lowest pre-retirement wage bracket have an average retirement savings shortfall of $30,000, while single women need another $110,000.

One big reason for the disconnect between what we will need and what we end up having is that many of us start to think about saving for retirement too late in life. We can't really fault college graduates with mounting student loans for not thinking much about retirement. After the expense of a new wardrobe, a car payment, ever-increasing rent, and health insurance, the average salary doesn't seem to stretch far.

Despite these real pressures, financial advisers advocate for early adoption of retirement planning. Why? Consider this example. Assuming a conservative average annual investment return of 8 percent, someone who sets aside $500 a month starting at the age of twenty-two will see well over $2 million when they retire at age sixty-five. But finding an extra $500 could be tricky on an entry-level salary, and the temptation to stave off investing for a few decades might be more appealing. The thing is, starting early in life rather than making up for lost time later on is generally a more lucrative rule of thumb. All else held constant, thanks to compound interest, a twenty-two-year-old who sets aside $100 a month will enter retirement with a larger nest egg than someone who puts in five times as much money each month but starts saving twenty years later.

Even to those of us who aren't actuaries, the math clearly shows the benefits of early investing, but the numeric nudge to invest earlier often still falls upon deaf ears. To get a better handle on why certain younger people set aside so little (if any) income for retirement, I took an informal poll of students I was teaching one semester who were on their way to graduating from college in the next few months. They all had jobs to pay their tuition and other bills, but fifty-five out of sixty said no when I asked them if they were saving for retirement. I asked how often they think about saving for retirement. They generally replied, "Not very often" or "Maybe once or twice a year." When asked why, many of them offered something similar to what one student, Victoria, said: "The future seems so far away." True enough.

Next, I tried to see if I could change their perspective. I wondered if I could find a way to get them to see their future retired self as somehow closer and more relevant to the person they are now. In the same way that runners who visually experience a finish line as being closer move faster than those who experience it as farther away, I thought that creating a visual experience that brought the future near might help these people pick up their investing pace. So I took photographs of my students' faces and, using computer-imaging software, blended each face with that of an older celebrity. Then I made an animation for each student, depicting the transition from current self to future self. Some women saw themselves acquire Betty White's hair and mouth. Other women saw themselves with Maya Angelou's eyes and jawline. And men watched as they transformed into Dan Rather. I thought that if I introduced them to their future selves—if they could plainly see themselves in their retirement years—maybe the future itself would not seem as distant.

Initially, the reactions mostly involved disgust, horror, and shock. When she saw herself with Betty White's hair, Elizabeth stopped breathing for a beat and then couldn't stop laughing. "That's terrifying," she eventually said. Marissa sweetly and softly said, "Oh no." Jessica proclaimed, "Oh my God, that's so scary." And Ratul just looked back at me and said, "Actually I look pretty good in that, I think."

Next, I gave them each a headshot of their future selves. In the white border, they wrote down what they hoped a typical day in retirement would entail, and how they would like to spend their time at that point in their lives.

And *then* I asked them if they'd start saving for retirement now. They all were open to the possibility.

My class project was based on a real experiment conducted by social psychologist Hal Hershfield, who found another way to introduce young people to their future selves. He took photographs of people in the community and morphed them into more realistic, non-celebrity-inspired aged versions. When he showed people what they might look like in forty-five years' time, they said they wanted to set aside 6.2 percent of their current salary for retirement. Those who saw photographs of their current selves set aside 4.4 percent.

In a second study, Hershfield created aged avatars of college students so that they would see themselves as forty-five years older but also interact with other people in a virtual environment. After a few minutes of taking on the form of their future selves, participants imagined receiving an unexpected $1,000. They were asked to decide how much of that money they would use to set aside for a checking account, buy something nice for someone special, plan a fun and extravagant occasion, or invest in a retirement fund. Compared to a group of students who saw an avatar depicting their current self, students who took on the role of their aged self set aside more than twice as much for retirement: an average of $172 out of the $1,000 windfall, compared to $80.

It's because of Hershfield's research that Prudential Financial created an ad featuring a jovial young man sitting on the couch next to an aged version of himself—his future "savings successor." They introduce themselves to each other and learn about how much they have in common. They like the same music, they root for the same teams, they have the same sense of fashion, and they have the same hairstyle, kind of. Prudential thought, based on the research, that encouraging us to envision our own savings successor would inspire us to save more. And they put a crack team of statisticians on the job of projecting what kinds of outcomes would be possible. Their models indicated that if each American set aside a mere three dollars a day (less than a cup of good coffee in New York City), as a nation we would have, collectively, $4.3 trillion saved for our retirement years.

Making the Future Brighter

Seeing our future as a part of the here and now helps us make choices in the present that are more aligned with the people we wish to become. When we focus on the future, and thereby contract the distance separating that far-off goal from the starting line we are standing at now, it is easier for us to make choices that can benefit us in the long run. This experience can also help us avoid decisions that have the potential for bringing immediate pleasure but distant pain.

The tension between short-term gains and long-term costs is one that adolescents have difficulty managing, particularly ones prone to delinquency. Because their cognitive abilities for risk assessment are still developing, teenagers may find themselves choosing a course of action that seems fun right now, but will prove detrimental in the future. The look of fresh spray paint on the community center may be appealing for all of a few hours, until detectives arrive at school to arrest the students who skipped class to graffiti the wall—or at least that's what my father told me when reflecting on his youthful exploits.

Again, psychologist Hal Hershfield wondered if this tension between short- and long-term gains could be reduced if students felt more connected to the future. So he and his colleagues partnered with a high school in the Netherlands. Students there made a new friend on a social media site—themselves. For about half of the students, the avatar looked uncannily like them. It had the same hairstyle as they currently did. It wore the same shirt and had the same freckles. For the other group of students, their avatar depicted themselves but aged by fifteen years. The eyes were a little more tired, the complexion a little ruddier. The eyebrows started to lighten. Subtle but noticeable changes matured each person's depiction.

Every day for a week, this doppelgänger messaged the student, asking about their day. A week before this new friendship developed and a week after it ended, the students confidentially disclosed how often they had engaged in delinquent acts in the past week. From these answers, the research team could calculate whether the new friendship had an effect on the students' behavior.

Students who interacted with the aged version of themselves felt more connected to their future self, and also curtailed their misbehavior. They were less likely to do things they were not allowed to and would later regret. They reported drinking alcohol less often. They intentionally broke fewer things. Seeing themselves in the future increased their sense of a shared connection with the adult they would become, and as a result they chose more productive ways of engaging with the world. This decline in misdeeds was particularly remarkable in comparison to the other group. The students who interacted with an avatar of their current self reported *more* frequent delinquencies.

The sense of connection with a future self did more than just reduce adolescents' misdeeds. College students on the brink of graduating who identified more with their future self reported procrastinating less often on their academic assignments compared to those who felt less connected. In another study, those connected to their future self were more disapproving of unethical negotiation tactics in business dealings, like trying to get a competitor fired, making concessions with no intention of honoring them, misrepresenting information to the competition, and bribing people to solicit insider information. In another study, almost three-quarters of future-oriented students were more likely to keep their professional commitments and attend meetings they'd agreed to; and among those who did, most were fair and honest even when at a financial cost to themselves. Indeed, future-connected individuals were two and a half times more likely to share information with another person, even when it meant receiving a smaller honorarium themselves for attending the session.

Narrowing In on Our Inspiration

In the mid-1950s in Montgomery, Alabama, public buses were segregated. When boarding, black people were required to pay at the front, leave the bus, and reenter through a separate door at the back. At all times, the ten front seats were reserved for white people and the ten back seats were reserved for black people. The sixteen seats in the middle were unreserved. Until the middle section was filled to capacity, white passengers sat in the seats front to back, and black passengers filled the seats from back to front. If additional black people boarded the bus, the law required them to stand. It was illegal for white people to sit in a row next to black people, so if additional white people boarded the bus, every black person in the row nearest the front had to stand in order to make a new row available for them.

On December 1, 1955, Rosa Parks was sitting in the first row of the middle section, where she was legally allowed to sit. The rows in front of her were filled when one white man came on board. Parks did not vacate her seat when directed to by the driver. She was arrested and found guilty of violating a city ordinance to obey a bus driver's seat assignments. She was fined ten dollars plus court costs of four dollars, and inspired a nation to rise up for civil rights.

The year 1956 saw nearly a full twelve months of Montgomery bus boycotts by almost forty thousand African Americans. They made up about three-quarters of the city bus customer and revenue base, and their actions crippled the economic structure of public transportation. Boycotters organized carpools. Those who owned cars volunteered to chauffeur others to work, back home, and around town. When the city pushed insurance companies to revoke the policies of those who used private vehicles in carpools, boycott leaders secured new policies with international companies. When black taxi drivers began charging riders just ten cents per trip, the equivalent of a bus fare, city officials ordered a fine be given to any cabbie who charged less than forty-five cents. Churches around the nation collected new shoes to replace the ones worn out by Montgomery's black citizens who took to foot.

Retaliation was swift. Civil rights leaders' homes and black Baptist churches were firebombed. Boycotters were assaulted. Ninety civil and community rights leaders, including Dr. Martin Luther King Jr., were indicted for conspiracy to interfere with business. King went to jail.

That year also saw civil rights activist Alice Wine pen lyrics that would inspire a nation. Wine was a resident of Johns Island, South Carolina, and a graduate of one of the first voter-education schools that taught African Americans how to pass the tests counties required citizens to take in order to cast a ballot. She learned how to register to vote, and how to respond nonviolently if attacked at the ballot box. She participated in the struggle for all citizens to join America's democracy. Wine wrote poems based on biblical verses and traditional folk tunes, and centered on issues of transcending oppression and persevering despite struggle and obstacles:

I got my hand on the gospel plow
Wouldn't take nothing for my journey now
Keep your eyes on the prize, hold on, hold on

Hold on, hold on
Keep your eyes on the prize, hold on, hold on

These lyrics were sung in South Carolina. They were sung in Mississippi by Freedom Riders from Jackson to Parchman, and then on to Albany. They were heard on the national stage when both Mahalia Jackson and Duke Ellington performed them in separate shows at the 1958 Newport Jazz Festival. Alice Wine's poetry would inspire those who continued to fight for justice in the years to come.

Her lyrics can also inspire us now, more than sixty years after their birth. Despite challenges and in the face of obstacles, we can stay focused. We can see a future that seems both far off and a part of our here and now. We can keep our eyes on the prize.

3

Plating a Full Plan

If you find yourself one weekend morning out to eat in London, or at the home of a culinarily inclined British friend, you could be squaring off against the full English breakfast. When you're confronted with a plate of delicacies warmed usually by way of the fryer, etiquette encourages consumption of the sausage links, smashed potatoes, eggs, mushrooms, tomato wedges, baked beans, bread, and black pudding. An indulgence to say the least, but the thing about this fry-up is that if you drop any two or three of the ingredients, you've lost the essence of the meal. It winds up just being meat and potatoes. Or eggs and toast. You've not had the complete experience. And the meal hasn't served its purpose, which is to make you full. Really full.

When we set out on a journey to accomplish something big, be it gastronomic or otherwise, the course we chart for ourselves is most effective if preparations are replete. Shipmasters don't cross the sea by just putting a pin in the map to mark where they want to end up. No, instead they take into account all the factors that impact their voyage, like speed, winds, currents, tides, water depth, hazards, and landmarks, all in advance of setting sail. Chefs don't conquer the behemoth task of plating the full English breakfast by simply laying a large serving dish on the counter. They do it by staging a mise en place that spans the full food pyramid. In the same way, we increase the odds of meeting our goal when we prepare for our journey in a full and complete way. We need to plan like we're settling in for the full English breakfast.

Marking the Destination

The first step in plating a full plan: Identify where you want to end up. Like those who spend their days in the kitchen or at sea, we too benefit by marking the destination before setting sail. Instead of a professionally printed menu hanging in the restaurant window or a tack on a nautical chart hanging behind the helm, identifying our own journey's end may take the form of something more common. For millions of people around the world, a variant of inspirational iconography does get placed in a prominent spot as they start off. In fact, this is exactly what one of the most popular self-help books of recent times—selling more than thirty million copies in fifty languages—advised we do when attempting to check off the items on our bucket list. It said: *Create vision boards.*

I'm sure you've seen one. There's a good chance you've made one. To craft a vision board, you compile a montage of visual icons, arranging the pictures like a page from a scrapbook. You choose images that depict how you want to look, what you want to achieve, or what success looks like to you—imagery that represents your loftiest dreams. And you hang it in a place where you see it every day.

Vision boards are incredibly popular, because people think they work. I recently surveyed nearly one thousand people from fifty-two different countries, ranging in age from sixteen to sixty-nine. Of these respondents, about half said they'd made a vision board themselves, and two-thirds said they knew a friend, colleague, family member, or acquaintance who had created one. Over 90 percent of survey respondents agreed that vision boards definitely, probably, or at least maybe help motivate and inspire people to figure out what goals are important to them in life. And over 90 percent said that they definitely, probably, or maybe help people complete a goal that's important to them. And if I'm being honest, my own photos folder on my phone sort of looks like a vision board, what with all the photos of me sitting behind the kit with Mattie at my feet holding a drumstick of his own, banging on the bass drum while wearing his polka-dotted headphones as oversized earplugs.

Celebrities spread the popular perception of vision boards. Famously, Ellen DeGeneres made it clear for months that she wanted to be on the cover of Oprah Winfrey's *O, The Oprah Magazine*. She created a vision board to remind herself and her audience of the goal. DeGeneres Photoshopped herself and Oprah into bikinis, with the two of them sitting on the beach and at the Playboy Mansion. She depicted herself and Oprah on Santa's lap holding a screaming child for what she imagined could be the Christmas edition. She placed herself between Oprah and the only other woman to ever have appeared on the cover of *O*, First Lady Michelle Obama. The dream was real, and so was the visual montage DeGeneres made of it.

Oprah caught wind of DeGeneres's fantasy and her mockups and said, "Ellen DeGeneres is a woman who can make things happen. When she decided she wanted to be on the cover of *O*, she pulled out all the stops. It worked—for only the second time in *O* history, this December, I'm sharing the cover with a woman I adore."

In 2016, TD Bank conducted a survey of five hundred small business owners, asking whether they use vision boards. Over three-quarters said that they think vision boards give their workforce an accurate sense of where the business aspires to be in five years. Within the group of respondents, millennials were the most likely to say they use vision boards. They have grown up in an era when people use visuals to tell the stories of their lives, and avail themselves of the digital and social media platforms at their disposal to do so. Nearly 60 percent said they'd used a vision board to decide whether to start their business, and almost 90 percent reported using them to develop business plans.

But is there really anything behind it? Well, the TD Bank survey found that those who used visuals when defining their business goals were almost twice as confident in their own ability to meet their goals than individuals who didn't use them.

Making vision boards can help us visualize where we want to be, and foster self-assurance that we can get there. Vision boards and other inspirational iconography strengthen our conviction in ourselves by formalizing our aspirations. They depict our hopes and dreams with concrete imagery. They are tools of materialization.

This process of materializing our goals applies to more than just financial decision-making, and can shed light on more than just the desired future growth of a company. It's a tool that we use quite often to our own advantage in many facets of life. We materialize when we write down our grocery list rather than rely on our memory of the contents of our fridge and pantry as we walk the aisles of the market. We're materializing when we create a list of chores our kids have to finish before they go out to play. We materialize when we leave a Post-it note affirmation on our mirror reminding us to be kind to ourselves, or to take out the garbage, metaphoric or literal. And the same goes for the checklist we create and cross off as we plan for a vacation or coordinate a team of coworkers at the office. Materializing can help us sidestep some of the common pitfalls that thwart our attempts to cross the finish line when racing toward our goals.

When I contemplated my musical journey from my place of total ineptitude to the one-hit wonder I hoped to become, my first thought was to cover the walls around the kit with pictures of legendary icons who had inspired generations. I hadn't ever been into showcasing my fan-girl status at any point in my life by covering my drywall in band posters or ticket stubs. But why not give it a shot now, I thought. So that poster of the rock band Rush my parents got my husband for Christmas a few years back found its way into a frame and onto the wall. As did a dozen or so other photographs of musicians Pete and I both liked, and a hundred or so ticket stubs from some of the greatest shows we'd seen.

Removing the Ambiguity from Our Aspirations

Unless we are Ellen DeGeneres and are friends with Oprah, to reach success we need to take another big step beyond materializing what it looks like with a vision board. Indeed, while the confidence this gave the small business owners in the TD Bank survey is great to have, the question really is whether confidence increases the likelihood of seeing results. Do vision boards help us find an actual path forward to accomplishing our goals? I wondered, *Would creating a wall of rock fame make a drummer out of me?*

Unfortunately, simply envisioning future success won't necessarily produce success, and creating images of ideal futures isn't usually enough to make our dreams come true. A study led by a colleague of mine at the time, Heather Barry Kappes, found out why. She asked people to think about what success would look like when they had achieved an important health goal. She measured the physiological changes that occurred in their bodies as they daydreamed, and found that heart rate and blood pressure dropped over the course of their visualization. Their bodies showed signs of giving up before they even really got started. They were responding as they would just before nodding off to sleep. When we contemplate how great it will feel to overcome some of our toughest challenges, like losing weight or finally getting that promotion, we are, in a very real sense, mentally savoring and vicariously experiencing success—and resting on our laurels. We grow sluggish even before we get off the starting blocks.

I experienced this myself. After tacking up those posters of rock drummers intended to inspire me, the next step I took was just to sit down and play. *Just do it,* I simplistically said in my own head. But I had fizzled fast, even before ever really catching fire.

I asked my husband if he would be my first (well, only) drum teacher. Pete was the natural choice for a few reasons, one of which was that he had taken a vow that, if memory serves, included the phrase "for better or worse." This would be a real test of his commitment.

He started my first lesson simply enough, with an explanation of the basics. Tuck your legs around the snare drum, he explained. Whack it on the upbeats, the second and fourth of each measure, to make a loud, sharp crack. Pull the hi-hat close enough to reach with your right arm crossed over your body. After a brief pause, I surmised he meant the pair of clapping cymbals to my left, mounted on a stand, like two flying saucers hovering in tandem. They were a complicated beast. With the strike of a drumstick, you can create a crisp crash. With a touch of the foot pedal under your left foot, you can close the cymbals, cutting off the metallic fizzle that would otherwise ring. And then there's the bass drum, also known as the kick drum. (One doesn't kick it directly, I learned the hard way, nearly falling off my seat in an early attempt.) It's the biggest one of the bunch, with enough surface area that it's often used for advertising purposes. For example, in case you happened to be at a Beatles show in 1964, but somehow in the moment forgot where you were, plastered on Ringo's drum was a British flag and the Fab Four logo. When you tap your right foot on the bass drum pedal, you get a strong thump that feels like the heartbeat of the song.

Then there are the optional accessories that build up and personalize any drum kit. Having no style, percussively or otherwise, of my own, I just used what Pete had already established. There was the ride cymbal on the right that you could use to drive the pulse forward with its punctuating *ting* every time the tip of the stick made contact. The splash and crash cymbals make a sound unironically mimicking their own names, to mark the beginning or the end of the chorus. The toms sat perched over the snare, a ring of drum heads and bodies of increasingly growing proportion off which a spirited drummer could roll down to the top of the beat. The rototoms off to the far left would remain an underappreciated trimming—like a green-leaf salad at Thanksgiving—because they were generally better for a Latin sound, and also too far away for me to reach.

Next, I took the sticks, but I soon realized I had options. The grip I used could be a traditional one, with the stick extending from my arm as if I were reaching out to shake hands while simultaneously holding a pencil. The grip could be French or German, depending on whether I felt like showcasing my palms. I opted against all of these. Instead, despite never having felt particularly nationalistic, I ended up using the American grip. With my hands assuming a 45-degree angle, I could use my wrists to get a powerful thwack, and my fingers to control what exactly got hit. There was the potential for a combination of both elegance and might—two qualities I had yet to demonstrate jointly or independently, on the drums or elsewhere.

After the drums and I had made each other's acquaintance, it was time for one of us to make the first move. Obviously, that was on me, not the drums, but I couldn't pull it together to get a sound out. I choked. I froze. I was overwhelmed by what the next steps would be, and I wasn't even sure where I wanted to end up. With the sticks still in my hands, having not yet hit a single head, I stared at Pete, got up, then walked away from the kit.

For me, what this first lesson made clear was that translating my dream into a reality was going to take more than just mentally Photoshopping my head onto Keith Moon's body and pinning that picture up on my imaginary wall of fame. Or ogling the drummer in that photograph of the sweaty Canadian rock band that I'd just pinned up at eye level. The vision board I had created by hanging that poster in a prime location was not a big enough step. But why?

There are two downsides of being a social psychologist. The first is that people don't know what that is, and assume I mean "clinical" psychologist when they ask at parties what I do. They instantly clam up or walk away out of fear that I can read their minds, or that I know how much they *really* don't like their mothers. I can't. And I don't. The second downside is that the tricks people try to play on themselves become easy to see through, and so are generally ineffective. So when I reflected on the flop of a first drum lesson I'd just experienced, I had some sense of why that was: I had been intentionally vague about what "learning to play one song on drums" really meant. I knew that I'd been trying to avoid accountability. I was just creating a loophole to give myself an out if I never really learned to play the song.

But being a social psychologist has at least one upside, too. I knew exactly what my own best advice to myself should be. I needed to define "success" concretely, and identify a definitive moment I could look back on and say *that* was when I knew I had done it. Which meant I needed other people to hear me. I needed an audience. I needed to count the number of people wearing shirts with my face on them. I decided to throw a party and invite all the neighbors. As a public proclamation of intention, I sent out invitations that heralded the main event: my drum solo. There would be no turning back.

I had met some of the people on the guest list before, but many of them were total strangers. Some had told me they had heard me practicing. None of them followed up with "and it sounded great!" Some weren't related to me in even the most remote of ways, and as a result bore no responsibility for making me feel good about myself. I knew one of them was a bass player and an original Deadhead. Another neighbor had dedicated a substantial portion of his living room to a permanent gig space in which friends could jam with him. Still another was a singer for a group that had required her to audition to join. These people were students of good music. They would be the real test of whether I had met my mark.

Removing the ambiguity of what qualifies as success, and clearly establishing when judgment day is, is an effective technique because it materializes what would otherwise be left vague. This is a lesson best exemplified by world-record-holding swimmer Gary Hall, who reached great acclaim by visualizing a concrete plan for success. In both 1969 and 1970, Hall was named Swimmer of the Year by *Swimming World* magazine. He was elected by all of the U.S. Olympic athletes to carry the American flag leading the Olympic team into the Opening Ceremonies in 1976 at Montreal, the only U.S. swimmer ever selected for that honor. But before all that, he was just another kid in the pool, practicing with a kickboard:

> *When I was 16 years old, training for my first Olympic games, my coach wrote all of my goal times down on the top of the kickboard I was using every day in practice. I couldn't escape them, but the result, after executing the plan, was that I made the Olympic team.*

The difference between Hall's kickboard and DeGeneres's vision board is the object of visualization. Hall and his coach didn't draw pictures of gold medals—well, at least not on his kickboard. They wrote down race times and splits. Hall and his coach materialized in a clear way where Hall wanted to be, but most important, they identified concrete action plans for growth. And pinned them down on a spot he would see every day in the pool.

Materializing a Concrete Plan of Action

Of course, there's more to Hall's remarkable success than a kickboard and a waterproof marker. He practiced, practiced, and practiced. Not haphazardly but intentionally, following a well-designed regimen that put that kickboard in his hands and line of sight often. The second step in plating a full plan: materialize a concrete plan of action. Inspiring real progress early on requires us to move beyond clearly identifying the destination. We must materialize *where* we want to be, of course—but also *how* we will get there.

There is reason to believe that literally seeing the particular steps Hall would have to take to get from the practice pool to the Olympic pool made a difference in his preparations. Shelley E. Taylor, a psychologist at UCLA, found that materializing the plan of action separates the metaphorical tadpoles from the sharks—the newbies from the pros. In the late 1990s, she and her team conducted an intervention with stressed-out college students prepping for their first midterm exam. The researchers contacted each student a week before the midterm and gave them specific instructions they expected would affect the student's performance. Based on chance alone, some students received instructions to materialize a plan of action. They were to visualize the concrete steps they would take to prepare for the exam in order to get the grade they hoped for. In addition to the hours they would commit to their review of course materials, they were told, it was also important to *see* themselves studying and to hold that picture in their mind. They were prompted to visualize themselves sitting at their desk or on their bed, studying the chapters and going over lecture notes. These students practiced this visualization technique each day leading up to the exam.

Other students received instructions to materialize the goal, much like people would do with a vision board. They conjured up the outcome to which they aspired, and imagined themselves getting a high grade. They were told to see themselves standing in front of the glass case where the midterm exam grades were posted, holding their breath, moving their gaze horizontally to find their score, finding out that they got the grade they wanted, beaming with joy, and feeling confident and proud. They also practiced this visualization each day leading up to the exam.

The night before the exam, the researchers called all the students. They asked them how many hours they had studied, when they had started studying, and the number of times they had reviewed each chapter and their lecture notes.

What Taylor and her colleagues found was that students who had materialized the plan of action reaped the biggest rewards. They started studying earlier and spent more hours preparing for the exam. They were more likely to do what was needed to meet their highest educational aspirations. And that translated into big outcomes. Students who had visualized the desirable outcome didn't do as well. Actually, they performed significantly *worse* than the class average. On the other hand, materializing the plan, compared to materializing just the hoped-for outcome, was the difference between passing and failing. It was that impactful. Even though all the students said they were quite motivated to study, the ones without a plan didn't actually do it. Visualizing academic success alone cranked them up, but failed to translate their desires into any sort of helpful action. The students who met their goal had turned it into a visualization that included the actionable steps separating where they were from where they wanted to be.

The same goes for inspiring voter turnout. The Center for Responsive Politics has estimated that candidates in the 2008 American presidential and congressional election spent a total of $5.3 billion, the costliest election up until that time. The hopes were, as they always are, that this was money well spent, that voters would show up at the polls. With the stakes so high, social scientists Todd Rogers and David Nickerson asked whether people follow through on their plans to vote, and what gets them into the polling stations. They followed almost 300,000 Pennsylvania residents through the end stages of the 2008 Democratic primary. The team called up one-third of them and delivered a typical get-out-the-vote script. Would-be voters were reminded that there was an election, encouraged to vote, and asked if they planned to. A second group heard the same script, but were also encouraged to talk about their concrete plans for the day of the primary. The researchers asked (1) when they would vote, (2) where they would be traveling from, and (3) what they would be doing before voting. The final group did not receive a phone call.

The researchers analyzed public voting records and found that about 43 percent of those who did not get a call voted in the election. But receiving the typical get-out-the-vote call increased voter turnout by 2 percentage points. Even more impressive, though, was that materializing a concrete plan of action upped voter turnout by more than 4 percentage points, compared to those who received no call. Adding those three simple questions to the phone call made a get-out-the-vote call more than twice as effective. Though 4 percent might not seem all that big a change, keep in mind that in the 2008 Democratic primary, Hillary Clinton's and Barack Obama's total popular votes were within less than 1 percent of each other.

Foreshadow Failure

So, we know that we are more likely to master life's to-do list when, in addition to visualizing what the moment of victory looks like, we materialize *what we need to do* to win. Effectively materializing our goals, though, requires that we push our preparatory visualization further. Because while visualizing the steps we must take to become our successful future selves produces benefits, the steps we choose might not always be the right ones. We might not fully know what to do to or how to do it. We'll likely stumble in trying to get to where we want to be. Materializing our way to the top involves accepting the possibility that we might make mistakes. The third step in plating a full plan: We must foreshadow failure.

Accepting the possibility, or even likelihood, of failure is becoming an embraced part of corporate culture worldwide. The Tata Group, a multinational holding company based in Mumbai, India, has a Dare to Try Award that recognizes audacious attempts at innovation that fail. Applications from employees grew over sevenfold within the first five years of the award's inception. Supercell (the gaming company behind the megahit *Clash of Clans*) cracks open a bottle of champagne every time a game fails. And Procter & Gamble confers its Heroic Failure Award each year. So does the Grey Advertising agency in New York. In 2010, for example, it created a commercial for E*TRADE in which a talking baby called Lindsay Lohan a "milkaholic." E*TRADE was slapped with a $100 million lawsuit by the actress, but the members of the creative team got their names engraved on the company trophy.

These aren't just cute gestures. They represent ways in which companies expect and embrace failure as a part of their overall strategy for success. When a corporate culture removes the stigma of flopping, it allows for employees and teams not only to fail faster but also to learn sooner. Discovery requires learning what does not work as much as what does.

Fostering an appreciation for mistakes—even major ones—is part of the reason why Google's X creates what others believe could only be moon shots. X is the secretive research and development facility founded in 2010 that has spearheaded inventions like driverless cars and contact lenses that monitor diabetes. At X, when a team kills its own project because members find a fatal flaw within it, their lemon is greeted with applause by peers and supervisors when presented at all-team meetings. As a part of the incentive structure, these groups are rewarded with bonuses, and some earn a few months of free time to work out what their next project will be. In fact, in a single year, X once killed more than a hundred ideas in which it had invested. This included one project that a team of thirty employees had been working on for two years.

What's effective about the corporate culture of X, Procter & Gamble, Grey Advertising, and Tata is not that they *plan* to fail. It's that they normalize failure. Their corporate culture anticipates the likelihood of failures and removes the shame of mistakes; as a result, teams can form contingency plans in advance of failure. When we allow ourselves to foreshadow failure, or communicate that it is acceptable for others to do so, we can anticipate the obstacles we may experience along the way and preemptively create a plan for attacking those problems head-on. If we were ever to find ourselves sinking in quicksand, running from killer bees, or standing eye-to-eye with a grizzly in the Canadian Rockies, we can probably all agree that that wouldn't be the optimal time to ping the Internet for escape solutions. Same with our goals. If we find ourselves thin on resources, short on time, troubled by a lack of progress, or stymied by the complexities of what we're working to accomplish, trying to troubleshoot solutions on the fly might not be the ideal approach. In other words, drowning in a sea of troubles is not the best time to begin searching for a life preserver. It's better if we already know where one is.

Consider the example of Charlie Munger. You might recognize him by name. You might know his backstory. But you may not know that he co-created the financial empire of Berkshire Hathaway by perfecting the art of finding faults in even the best-laid plans that he himself generated. He quite literally wrote the book on foreshadowing failure.

Munger is a college dropout. He went to school to study mathematics, found himself most passionate about physics, but left university before he completed a degree. After the outbreak of World War II, he served as a meteorologist in the U.S. Army. Following his military stint, he went on to study law. And did a pretty great job at it. Without having completed his undergraduate education, he found his way into Harvard Law School, no less, and graduated magna cum laude. His legacy is not in the sciences or legal studies, but in finance—though he has never taken a course in business, economics, or accounting. We might be more familiar with his friend and business partner, Warren Buffett, a frequent rival for, if not holder of, the "richest man in the world" title. As of 2018, Berkshire Hathaway, the holding company for which Munger has served as vice chairman for multiple decades, was tied with Apple as *Forbes* magazine's top-listed company in the United States based on revenues, profits, assets, and market valuations. In the last thirty years, with Buffett and Munger leading the charge, Berkshire's share price has risen by more than 4,000 percent, outperforming the S&P 500 Index six times over across that same time frame. And that's not counting dividends.

Warren Buffett gets written about a lot. We read stories about his Giving Pledge, which encourages billionaires all around the world to give away at least half of their wealth, and to do it before they die. (He's well on his way to meeting his commitment to give away 99 percent of his own worth.) Buffett lives in a modest ranch-style home in Omaha, Nebraska (incidentally, a couple of miles away from where I grew up). He eats a McDonald's breakfast every morning that costs less than a latte at Starbucks. And he bought the local ice-cream shop that was going bankrupt because that's where he likes to take Bill Gates when he comes to visit.

But Charlie Munger gets less attention. Why is that? Well, of his own accord, he stays in the shadows more than Buffett does. His most common response to questions asked generally of the chairman sitting on his right during the company's yearly shareholder meeting is "I have nothing to add."

But Munger's words elsewhere offer tremendous value. People want to know how he came to amass such an incredible fortune and to co-create one of the most lucrative companies in the world, despite no formal training in business. Munger was basically self-taught. He recalls that in his early years as a lawyer, he decided to invest in himself. Back then, Munger charged clients twenty dollars an hour, and decided that he could afford one hour of his own time each day. He spent that hour reading a lot from everywhere. And what this process brought him, he has said, is not the genius so many people ascribe to him, but instead an understanding of just how much more he needed to learn. In an interview with the *Wall Street Journal* reporter Jason Zweig, Munger said, "Knowing what you don't know is more useful than being brilliant."

Munger claims that throughout his life he has *not* tried to be smart. Working toward that goal proves more challenging than it's worth, he explains. Instead, he worked to uncover the flaws in his own thinking. "I am very interested in the subject of human misjudgment. Lord knows I've created a good bit of it. But I don't believe I've created my full statistical share. And I think that one of the reasons was that I tried to do something about the terrible ignorance I left the Harvard Law School with."

Across the decades, Munger accumulated knowledge and wisdom from what he read, people he met, what he saw happen in the markets, what he saw happen with his own investments, and what others taught him. He read historical records of the organizational dynamics and process that created the U.S. Constitution to understand how the Founding Fathers agreed on the principles of our system of government. He conducted case studies of the communication strategies used by the CEOs of the most lucrative oil refineries. He studied the motivational principles of Alcoholics Anonymous, airline pilot training, and clinical instruction in medical schools. He noticed patterns of rationality and irrationality in people's judgments that contributed to their success and failure across all facets of life. He took this information and created a system of behavioral economics even before the field existed as an academic discipline.

In 1995, Munger delivered a speech at Harvard University. The lecture hall was packed far beyond capacity. This was as close to a financial genius as many attendees had ever been. In his remarks, for the first time ever, Munger formally articulated what went on in his head as he made some of the biggest decisions of Berkshire Hathaway's history. It all boils down to a checklist that he created to help him foreshadow failure.

Munger described how he puts his tentative plans on the metaphorical hot seat. He spins a plan around, turns it over, and investigates it from all angles. He looks for its weaknesses and shortcomings, and tries to determine how the plan won't work. He also recognizes that his own ability to detect the possible shortcomings is suspect. To overcome this inability to objectively assess a plan he created, Munger formally tests it against what he has determined are the twenty-four standard causes of human misjudgment. His checklist. He explained, for example, that psychological denial affects people's ability to judge the credibility of a source of information. He noted that people's drive to do something, rather than do nothing, leads to rash decisions that ultimately prove to be wrong. He explained how the connections and associations people hold in their minds, the over-optimism they can't let go of, and the need to reciprocate impact the efficacy of the choices they make.

The Harvard audience sat riveted in silence for over sixty minutes, except for the occasional chuckle at the quips that lightened Munger's delivery. At the end of his oration, Munger opened the floor up to questions. The very first remark from the first person up to the microphone was "Will we be able to get a copy of that list of twenty-four?" To which Munger replied, "Yes. I presumed there would be one curious man" (I'm sure he meant to add "or woman").

What Munger did in that seminal lecture at Harvard was formally articulate the collected knowledge that emanated from his decades of study. And after presenting that first checklist, Munger went on to put pen to paper in *Poor Charlie's Almanack*, a book he coauthored, condensing his list of cognitive biases into a ten-point guide. In both accounts, Munger took the component parts of those theories of human behavior that had been brewing in his brain for the extent of his career and crafted a concrete product—something real and tangible. He created a visual manifestation of his set of cognitive biases, organized as the checklist against which he evaluates his own plans.

———

Despite the fact that he is the most decorated Olympian of all time, Michael Phelps is—just as Munger could also be described—a doomsayer of sorts. He foreshadows failure as a part of his routine. Back in Beijing in 2008, Phelps was on the doorstep of making history. In that year's games, he had won seven gold medals. Only the 200-fly sat between him and winning more gold, which would make him more decorated in a single Olympic Games than anyone else in history. But right as he dived in for the start of this race, his goggles started leaking. By the 150-meter mark, they were almost completely full of water and he couldn't see. But he didn't panic. He was prepared for this incident because he had long made it a habit to visually simulate all obstacles he might encounter. He materializes each possible failure, crafting a vivid, concrete, and tangible image in his mind of how his plan might go wrong. Then he takes it a step further and devises the solution. In this case, he calmly switched his concentration to his stroke count—which he could do because he knew exactly how many strokes would get him across the pool as fast and efficiently as possible. As a result of practicing the art of visualizing success *and* troubleshooting solutions to major obstacles, he knew exactly what he needed to do when disaster struck at those Olympic Games—and did it to win his eighth gold medal. Eventually, he'd have fifteen more.

Materializing obstacles and solutions benefits not only elite athletes. Scientists have found that people who incorporate this tactic into their daily routine accomplish more of what they set out to do. A team of psychologists from the University of Chicago and the University of Cologne set up 110 adults' smartphones to ping them four times a day for one week. Each time, respondents jotted down a description of one thing they wanted to get done that day. About a third of the time, it was something that would be fun, like reading a book. A quarter of the time, the goal involved school or work. Another quarter of the time, it involved health and fitness. Other times, the goal was aimed at relationships, managing finances, spiritual health, activism, or other pursuits. Sometimes, they were asked to think about what might make it difficult to achieve a goal, and how they might overcome those challenges. In other words, they were prompted to anticipate obstacles and foreshadow the solutions. At night they noted whether they had met the goals they mentioned pursuing throughout the day and how happy they felt. Other times, they listed a goal they were working on, but they received no follow-up prompts to help plan its pursuit.

When the goals were difficult to meet, considering the challenges and planning solutions preemptively led to over 50 percent more progress on those specific goals. This was in comparison to the progress made on stated goals for which no planning prompts followed. Moreover, when they had anticipated the challenges and solutions, participants reported feeling much happier that day. Materializing the hurdles and planning how to handle them improved productivity and mood.

Our brains actually respond to events differently when we foreshadow failure, as Michael Phelps did. Inge Gallo, a researcher at the University of Konstanz in Germany, investigated why some people can overcome their fears and others can't, even when they all want to and are trying to. In this study, she focused on fear of spiders. Arachnophobes were shown a series of photographs that included some pleasant items, like delicious-looking food, and some mundane items, such as a telephone. The occasional photograph of a spider was thrown into the mix. Some participants adopted a simple strategy to cope with these images. They just reminded themselves of their goal: "I will not get frightened." Another group took it a step further. They stated their goal to not get frightened but also acknowledged the difficulty of this aim, and made a plan for what to do when they did see one of the forbidding images. In this case, the plan was as basic as "I'll ignore it." It seems like the slightest change and only a minor addition, but it had a big impact.

The participants who anticipated the challenge and planned for how they would handle it didn't have nearly as bad an experience. We know this because Gallo used electroencephalographic recording—caps with electrodes—to study what went on inside the participants' brains when they viewed the photographs. She measured the electrical signals sent from the visual cortex, the part of the brain that specializes in processing information we take in through our eyes. Her investigation found that volunteers who simply formed the goal to withhold fear displayed brain activity that looked just like that of the subjects who viewed the pictures without establishing any kind of goal at all. On the other hand, those subjects who had visualized a concrete plan *and* foreshadowed failure showed less activity in the visual cortex within one tenth of a second of seeing a spider. In other words, planning for how to react led to a sort of adaptive blindness. The visual cortex of their brains responded as if the spider wasn't even really there, like they didn't really see it. As a consequence, the participants didn't feel as scared when they came upon one.

Materializing the goal coupled with the plan of action and contingencies can also help people avoid slipping back after achieving success. Traci Mann, a research psychologist at the University of Minnesota, conducted a meta-analysis asking whether diets are effective in the long run. She reviewed the results of over thirty separate diet studies—twenty years of data—and asked: Of the dieters who had met their target weight, how many had kept the weight off five years later? Unfortunately, for every one person who met their weight-loss goal, two others gained back more weight than they had originally lost. Her conclusion: Diets—and, in particular, having achieved success in dieting—can backfire.

This makes sense in the context of what we just learned about visualization and motivation. Meeting a weight-loss goal can feel like a major achievement. And it is. But the goal is never really fully accomplished, because maintaining an ideal weight requires sustained effort. Preserving a healthy credit rating requires routine monitoring of bills and finances. Keeping a steady beat requires routine practice at the drums, which is why I sounded as unsteady as the snores coming from the guy just on the verge of falling asleep next to you on the plane: sporadic, and maddeningly so.

The three-step process of materializing can sustain progress, even after initial success. Researchers from the University of Zurich looked at weight gain on an ongoing, week-by-week basis. They found that dieters who met their mark one week felt like they had earned a treat or could, in a sense, ease off the pressure during the next week. And when they did that, they gained back the weight they had lost the week before.

Not everyone saw their progress slip away. Some dieters reported engaging in the three-step process of materializing. They took time to consider how they'd met their goal, what they'd overcome to lose the weight, and how they'd mastered those challenges. And those people generally kept the pounds off the week after they lost them.

Chocks Away

Before takeoff, British airmen during World War II would check that the compass and altimeter were set, flaps up, bomb door closed, oil pressure at the right level, intercom working, radio functioning, bombs unfused, windows clean, and all instruments functioning, among a few dozen other things. Anything missed could mean disaster. But when all checks were complete and everything was in order, a pilot could run the engines up and then signal to the ground crew "chocks away." The crew would remove the blocks around the wheels before the pilot taxied to the runway.

Many of the goals we set require steps that are likely not a matter of life or death, as the procedures were for the wartime pilots before they set off. But they may still be just as important to our health, happiness, and well-being. Before we take off on our own adventures in goal pursuit, it's clearly advantageous to run through our own checks to ensure we've set ourselves up for success.

Foreshadowing failure comes pretty naturally to me. When I'm working on big projects or planning something major in my life, I chronically think about the ways things could go wrong. I end up spending more time than I'd like to admit preparing for these worst-case scenarios. Applying this talent, if you could call it that, to figuring out what aspects of my practice regimen might complicate my progress was easy. My work responsibilities would surely curtail my practice time. Mattie's need for naps—some of the only "me time" I could count on—meant that I would not be able to practice when my hands were, literally, free. Nearby neighbors on the other side of thin walls were—at best—uninterested in monitoring my progress.

Simultaneous with my issues of finding the time and soundproof space to practice, Pete and I were also trying to troubleshoot a few other predicaments. All of our ears needed a break from the construction noise and sirens in Manhattan, and we wanted Mattie to be able to sniff the flowers without meeting one of New York City's resident rats eye-to-eye. They seemed to be just as frequent visitors to our nearest playground as were we. In addition, on one previous visit out to the country, we had talked to Mattie about what farmers can plant in a garden. "Cheese," he emphatically insisted, time and time again upon inquiry, which only reconfirmed our belief that all of us needed to get back to the land.

The solution we conjured killed all these proverbial birds with one rural stone. We had access to a family home in Connecticut, and so we doubled down on our regular sojourns. We jumped on a train out of New York on Friday evenings and came back to the city Sunday nights. On each whirlwind visit to the country, we spent time finding cows on the nearby farms, and trying to explain the origin of milk and its creative potential. And for a couple of hours over the course of each weekend, while Pete had Mattie out and about, I was able to get in a practice session or two without neighbors banging on the walls for silence.

To the best of my ability, I had materialized the goal I was aspiring to achieve. The invitations in the mail and now taped to my fridge door were a pestering reminder of the goal I had set. And I had concretely mapped out my route for getting there. I had considered the obstacles that could come my way—chief among them the problem of finding time and space to practice—and designed a plan for circumventing them. Chocks away!

4

Becoming Your Own Accountant

One night, Pete put a surprise date on the calendar for us. For such evenings, he usually gave me a time to show up, a location to meet at, and the type of shoes to wear. That night, it was the Blue Note jazz club around the corner from our apartment, to hear McCoy Tyner with his combo. It was one of the first times we left Mattie with a babysitter he didn't know. The taste of freedom for those few hours was delicious. The club was packed, but we still got a table right behind the grand piano with a perfect view of Tyner's hands as they filled the club with those complex and luscious chords. But as legendary as those sounds were, it was the drummer who caught our ear that night.

Francisco Mela was behind the kit. He was forty-nine years old, and with his fedora cocked just off to the side of his head, he looked like the baby of the group. But his appearance was irrelevant just as soon as he laid down the beat. His drive electrified the room. His hands moved so fast that all we could see were blurred sticks and the shimmer of quivering cymbals. His energy was addictive. This drummer knew what to do.

After the set, Pete and I found Mela backstage. That's not hard to do. "Backstage" is really just a space off the restrooms for club patrons. I asked what had kept him interested in practicing when he was just getting started. He told me, "Ah yes, yes. To leave Cuba. Only the best got out. I had to be the best. I had to."

Mela was born in Bayamo. And a quick look at history would tell you that growing up there at that time was rough. In Cuba, the ration book for 1968, the year of his birth, for example, allowed each person to buy two shirts and two pairs of shoes a year, three pounds of rice and twenty cans of evaporated milk a month, three-quarters of a pound of meat and three ounces of coffee a week, and a liter of fresh milk a day for each child. Chicken was scarce on the island. The wait, if you wanted to buy new tires for your car, had been as long as a year, and spare parts were available only through the black market.

The embargoes led by the United States hit musicians hard too. As a form of retaliation, Castro seized control of Cuban recording studios that were owned by American companies. RCA, for one, then refused to pay Cuban musicians for their performances, or to turn over the royalties they deserved for their published work. Musicians who defected from the country were dubbed *gusanos* (worms), and the Castro government banned their music or any rising musician's formal study of it. This was the Cuba that Francisco Mela grew up in.

Mela was determined to be the best, and he got there through practice. Lots and lots of practice. When the opportunity came, he left. He started first by playing in Mexico, then moved on to Boston, earning a degree at Berklee College of Music, one of the nation's top conservatories. The faculty recognized Mela's incredible perseverance and talent. They hired their new grad to teach during the day, and gave him the time to play at Wally's Café Jazz Club at night. In those first few years, Mela was honing his own sound, blending modern jazz with the traditional music he'd grown up with in Cuba. Soon he released his own debut album, which *The Village Voice* called the best album of the year. Then he joined up with the world-

renowned saxophonist Joe Lovano and recorded an album that aficionados considered Lovano's most adventurous to date. For that
album the band, including Mela, received a Grammy Award nomi-
nation. Then McCoy Tyner snapped him up. Today Mela is one of
the most important Cuban drummers in jazz, according to *Jazz-
Times* magazine.

It wasn't the family business. It wasn't luck. It wasn't being born
at the right place at the right time, because Cuba then wasn't. Mela
made it, and made it big, through sheer force of practice. Despite the
political odds and societal difficulties, he aspired to find an audience
outside a country that did not want its people to leave. To be the best
in Cuba, he dedicated himself to working up his chops. Mela spent
hours practicing solo, rehearsing with bandmates, and performing
live. Every day.

I'm not Cuban, but part of Mela's story resonated with me. I
wasn't going to become a rocker (or a pastry chef, or an at-home
barista capable of making a coffee that didn't taste like dirty water,
or any of my other aspirational conquests) by dabbling in the art
once every few months. Watching Mela that night hammered home
for me that the thrill of making it would require consistent and frequent effort.

I was self-aware enough to understand that moving my kit to
Connecticut (to protect myself from noise complaints) was not going
to create a routine or make drum practice a real habit. I wasn't finding myself sitting in front of the kit often enough. I needed to take
my efforts to another level.

I came to this realization at about the same time I met up with a
longtime friend. Giorgio Piccoli is an accomplished entrepreneur
and a master of habit. At twenty-seven years old, he created Americanflat, a curated gallery of museum-quality art collected from more
than two hundred artists it represents all over the world, marketed
to "art lovers, not investors" just starting to cover their walls. It established global on-demand printing capabilities in all countries in
which it operates. Within seven years, Americanflat did $20 million

in sales, in all continents but Antarctica, and proceeds of every sale are returned directly to the artists to support their craft.

At one point in our conversation, Piccoli pulled out his phone and on it I saw something unusual. It was his list of lists. Every day, for almost five years now, he had been making a list of ten things. Anything. He makes lists of ten ways to improve the experience of flying for people in wheelchairs, ten things people don't like about picture frames, ten ways to grow basil. On one list he shared with me, I saw ten proposed business partnerships that resembled a game of celebrity hookup. What if Google and Amazon had a baby? What if Rosetta Stone and Lonely Planet got together? Could Instagram and GoPro revolutionize live streaming?

Piccoli was scrolling through his notes when he offered a quick example of how he finds inspiration. "We're at Rosemary's Restaurant, Emily, and you wanted a cocktail with rosemary but didn't see one. If I was doing my list thing now, I'd write down ten menu items with rosemary they could add." I asked him if these lists ever turned lucrative. Had they become the basis for some business venture? "Sometimes, yeah," he said, "but more often than not, no." Despite the lack of fiscal outgrowth from his habit, Piccoli says, they are a workout for his brain. He practices creative problem-solving and delving into new mental territory with each attempt. As he explained, I interrupted: "You've done this every day? That's more than, like, eighteen hundred lists! That's more than eighteen thousand things," I said, astounded both that he'd stuck with it for so long and that I'd done that kind of math in my head after a glass of wine on a very empty stomach. "If most of the items on those lists aren't going to be the next big thing, do you have to write them down?" "Oh yeah," he said incredulously. "You *have* to write them down."

That the written form is obligatory seemed so evident to him, but so dispensable to me at the moment. I have never been one to make to-do lists. The few times I've tried, crossing things off when I completed them didn't rev me up. I put *make to-do list* on my to-do list, and crossed that off too. Didn't do it for me either. My nonplussed reaction aside, plenty of other people feel empowered when they chronicle their responsibilities in this way. Maybe I was missing something of value in this organizational exercise.

Indeed I was.

Anecdotally, Piccoli's daily lists reminded me of the only thing I ever tried to do daily in my life (except for showering, brushing my teeth, and flossing): practicing my saxophone. Back in grade school, I had made it a routine to practice nearly every day. How did I make that happen?

Rather than digging through my own memory vault, I called up my high school assistant band director. It had been twenty years—I knew because the reunion planning committee's announcements were becoming a reminder of just how long it had been, and just how old I'd gotten. Would Bob Patterson even remember me?

He did. And the conversation was a great skip down memory lane. We talked about state marching band competitions and the perennial rival we could never quite topple, and reminisced about how bad the bus smelled on long road trips. After a while, I asked him how he got kids into a routine of practicing every day, or as close to that as possible. He reminded me of the time sheets we, the sprouting virtuosos, had filled out and turned in each week at our music lessons. We wrote down on a quarter sheet of paper how many minutes we practiced each day. I thought those weekly journals were for me, as a student, to prove to him, the teacher, that I had done the homework. Not so, he told me. It was really for the parents.

The power of materializing, here, came from keeping that now-old-fashioned handwritten time sheet. With this weekly review, parents verified and signed off on their children's practice sessions before those reports were turned in to teachers. This visual aid told parents if and when they'd carved out time in their family's schedule for their children's practice, and how often or how infrequently that goal of daily practice had been met. By writing it down, parents could visually take stock of how each week went and whether the goal was met, making them accountable not only to the band's director but also to their children and themselves.

I was far from a high school teenager anymore—the wrinkles on my face gave that fact away. But back then I'd been a pretty good sax player, and my teachers' scheme for increasing the number of practice sessions was likely a part of the recipe for musical success. I decided to sample that strategy again—with the added adaptation of my mother's approach to getting me to do chores as a child. Every time I carved out time to practice, I gave myself a gold star. I took one of those free calendars that come in the mail around the time nonprofits are soliciting year-end donations, and I slapped a sticker on each day to commemorate my scheduling victory. *Found a chunk of time to practice drums? Way to go, me! Give myself a sticker.*

The technique that school music teachers use to motivate budding instrumentalists, and what I was doing with my gold stars when returning to the craft, share commonalities with other practices like journals, diaries, logs, lists, and report cards. They make what we're doing concrete and apparent, and create a visual manifestation of our otherwise haphazard pursuits. Notating our personal data makes us responsible to ourselves and our aspirations. By materializing our progress, we become our own accountant.

Automating the Accounting

Even economists at times need help with accounting, or at least this form of it. About ten years after he earned his degree in economics from Yale, Mike Lee was planning his wedding. He and his fiancée set their sights on a beautiful beach celebration, and both felt that being in better shape would complete their picture-perfect day. Lee went to a trainer, who handed him a book listing the nutritional values of about three thousand foods and a small pad of paper to write down what he ate each day. Perhaps this trainer had followed the scientific breakthroughs made by a team at the Kaiser Permanente Center for Health Research. Doctors recommended to a group of 1,700 individuals at risk for or experiencing diabetes and hypertension to follow a diet rich in fruits and vegetables and low-fat dairy products. The subjects exercised as prescribed, pushing themselves to moderate levels of exertion for at least thirty minutes a day. After six months, the average person had lost about thirteen pounds. A pretty remarkable feat. But those who also kept daily records of how much food they ate lost *twice as much* weight as those who kept no records. To Lee, though, the effort required to look up food values and do the math to determine the caloric value of what he was eating seemed tedious and impractical. So he did it one better. He created a Web application that would allow him to track his calories automatically online. This was the beginning of the wildly popular app MyFitnessPal.

Drawing from the largest nutrition database in existence, MyFitnessPal allows users to create an electronic food journal. By its ninth birthday, MyFitnessPal had amassed more than 80 million registered users who, combined, had lost more than 100 million pounds. In 2015, Under Armour purchased MyFitnessPal for $475 million. In the next three years, membership grew to 150 million in what Under Armour described as the "largest digital health and fitness community in the world."

And, from what I read, Lee and his wife had a pretty great wedding.

Unfortunately, just like the organizational state of the toys in my bedroom growing up could illustrate, my gold-star system wasn't working as well as desired. But I didn't think that somehow devising a more technologically sophisticated star system (à la MyFitnessPal) was the answer. With the flip of a page from one month to the next, the ratio of days to stickers grew. The stars weren't sustaining the motivation, and to be honest I had no idea whether I was getting any better on the drums. The key to practicing more often and more effectively, I was realizing, was not just in materializing whether an effort was made that day. There was more to the secret recipe than that—but what was the special ingredient?

Nathan DeWall is particularly remarkable at materializing his way to success. He started training for his first marathon when he was four years old. His father planned to run one in Sioux Falls, South Dakota, later that year, and DeWall wanted to follow in his footsteps, literally and figuratively. His dad got him his first pair of running shoes and a green T-shirt imprinted with the word JOCK. They ran together for two- and three-mile stretches at a time, talking about life, and likely about *Sesame Street*, with each passing stride. Of course, DeWall didn't actually run a marathon as a child, but the itch started then.

By the time he hit middle school, DeWall had switched out his sneakers for cleats. Like many boys growing up in Nebraska, he decided that he wanted to be a football player, an All-American on the university team like one of his uncles had been. A few years in, DeWall was on his way, playing on his high school football team. But that dream quickly turned into a nightmare. In one game, DeWall cracked a vertebra in his neck. The paralysis was instant and fierce. For forty-five minutes, DeWall couldn't feel or move any part of his body below his neck. He was certain he would be in a wheelchair the rest of his life.

Thankfully, he recovered. But his athletic aspirations took a back seat to more creative, mental, and artistic ones thereafter. At Saint Olaf College in Minnesota, he was accepted into the choir, the top a capella ensemble in the United States. Later, while working on his PhD, he focused on scientific writing. By the time he got his first job as a university psychology professor, he had published more articles than most people with twice his experience in the field. By all accounts, DeWall was well under way, charting his new career. Each aspect of his life seemed to be going well. Every goal he set out to accomplish, he did.

One day, for no reason other than to be supportive, he joined his wife, Alice, on a visit to a weight-loss clinic. Sitting in a private room with his wife, a nurse, a scale, and a chart, he started thinking about his own health profile. The nurse said, "Nathan, do you want get on the scale?" "Sure," he said. He stepped on. The nurse looked at the numbers, then at the chart, then at him. "Well, you're obese." "No, I'm tall," DeWall replied. "How tall?" the nurse asked. "Six feet, two inches." The nurse put her finger on the chart at the mark for his height. She slid it over to DeWall's weight and replied, "You're tall. And obese."

Before that day, DeWall had not thought of himself as over-weight or even out of shape. But seeing where he placed on that chart shook him, and awoke a determination to lose the pounds. A new goal took hold.

He started to walk. He was mindful about his eating, following the mantra "If I bite it, I write it," and he kept food logs. A few months later, Alice said she was going out for a run and asked him to join her. He said he couldn't because of his bad knees. She called him on the excuse, reminding him he'd never had bad knees, and they likely hadn't turned bad that very day. He laced up his shoes and joined her for a two-mile run. Three-quarters of the way through, Alice turned to DeWall and said, "What's the matter with you? You look and sound like you're about to die." "Thank you," DeWall replied sarcastically.

But within a year, running from his house to the gas station was no longer a near-death experience. DeWall ran his first fifty-mile ultramarathon in Missouri less than twelve months into his new lifestyle. It was rough, he acknowledges. Counterintuitively, he gained ten pounds training for the race. After crossing the finish line, he looked down. His feet had swollen so much that his ankles had disappeared. From the waist down, he looked pregnant. But he kept at his running, learning the chemistry of his own body and how to balance the calories he ate versus what he burned off.

Four months later, DeWall ran his first 100-mile race. Soon after that, he ran another. And another. He ran 75 miles from Lexington to Lousiville. Then he ran 378 miles from the northern end of North Carolina to the southernmost tip. On foot, DeWall crossed the state of Tennessee in six days, running 314 miles. Nonstop. I asked him, "What does 'nonstop' even mean, Nathan?" He explained that in the first twenty-four hours, he ran 77 miles. Then he lay down on the side of the road and slept for two hours, before getting up and running another 60 miles. He found a hotel and slept for three hours in a bed. Left. And ran another 50 miles. "You get the picture," he said. *No. No I do not,* I thought to myself.

"How do you eat?" I asked, my jaw hanging down in amazement. He explained that it's really about managing salt. Especially in Tennessee, where the humidity hovers near rain-forest levels, runners sweat out the salt that they need to make their muscles function properly. And after the first twenty-something miles, a runner's body has used up all the calories it could have stored from any meals before. "Pop-Tarts are gold. I love Pop-Tarts," DeWall proclaimed. Gatorade, instant mashed potatoes, peanut butter and honey sandwiches, beef jerky, and nineteen Red Bulls were his other answers. Basically, the diet of a teenager who didn't pass health class.

It wasn't his on-the-road diet DeWall was most proud of, though. It was what he accomplished in the spring of 2017. Within a span of three months, he completed two of the hardest ultramarathons in the world.

In April, DeWall ran 147 miles (the equivalent of five and a half marathons) in six days across the sand dunes of the Sahara in the Marathon Des Sables, where midday temperatures top out at 130 degrees Fahrenheit. Feet swell so much that runners have to train wearing shoes that are several sizes too big. The heat, the distance, and the friction of the sand break down the rubber on their soles. DeWall figured out that if he started each day complaining to the staff doctors of shoulder pain, he could receive enough extra medical tape to repurpose for covering the mesh on his shoes, to keep them from filling with sand. He ran carrying on his back his sleeping bag and all the calories he needed for the race. You poop in a plastic bag. There are snakes. And runners carry their own venom pump to combat nips from scorpions. The upside of running in a desert, you wonder? You won't get bitten by mosquitoes. It's too hot for bugs to live.

Only three months later, when July hit, DeWall flew over to California for the Badwater 135. He heard the starting pistol at 9:30 p.m. in Death Valley, the point of the lowest elevation in North America and the hottest temperatures. He described the 117-degree thermometer reading as "cool; it was nice." He ran the first leg of the race in forty-eight hours, without stopping for a rest. He wore a reflective neon waistband so drivers could see him running alone on the roads in the middle of the night. The race traversed three mountain ranges and, true to its name, covered 135 miles, ending at the trailhead for Mount Whitney, 8,300 feet above sea level. Runners climb almost 15,000 feet cumulatively and descend over 6,000 feet. A hundred and ninety-six people ran the race. You have to be invited to even try.

How did DeWall transform himself? Of course, the ways are many. He is remarkably regimented and scheduled, as you might expect of someone who has accomplished—repeatedly—such incredibly difficult feats. Take, for example, the pair of sneakers he was wearing when we chatted. They had the number *10* written in Sharpie on their sides. "I need to keep track of which ones I'm wearing. I bought a lot of the same type of shoe. I stick with what I like."

As a scientist, he naturally gravitates to numbers, but his interest in data is not unique among athletes of this caliber. DeWall tracks his life electronically. One of his online apps tells him how much he runs. He clocks seventy minutes of easy running every day when he's in between training cycles, and hits the pavement six days a week regardless of what race he's just finished or what is coming next. He told me, "I would be sad if I didn't run at least two thousand miles a year." It was three-quarters of the way through this one, and he'd already hit 2,055. "Sometimes I wonder whether I'll learn to live without the pretty graphs that chart my progress. I doubt it. Plus, who wants to live like that?" he emphatically proclaimed. "Before a big race, I often go back through my visual training logs to assure myself that I've done the necessary work to achieve my goal. Before running the Badwater 135 ultramarathon, I looked at my Strava data to remind myself that my training had included running five marathons in five days. Those visuals built my confidence and helped me accomplish my goal of finishing the world's toughest footrace."

Of course, DeWall is a great storyteller, and the details of those competition memories are far from lost to him. But he does not rely on his memory. Instead, DeWall psychs himself up by visualizing how he has prepared. For him to feel self-assured, he needs to see it for himself.

And this is the difference between my gold-star system and the process by which Lee built a fitness empire and DeWall crossed two deserts on foot. We all collected data on ourselves but, importantly, those guys went on to reflect upon their visual logs. They reviewed where they had started and where they were currently, to ignite some motivational fires. They materialized their actions to bring about a better understanding of their own progress.

Materializing progress can also bring awareness to where we have fallen short. Just as creating and routinely reviewing a log that materializes what we put on our plates can curb mindless snacking and overindulgence, materializing what we've spent our money on can prevent excessive purchasing from eating away at our wallets.

Consider the fact that the rate of Americans filing Chapter 7 bankruptcies each year steadily increases. In 2007, less than half a million Americans filed with the courts to liquidate their assets in order to pay their debts; by 2010, that number had more than doubled. As of September 2018, total American household indebtedness stood at $13.51 trillion. One big reason was credit-card purchases. At about the same time, Americans held just shy of half a billion accounts with credit-card companies. And they use those cards.

Numbers released from the Federal Reserve show that the outstanding debt that credit-card holders carry from one month to the next—balances that they can't pay off—is on average $9,333.

The ease of swiping a credit card was part of the reason that Carrie Smith Nicholson, a thirty-five-year-old former small business accountant with an inspirational story, found herself in a financial predicament she'd never expected. Recently divorced and now flying solo fiscally, Nicholson was saddled with credit-card and auto-loan debts that amounted to a third of her salary at the time. "It was not exactly what I pictured for myself at twenty-five years old," she says.

But, once she'd set her sights on financial freedom, Nicholson paid off her $14,000 debt entirely in fourteen months. How? She, too, turned to tools that materialized her expenditures. Nicholson used an online payment-plan calculator called ReadyForZero. This web app creates a timeline and displays a chart of past progress and a balance that moves closer and closer to zero. It showed her credit score as it increased along the spectrum from red to green. Creating a plan to attack the balance and using a tool that helped her to visualize her progress enabled Nicholson to do what so many people struggle to accomplish. She parlayed her experience and knowledge into entrepreneurship, creating an online community in which she curated information aimed at improving fiscal health, writing for media outlets with international reach, advising clients connected to major banks, and inspiring others' sense of personal financial efficacy through her own story of success.

The visual log of monetary flow brought Nicholson awareness of where the leaks were each month, and what expenses could be curbed. The same applies to time. Struggling with procrastination or a lack of productivity? Taking a few days to record how you *actually* spend your time during the day can bring insight into where the hours go.

Dan Ariely is a behavioral economist who specializes in understanding our errors in judgment. In 2014, he partnered with a tech entrepreneur and a data scientist to create an app called Timeful, an artificial-intelligence system capable of discovering when users are most productive, finding windows of time to complete tasks, and suggesting a schedule that could get the job done. The more you use it, the smarter the app gets at finding lost time. A year after launch, Google acquired the app and has integrated it into its products as a feature called Goals.

Fittingly, Goals invites you to create a goal—for example, to meditate, drink more water, or write a book—and asks you how much time you want to spend on that goal, and when you think the best time of day would be to do it. The app then automatically schedules time for it and puts it on your online calendar, based on an algorithm that predicts when you're most likely to do it. If a conflict comes up, the app can also reschedule that "session." It follows up by asking how you did during the goal-allotted time, and your response teaches the app whether it made a good choice for when to squeeze it into your schedule. If you tell it enough times that you didn't bliss out, hydrate, or type away when it scheduled the activity during happy hour, for example, it will try scheduling a different free window the next week. It also materializes the progress you've made on your goal: circular trackers at the bottom of an overview window portray your progress from week to week.

Goals is capable of helping us find lost time and scheduling our activities better than we could ourselves, for a few reasons. First, it materializes what we might otherwise leave in the abstract. As Ariely explains, we give precedence to scheduled events "and all the short-term things we agree to do in our calendar." Longer projects, which might not be completed in a single appointment—like losing ten pounds, refinancing our mortgage, or getting more me-time in—take a back seat to the concrete, specific, and scheduled events of our lives. We think we'll work out in that blank space between our alarm clock going off and our first meeting at the office. We anticipate going over our bank statements after the dinner date but before bed. But that doesn't happen. Instead, says Ariely, "Empty time where you think you'll do something loses precedence to things on the calendar that are concrete and specific." Materializing our priorities—mapping them out over the course of our day—increases the likelihood we'll get them done.

The idea of outsourcing our scheduling to someone else might seem unappealing. We like being in control, and believe we know ourselves better than other people or apps know us—which leads to the belief that we know best how to design our day. But in his research, Ariely found that people actually benefit from delegating this responsibility to someone else. Massachusetts Institute of Technology students taking one of his courses did better when he scheduled the deadlines for their coursework rather than leaving it up to them to decide. He put deadlines on some students' calendars, telling them when they had to submit each of three required papers. These deadlines were evenly spaced across the semester. He gave other students the opportunity to set their own deadlines. They were free to choose the dates by which they wanted to hand in each of the assignments, as long as all the deadlines were set on or before the last day of class. Despite our intuition that we know our own schedule best, the students whose schedules were set for them by their professor wrote better papers and received grades that were about three percentage points higher, on average. That's the difference between a solid B and a B-plus. Performance on the final paper was affected to an even greater degree. Students who imposed their own deadlines received on average a solid C. Those whose schedules were decided for them by Ariely earned on average a solid B, nine percentage points higher. This difference in performance was not because the students who chose their own deadlines decided to set all three for the final day of class. In fact, three-quarters of them chose to spread the deadlines throughout the semester. The difference was in precisely when they set them. They did not choose to evenly space them, and they did not set them soon enough—factors that Ariely knew contributed to better performance, but the students did not. Despite our preference to be in control of our own time and our intuition that we might better plan our days, when we act as our own secretary, we might not be able to find the time we need to get the job done well.

Ariely's work also shows that we spend the precious resource of our time in the wrong ways. Before creating the app that Google gobbled up, Ariely ran experiments to measure whether people needed such assistance in the first place. He found that we're pretty inefficient at using our time when left to schedule our day ourselves. Nearly 80 percent of the people he surveyed start their day off by doing things like responding to email or catching up on their social media feeds for the first two hours in the morning, even though this is the most productive time of our day, when our energy and ability to focus tend to be at their peaks.

It's also the case that, on the whole, we humans are pretty poor time predictors. We tend to think we can get a job done much faster than we really can. In one study, amateur chefs predicted it would take them about twenty-four minutes to prepare an hors d'oeuvre tray of sliced fruits and vegetables, finger sandwiches, skewered meat and cheese, and shrimp, when in reality it took them ten minutes more. When the job gets harder, our forecasting error grows. Typesetters tasked with formatting dictionary entries were right when estimating how long it would take to bold and italicize some parts of the definitions. However, when the job ahead of them became more challenging, requiring four times as many changes to double the number of formatting considerations, the amount of time it took was more than twice what they'd estimated. And when we want a project to yield a specific result, our ability to accurately predict the time it will take gets even worse. People who believed that the IRS owed them money anticipated submitting their tax returns about a week and a half earlier than those who did not foresee a refund expected to file. As it turned out, it took these hopeful citizens two weeks longer than they'd predicted to get their documents submitted, while those without the expectation of receiving a refund were off by only a few days.

Paradoxically, the strength of our intentions to meet a deadline impact not only how accurate we are when scheduling our time but also our decisions about what would help us do the job best. Scientists from the University of Waterloo found this to be true when probing why college students have problems saving money. In this study, students set financial goals they hoped to achieve in four months' time, knowing that they would be rewarded financially by the researchers if they saved what they hoped to. To help them meet their goals—and get their reward—the researchers also offered a low-priced subscription to a weekly newsletter that gave the students individualized financial progress reports and tips on how to save more. The service was effective. Students were more likely to meet their savings goal when they received it. And they knew the publication would be helpful; they accurately predicted that their peers would be better savers if they received it. But the research turned up something interesting: very few would pay the fee of a few dollars to receive that newsletter. Now, I understand the frugal nature of a college student—I was one for nine years. But the fee would have been deducted from the compensation they received for participating in the study, and it was significantly smaller than the bonus they would receive if they met their goals. They would come out ahead if they ponied up for the publication. But strong intentions can lead to the mistaken belief that we are capable of optimally planning, and this belief can keep us from capitalizing on techniques—even ones we know would work—that could help us plan better.

How can we shortcut these missteps that undermine our efforts to plan our days strategically and effectively? Either with or without the help of Google and its apps, one solution is to materialize the process through what behavioral scientists call "unpacking," or breaking down a large task into its component parts.

Here's an analogy. About half of the people who wear glasses or contact lenses to correct their vision do so because they experience hyperopia. You might know it as farsightedness. Some kids develop hyperopia as early as in their preschool years, and teachers sometimes mistake their inability to (literally) focus on the schoolwork on the desk in front of them with hyperactivity or behavioral problems. But simply by getting the right pair of eyeglasses, these young children can suddenly sit in their seat, listen and concentrate, and do better in school. The glasses make the details of what's before them clear and concrete, and the kids are better equipped to excel.

Like those now-bespectacled children, we all increase the odds of success when we make ourselves accountable to not only our goal but the path to it as well. We must see the details that stand between us and what's further off. On the other hand, we decrease our odds of success if we just focus on what's to come in the future. It's not enough for us to say, for instance, that we want to graduate from college, move across the country, or switch careers. We have to take that large and long-term interest and break it down into manageable mini-goals. We have to see the details of the path underneath and in front of us. Receiving the mortarboard and diploma requires planning out each semester's course load. Uprooting a family and transplanting to the other coast demands deep investigation of schools, career opportunities, and housing options. When we unpack our distal aspirations, we better appreciate, plan for, and navigate the difficulties of getting from here to there. When we track our progress at the micro level and review the advancements we've made, we make ourselves accountable to our own aspirations.

5

In Sight, In Mind

Photographers swarmed like flies around cut fruit in the tropics, snapping at the beautiful and creatively clad patrons at the opening for the Museum of Modern Art's *Items: Is Fashion Modern?* Chunky neon eyeglasses on slim faces. Sequin skirts under shaggy sweaters. Flower headdresses. The costumed panoply was clickbait for the cameras. It was dress-up for the chichi crowd who came to see what 111 objects the curators had selected to comment on contemporary society. Superficially, the pairing of selections seemed as unusual as my choice to start this book while pregnant with my first child. A burkini sat in the same space as a WonderBra. A fanny pack alongside a fur coat. Leather pants up against loafers. What connected these items, though, was that they all revolutionized culture, politics, identity, economy, technology, and of course fashion—and still hold currency today.

I was lucky to snag a ticket to the party while in some intense throes of evading a much-needed music lesson, and invited my friend Carly, who is always—and certainly was that night—far better accessorized than I. We set out on a mission to find one piece in particular. I had read about Giorgia Lupi and knew that her art appeared in the show. I didn't know what form it took, or in what artistic medium it appeared. We were running blind in this operation, but that night I was Indiana Jones and this was my holy grail. The two of us went through the galleries, searching each placard for the artist's name, as methodically as two women whose hands had just been filled with (then drained of) prosecco could. We went through the show front-to-back, back-to-front, then front-to-back again. We asked a few people. But with an open bar and a lively social scene, no one was really there that night to offer curatorial guidance.

When the festooned revelers started to run thin and the party was nearing an end, Carly begged off from our hunt. We left the gallery space and turned the corner toward the museum exit. Only then were we smacked in the face with the capstone exhibit—Lupi's mural! It wasn't clothing. It wasn't a handbag. No fashion house had designed it. This single piece of two-dimensional art comprised easily a hundred times more surface area in the show than any other piece. Envision a wall three stories tall on which appears a freely flowing set of musical staffs, on which are artistically rendered clutches of notes. This wasn't a show about sound or harmonies. The notes on the staff were not intended to represent particular acoustic frequencies or durations. Instead, each of the 111 musical notes represented a piece of clothing or accessory that appeared in the show. The relevance of the garb to history and contemporary society was symbolized by an element of Lupi's composition. The color of the note's head and the size of its flag signified something about the origin of the corresponding item or its consequence to society. There was a red quarter note drawn as part of a phrase. Rather than suggesting a change in the melody of the piece, that red note stood in for the Converse All-Star sneakers that Carly and I had seen on the feet of a mannequin a few rooms back. The red paint signified the shoe's role in rebellion. The note's location in the middle of the piece identified its temporal place in fashion history. As the score unfolded from left to right, I noticed whole notes representing hijabs that were placed well before the sixteenth notes standing in for headphones.

Like a clutch of windswept dandelion stamens, several notes gathered together. One stood in for red lipstick, another for Chanel No. 5 perfume, and a final one for men's ties. The mural's legend offered the theme that bound these three together: power. Each wardrobe element and its trimming told a story about society. Lupi had extracted that story and synthesized, quantified, reprocessed, and reproduced it in this schematic form, which resembled modern art itself. This gorgeous, sprawling mural was, essentially, an infographic: data made visual.

I first came upon Lupi and her professional partner Stefanie Posavec through a different, though no less astounding, project. I found them in their diaries—or their project *Dear Data*, to be more precise. Lupi is Italian and lives in New York. Posavec is American and lives in London. They met at an event that mixed graphic designers, engineers, journalists, and scientists. Virtual strangers to each other, they clearly clicked, because a plan was hatched to embark on a relationship that required daily maintenance, constant monitoring, and weekly reporting. Every Monday they chose a theme they wanted to quantify for the next seven days. The number of times they smiled at strangers. The types of doors they passed through. What, when, how often, and with whom they drank. The frequency and sources of their feelings of jealousy. Every compliment they gave or received. The sounds they heard in their vicinity every hour they were awake. All the times they laughed. The urban animals they passed by.

Each week was a different theme, and at every moment of the day they remained vigilant for and recorded instances related to the theme. They tallied up their results and shared them with each other. But not in the form of a spreadsheet or as numbers of any sort. Each drew her results by hand on a postcard, producing translations of her experience into a miniature Kandinsky-like painting worth, at that time anyway, the cost of the postage stamp it took to mail it to the other.

Like the mural at the Museum of Modern Art, the imaginative

renditions of their week in data were intricate and complicated. Each was accompanied by a legend supplied by the artist for decoding the meaning of every squiggle, color swatch, doodle, and form. Lupi learned that Posavec's husband inspired feelings of love in her more than three times as often as feelings of annoyance. And Posavec learned that Lupi sees far more dogs than rats in her wanderings, which is remarkable given how many New York City subway platforms she waits on. But more than these details about the nature of their days, they learned how they are each connected to a bigger social sphere, how they engage with their emotions, the patterns of their behaviors that create how each perceives and is perceived by the world. The minutiae of their data transformed into pictographs made them intimately human to each other. At the close of every week, and at the completion of their artistic renderings, they jotted down their pen pal's address, plunked a stamp on it, and sent it off in the post to travel across the ocean.

Two strangers with no formalized commitment to each other set and succeeded at a goal that required daily maintenance for a full calendar year. Before I met Pete, I was single in New York. I admit to having met a few people in bars, strangers at the time, as Lupi was to Posavec. But the vast majority of my consorts were impossible to commit to for even fifty-two minutes, so the fact that these strangers sustained their arduous enterprise for fifty-two weeks amazes me. And it's a feat that has been noted by far-harder-to-impress bodies than me. Lupi and Posavec cataloged their enterprise in *Dear Data,* a book that reproduced their postcards along with insider notes on their experience. It was published in 2016, the same year that the Museum of Modern Art acquired all 106 original postcards for its permanent collection.

I needed to know more. I started my query by video-chatting with Lupi. She sat at home in Brooklyn. I sat in my office in Manhattan. I asked all kinds of questions, and she gave the most interesting answers. She told me about the coincidental similarities between herself and Posavec—they're both only children, of the same age, who crossed the Atlantic to pursue their artistic dream. She commented on the way that their drawing styles started to resemble each other over time. She told me about how she now teaches children about the *Dear Data* project, and how exciting it is to see middle schoolers illustrating the data from their own lives, and eagerly anticipating the math class they did this in—an elusive enthusiasm that practically achieves unicorn status. And she chuckled at the "data voids" that appeared because of a husband's protests, three boozy Christmas parties, and other reasons.

I asked her my big question. "Giorgia, you and Stefanie did something that is really hard for lots of people. You set a goal and saw it through for an entire year, and by the end of that time, you actually finished it. How did you do it? What tricks did you use?" There was a pause. I used that moment to check out the room she was in, what was behind her and on the sides. And I knew then that the answer Lupi was about to give me would be totally unsatisfying.

What I saw was this. Behind Lupi was a glass wall. On which were more than a dozen Post-it notes. I meant for my attempt at sleuthing to be a surreptitious one, so I squinted with hopes of snooping as covertly as possible without being pegged as a weirdo. I saw sketches that seemed to evolve gradually from one square to the next, down the length of one column and across the rows. It was a storyboard documenting the evolution of Lupi's work. I took the next moment to consider what her view was of what lay behind me. On a console in my office, behind my chair, was a mess of papers so scattered that she surely couldn't see where any one pile ended and the next began, nor the counter underneath.

And my suspicion was right. From her response to my request for advice, it seemed that Lupi did not struggle to meet big goals. She didn't seem to have doubted her ability to sustain the project or see it through. She didn't have to change her life to realize her dream, even though she had to have been thinking about it almost every waking moment, because she was counting something in her daily experience all the time or drawing a picture of it.

I asked Lupi about that storyboard when I connected with her again later on. "I like remembering the first ideas I had for projects," Lupi explained, "and having them around can be a nice reminder of how things evolve during a project." I told her I thought this was genius, that posting her work on the walls she looked at every day rather than archiving them in file drawers may have been an intuitive system of materializing. She laughed. "The real truth is that I just like my sketches." I don't doubt that her choices may be aesthetic ones, but I'm convinced that what seems like personal style to her may actually be a key ingredient in her success. The storyboard collection was a tangible form of accountability, whereby ongoing projects are kept in sight and progress is visible. As second nature, Lupi surrounds herself with the visuals of inspiration and evidence of progress.

I decided to hit up Posavec for advice next, thinking I might relate to her approach a little more. The legends on her postcards had smudges where life got in the way of perfect penmanship. She crossed out mistakes. She included footnotes to her drawings, expressing her frustration in misspelled words. The vertical lines she drew strayed from plumb, which seemed metaphoric of how my life seems to generally unfold. *She'll get me,* I thought.

I sent an email to Posavec asking to talk about *Dear Data*. I included in my plea an embarrassingly detailed account of my own organizational disasters, and described my envy of Lupi's Post-it note grid. Posavec was half a dozen time zones away, juggling life with a new baby herself, but perhaps my self-deprecation worked. She wrote back, and we arranged a conversation. For starters, I asked her where she might place herself on the Giorgia–Emily spectrum when it came to formulating and enacting a plan for completing a goal, and (if she were more toward the Emily side of things) whether there was anything she used to help her visualize her plan of attack for *Dear Data*. She's a really nice person, so I am nearly certain her answer was more to appease my ego than anything else, but she claimed, "I am definitely more on the Emily side of things, though over time working with Giorgia I have moved (just a little) more to the Giorgia side." We all need a little Giorgia in our life.

Posavec offered another thought, however, which has stuck with me. She said that one thing that motivated her from week to week, and inspired her to keep going, was seeing Lupi's postcard from the previous week—having been stamped and put on a plane in New York, flown across the ocean, carted to a flat in London by Royal Mail, and framed by her doormat for her to find. "There like clockwork after every weekend . . ."

That doormat deserves more credit than you might think. Knowing what I do about how a frame can highlight and direct our focus onto something that really matters, I realized that the doormat is in great part responsible for Stefanie's motivational stamina. Her doorway contained her shoes, her umbrellas, her keys, and her bags. One little postcard dropped in the middle of all that could easily get lost. But that doormat highlighted that postcard's arrival each week, bringing focus to it and to the goal it was serving. That doormat was framing up the thing that inspired this duo to persevere. In addition to the tool of materializing, we have the visual strategy of framing available for our use. And much like a horse and buggy or a pestle and mortar, you can have either on its own, but together you can get a lot more done.

The Power of a Visual Frame

Lorraine O'Grady isn't a postal worker or a data monger. She isn't known for her skills as a pen pal, though I'm sure she would be a really cool one to have. She is a visual artist, and an accomplished one at that. Her pieces appear in the permanent collections of New York City's Museum of Modern Art, the Art Institute of Chicago, and the Los Angeles County Museum of Art. She had a one-person exhibit at Art Basel in Miami Beach, the United States' most important contemporary art fair. She was selected for the Paris Triennale, and was one of only fifty-five artists selected for inclusion in the 2010 Whitney Biennial.

But O'Grady's career was dressed in these accolades only after she framed up northern Manhattan as a piece of art. During the African American Day Parade in September 1983, O'Grady positioned a giant, antique-style gold frame atop a float. On the platform supporting the frame, O'Grady painted the words ART IS . . . The streets of Harlem with their rusted signs of the Jazz Age, Nubian delis, blue-painted wooden police barricades, and once luminescent signs advertising hotel rooms for rent were outlined in gold as the float rumbled past. The black children, their parents, and their neighbors passed through the large frame for a moment. In the spirit of celebration and inclusivity, this gilded piece framed everything it passed and labeled it as art.

O'Grady didn't know it at the time, but that gold frame changed the art world's thinking on who could act as a muse. The piece, *Art Is . . .* , brought attention to issues of racial inequality in the contemporary art world. Poorer neighborhoods like Harlem didn't qualify as art back then. What appeared in museums was not normal people in everyday clothing, sitting along the street on the weekend watching a parade through their neighborhood—a neighborhood that wasn't white. In reflecting on her piece, O'Grady said later, "I guess I didn't understand what the power of a frame and a camera were."

But that frame is powerful. Just ask the anxious U.S. representatives to Congress on hand for the first workday in January. You might think that with the start of a new year, anxiety might come from the legislation that is set to expire with the turn of the calendar page or the countdown to Tax Day that has officially begun. Not so. The angst is over a seating chart.

At the start of each congressional session, U.S. senators vie for the best-placed desks in the Chamber. They mull over and strategize where to plant themselves during debates, angling for the exact spot they want. Each congressional desk is uniquely numbered and comes with its own historical record. Inside each desk's drawer, you can find the names of senators who squatted there before, dating back as far as the early 1900s. Some names are in marker, some in pen. And others, like that of Republican senator Lamar Alexander, were etched into the wood with a paper clip.

Some senators choose their desks based on history. Republican senator Susan Collins of Maine wanted the desk formerly held by Margaret Chase Smith, the only woman in the Senate for most of her years in office.

Some choose based on snacks. Senators cannot eat in the Chamber. Regardless, desk 24 has been stocked with chocolates and candies that senators snag on their way out, ever since California's one-term Republican senator George Murphy started the tradition fifty years ago.

But more commonly, senators choose for the view. Not the view they have when looking out, but whether they are in view of others. Orrin Hatch has served in the Senate longer than any other Republican in history and has inherited the right to sit wherever he pleases. He has chosen a spot directly behind the majority leader, an aisle seat in the middle of the action.

"I'm closer to the aisle, which I've always tried to be so that you can get recognition," the Utah Republican said. "In a very serious situation, sometimes getting recognition is the difference between winning and losing."

Like executives at a boardroom table, eager students in a classroom, or the artist Lorraine O'Grady, what Hatch knows is that what appears inside the frame matters. As if it were an old Broadway theater, the worst seats in the Chamber are the two outermost back corners. From the press area, a reporter must stand up and peer over the railing to see the most junior members, who usually end up there. But the best seats are off the center aisle in front. These seats are right in the line of vision of the presiding officer, who decides which senator gets the right to speak. Political real estate, just as with urban apartments or a first home in the suburbs, is all about location, location, location. Where senators sit positions them either within the line of sight of the most powerful entity in Congress or far from it. In the frame or out of it.

Similarly, inside the gilded edges of O'Grady's piece of art, or surrounded by the confines of the doormat just inside an apartment, what appears inside the visual frame is a game changer. We all look at the world around us through a frame. We deem what appears inside a frame as important. What's outside the frame, well, that's not. Whoever the Majority Leader perceives as being inside the frame is acknowledged and gets the floor. What an artist places on canvas inside an oak frame is appraised monetarily and valued socially. Frames highlight some information and cut out the rest. They shape our perceptions of what matters, and quite literally move us.

The Biology of Blind Spots

We all experience a natural form of framing that leaves us blind to some of the things that surround us. This is hardwired in us. As you may recall from anatomy class, the insides of our eyes are lined with the retina—a super-thin sheet of cells that are sensitive to the light that enters our eyes from the outside world. There's a small spot on our retina where it connects to the optic nerve—the conduit by which our eyes send messages to our brain. At that point of contact, we lack cells that can detect light. And without those cells, any information hitting the retina in that place is lost. This is a blind spot; we have one in each eye.

To find one of your blind spots, you can try the following exercise.

On the next page, you'll see an X and a circle. Hold the page up so your nose is pointing at or even touching the page in between the two of them. Close your left eye. With your left eye closed, focus your right eye on the X, but take notice of the dot off on the right side. (It may be difficult to keep from peeking directly at the dot, but keep your right eye focused on the X.) Then, move the page closer to and farther away from you. At some point, that dot you noticed in your peripheral view will disappear. That's because it's lined up perfectly with your right blind spot.

Our blind spots are rarely a problem in our everyday life, because our minds go out of their way to hide them. Even when we're not trying, and without us being aware of it, our eyes jitter around several times a second, framing up different parts of our surroundings. Then, our brains stitch together all of the slight variations in what our eyes have framed.

While our bodies have evolved to shift our frame intuitively and automatically, we are also capable of controlling our visual frame. We can teach ourselves to use our framing tool to change our behavior, because what we see affects what we do. Our voices rise in pitch when we greet a tiny baby. When we look at our electric bill, and we see how little energy our neighbors have used compared to us, we turn off the lights and turn down the air-conditioning. Our cheers grow more enthusiastic after watching slugger Aaron Judge make another home run in his rookie season, and our cries become more dejected when Red Sox outfielder Mookie Betts hits one out of the park himself—assuming we root for the Yankees. When it comes to who or what we see around us, our perceptual experiences bear directly on our actions.

In fact, our eyes and brain are specifically designed to pair what we see and what we do. There are neural connections in each of our brains—scientists refer to them as the dorsal pathway—that are designed to quickly translate our visual experience into movements other parts of our body can make. The sensations we take in with our eyes travel to the primary visual cortex. Here, the brain notes all the basic bits of what's in front of us, like the sharp edge of a table or the rounded arm of a chair, and makes a detailed map of what's out there. Importantly, it's also taking note of where each of these bits is located with respect to one another and ourselves. *The sharp bit is close by,* the brain notes, *and that round edge is farther off to the right.* Within hundredths of a second, the brain sends this information along to the parietal lobe and then on to the motor cortex. The parietal lobe, one of the four major quadrants of our brain's cortex, integrates information from across all of our senses. This also happens to be the part of the brain that does the most work to make sense of what we are touching. The motor cortex helps us actually move our limbs. What this means is that what we take in through our eyes nearly instantly engages with a part of our brain that is responsible for how we move our arms, hands, and legs—perhaps to avoid the sharp table edge, or even to coordinate our flop onto the more comfortable corner of the chair.

In 1909, a Hungarian physician named Rezső Bálint described an interesting case of a man who experienced a neurological impairment called ataxia, which disrupted his dorsal pathway. Imagine that the dorsal pathway is a set of train tracks; what this patient experienced was like an earthquake that severed the line. Bálint's patient came to him saying that his right hand was clumsy. He would try lighting a cigarette at its middle instead of at its end. This was especially weird because with his left hand, his reach was accurate. He tried to cut a slice of meat. He would hold the meat down with a fork in his left hand, but he couldn't seem to get the knife in his right hand to connect with the steak on his plate. He would look down and see his knife sawing somewhere on the table off the plate's edge. Weirder still, it did not seem like his right hand was the problem. If he closed his eyes, he could reach with his right hand to different parts of his body as the doctor directed him to. This discovery meant that Bálint's patient didn't have problems with his muscles or body movement. It was just something about how his eyes coordinated with his body inside his brain to interact with the objects he saw.

For those of us fortunate enough to have healthy visual systems and properly functioning neurological connections, what we see does a good job of determining what we do. This is called automaticity, and it can pose a challenge for our best-laid intentions—but can also be a solution to motivational struggles. Certain behaviors can be spontaneously triggered by prompts or cues that fall within our purview, sometimes with and other times without our awareness. When these actions contrast with choices we wish we had made, or contradict goals we're trying to pursue, we can find our plans foiled. For instance, when we're out for dinner with our mother, just looking across the table at the person who for years goaded us to finish the food on our plate might lead us to overindulge and eat the portion of the entrée we had intended to set aside for lunch tomorrow. Passing by someone tucked away in an alcove lighting up a cigarette might tug at the fingertips of the smoker trying to quit. Seeing the illumination of a text alert just as our head has hit the pillow might beckon us to pick up the phone one last time, even though we're trying to scale back on what feels like an Internet addiction. We might find ourselves yelling more loudly or pushing our children too strongly from the sidelines of a Little League game when we see other parents doing the same. If we go out for drinks after work, just watching a co-worker belly up to the bar might encourage us to do it too, even though we know we've already hit our limit. Again, how we position our visual frame affects what we see, and can bear directly on the actions we take.

Which brings us to the mystery of Walmart. In the immediate wake of the economic collapse of 2008, Americans suffered. Almost one million people lost their homes to foreclosure before New Year's

Day. More than 2.5 million people lost their jobs. The recession pinched most Americans' wallets in ways few people had ever before felt. The Dow Jones Industrial Average fell over 50 percent from its pre-recession high. Though the recession hit the working class hardest, the nation's largest retailer, Walmart, was reporting record valuation. In fact, it was one of only two stocks in the Dow Jones that increased in value during 2008. Though the net worth of the average American dropped by one-third, the number of blue plastic shopping bags they were fitting into the backs of their cars was growing. Why?

Clutter.

By design, Walmart has always dropped pallets of products— oversized boxes of dishwashing detergent or discount leggings—in the middle of aisles, like shopping speed bumps. Just as intentionally, Walmart shelves brim with stuff: juice boxes in the juice aisle, candy corn in the candy aisle, and even at one point bacon-scented pillows in the home goods department. The strategy has been to have shelves teeming with items that shoppers don't even know they want before seeing them (and often wonder, after purchasing them—if my own experience is any indication—whether they actually do). The displays are a visual cacophony that tempts even the most discerning of bargain hunters.

There was a brief period in Walmart merchandising history when the company tried adopting a slimmed-down visual experience— fewer things and fewer pallets and fewer options. Perhaps not surprisingly, customers reported enjoying their shopping experience more. The place was easier on the eye. But shedding the oversized shelving and whittling down inventory made customers buy less. So back came the pallets. Restocked were the endcaps. Ben DiSanti, senior vice president of planning and perspectives for a retail marketing consultant, explained, "If you have the temptations there, it will lead to additional sales."

The pull of temptation impacts more than just our pocketbook. Waistlines, too, feel the effects of these visual displays. Researchers went door-to-door surveying about a thousand shoppers in Pittsburgh who live in areas considered "food deserts," typically lacking easy access to fresh fruits and vegetables and healthy alternatives. Participants agreed to have their height and weight recorded, and to report on the types of places they shop at. The researchers then audited all these neighborhood stores. They looked in particular at the types of food in the end-aisle displays, special floor displays, and cash-register displays. They took note of whether the foods were sugar-sweetened beverages, candy, snacks high in solid oils, fats, and added sugars. They also noted whether the displays had whole-grain products and fresh produce. The researchers found that residents of these communities saw about fourteen or fifteen displays of sugar-sweetened beverages, and more than four price reductions for these drinks, on their visits to the grocery store each month. They also saw twenty-eight displays of high-fat and added-sugar foods. Not surprisingly, the foods that appeared in these highly visible locations impacted the overall health of the average shopper in these neighborhoods. Statistical analysis showed that the more these household shoppers were exposed to end-aisle visual displays of sugar-sweetened beverages, the higher their body mass index. Since the average shopper was visiting a store a little more than three times a week, the impact of exposure to these unhealthy foods placed in highly visible locations was the equivalent of gaining up to two and a half pounds per month.

Of course, companies know what DiSanti explained—what people see is what they buy—which is why commercial industries use the architecture of the shelves to frame up the products they hope to move, even if those products pose complications to the good health of their customers. This is why, in 2011, the U.S. tobacco industry paid retailers $7 billion, representing over 80 percent of the advertising budget, to display their products in highly trafficked areas in stores: near the cash registers and in eye-level displays. This product-placement strategy also worked for carbonated-drink companies. In a one-year analysis of sales in a major supermarket in northern England, researchers found that getting soda into aisle-end displays increased annual sales by over 50 percent. This kind of increase was matched only by "buy three, get one free" promotions.

Of course, regulators know all this too. And some governments have taken counteraction. For instance, by 2009, most states in Australia had banned tobacco displays near checkout counters. This legal shift preceded a downward trend in youth smoking rates. Among Australian youths ages twelve to twenty-four who had never smoked before, the odds that any one of them would become a smoker dropped by 27 percent after the government banned advertising near the registers in stores.

Coming Eye-to-Eye with Good Health

Frames and their impact on choices are not all bad. Our visual environment—what appears both within and outside our frame—also nudges us toward decisions that improve our health and well-being.

In 2010, Anne Thorndike and her research colleagues turned the cafeteria at Massachusetts General Hospital into a testing ground. They examined how visual frames affect the choices we make at mealtime. The first phase of the study was covertly deployed. Three months before anyone knew it, cafeteria cash registers began to identify and record the types of foods purchased by people visiting the cafeteria. Then the researchers started tagging foods with different-color labels. Green-tagged items, like fruits, vegetables, and lean proteins, were the healthiest. Yellow tags were placed on less healthy items, and red tags on foods with little or no nutritional value. A few months later, the researchers rearranged the shelves in the cafeteria. Green-tagged foods were moved to shelves at eye level. Yellow- and red-tagged foods went higher or lower, out of an easy line of sight.

When the team analyzed the purchase patterns twenty-four

months after these changes, they found something astonishing. Overall, purchases of the green-tagged items—the healthiest options—had increased by 12 percent compared to the first covert testing period. Beyond that, purchases of red-tagged unhealthy items had dropped by 20 percent. The most frequently avoided item became the sugar-sweetened beverages. Purchases of these non-nutritional drinks dropped by 39 percent. Placing the yellow- and red-tagged foods on harder-to-see shelves gave a visual warning to consumers and helped to keep those products on the shelves.

Google discovered this same phenomenon through slightly different means. Not long ago, it had a big problem. Just as its employee roster was growing, so too were employees' waistlines. Employees at Google have access to many amenities; perhaps the most talked about is the free food. The company has its own fleet of food trucks, creating sinfully delicious dishes like burrata salad with stone fruit, or naan with smoked salmon and dill cream. Inside the office walls, cafeterias offer seared diver scallops with Parmesan, squid-ink rice, and maitake mushrooms followed by banana cheesecake. And the snacks in between the usual three meals are abundant enough to count as a fourth. The New York office, for instance, had beverage stations all over each floor, and these stations were all stocked with treats like M&M's, chocolates, nuts, cookies, granola bars, chips, pretzels, and beer. Getting a bottle of water, at the time of this study, generally wasn't a calorie-free experience, because employees inevitably took a handful of something sweet or salty when popping in for a drink.

The problem was that these offerings were *too* tempting, in part because they were always in view. So Google tried to change the allure of the unhealthy options by altering what fell into employees' visual frame. At the snack stations in New York, the pantry crew stocked the eye-level shelves with bottled water, and put sugary sodas at the bottom of the refrigerators or behind frosted glass. By comparing what needed restocking now to what needed restocking before, the pantry attendants reported that employees were 50 percent more likely to snag a bottle of water than before. And to choose a sugary drink slightly less often.

The pantry attendants also made the unhealthy snacks harder to see, obscuring the line of sight employees had on them. They stored the chocolates in opaque containers while putting healthier options, like dried figs and pistachios, in transparent glass jars. Google's New York employees alone consumed 3.1 million fewer calories from M&M's over the next seven weeks. By placing the temptations outside the visual frame, Google had, in effect, decoupled the link between focused attention and action.

Knowledge that a visual frame can inspire healthier choices is not unique to Google, and the impact on diets is not special to the tech community. In Philadelphia and Wilmington, Delaware, for instance, researchers, nonprofit health advocates, and supermarket managers have banded together to try to nudge healthier choices among shoppers in low-income neighborhoods who aren't working in companies that prepare their meals. These influencers brainstormed the creation of a visual environment that would frame up healthier choices and, in particular, inspire sales of water. To craft their visual landscapes, they used two marketing techniques: cross-promotion and prime placement. In the dead space within the soda aisles, store employees stacked up bottled water. In the coolers at the ends of the checkout lanes, water now appeared on the top shelf, easy to see and access, while sodas were moved lower down and out of sight from most adults.

To know whether the placement of water made a difference, the research team needed a group of stores to compare sales against. They selected stores that were in the same neighborhoods and attracted the same clientele. Within these stores, managers were not given any special instructions on how to display their bottled water. They just used the techniques that they always had and that their customers were accustomed to.

Then managers took note of how many cases of water they sold. During the time they were tracking them, water sales decreased by 17 percent in the stores that stocked their aisles and their coolers as they wished. But the stores that put water in shoppers' visual frame saw sales of water increase by 10 percent. Another study of supermarket produce sales found something similar. When managers put fruit closer to the cash registers, fruit purchases increased by 70 percent. When the fruit appeared within the visual frame, consumers went for it; when it remained outside the frame, they didn't.

Michael Bloomberg is the eleventh-richest person in the world, with a net worth of over $50 billion, half of which he has promised to give away as part of Warren Buffett's Giving Pledge that I mentioned earlier. He created a global financial services and mass media software company that bears his name. His profile in business is legendary, and so is the mark he's made in politics. He was elected mayor of New York for three consecutive terms. While mayor, he focused on public health campaigns, reforming laws where possible to improve life expectancy for city residents. He enacted a new bill that applied to all restaurants operating in the city with fifteen or more outlets there or across the country. Think chains of all sizes. This bill required that calorie counts be posted as prominently for the eye to see as the price of each menu item. Venues like McDonald's and Starbucks already provided calorie information on websites, posters in dining areas, and tray liners. But now the caloric cost of each item had to be as easily seen as the monetary cost. If people can see the calories, he explained, they'll make different choices.

Just as Bloomberg worked to increase the visibility of information that would dissuade consumers from making unhealthy choices, he also worked to decrease the prominence of other hazards. He banned smoking in city restaurants and bars, parks, plazas, and beaches. After the success of these measures, he pushed the city council to adopt measures that would ban the display of tobacco products in stores. Bloomberg aimed to make sellers keep tobacco products out of sight, except during a purchase by an adult or during restocking. They had to be stored in cabinets or drawers, under the counter, or behind a curtain. Though the city did not move forward with that product-display restriction initiative, the mayor wanted to push sellers to deglamorize tobacco, to decrease how appealing it looked. "Don't make it look like it's a normal product," Bloomberg said. "Cigarettes are not a normal product."

Bloomberg's rationale in all of these initiatives was based on numerous studies backing up the idea that what falls in our line of sight can nudge our choices, even despite our best intentions to the contrary. A survey of nearly three thousand smokers, ex-smokers, and smokers trying to quit found that a quarter of them said they'd bought cigarettes on impulse after seeing a tobacco display at a cash register, even though they weren't shopping for cigarettes. And one in five smokers trying to quit said they'd stopped going into stores where they usually bought their smokes because they knew if they stepped inside, they'd buy them.

We may be unable to change the types of products managers place next to the cash registers. We likely can't decide whether soda or cigarettes are sold in the cooler or on the counter at eye level or high above our line of sight. But awareness may be one way to decouple the automatic impact of visual frames on our actions. If we know that the aspects of our visual landscape that fall inside the frame shape our wallet's bottom line as well as our health, we can intervene on what might otherwise be an automatic response to what we see.

At the same time, if we are aware that how we frame things can directly influence the choices we make, we can intentionally choose to structure our home, office, or wherever we spend our time in ways that can promote better choices. Because what falls inside our visual frame shapes what we do, we can be conscientious about what we see in the spaces we live in. We draft plans and form intentions, of course, but we still need to catalyze actions that push us closer to meeting our goals.

Psychologist Wendy Wood discovered just how powerful the contents of a frame can be. She calls these framed-up instigators of automatic action "visual sparks." Wood studied students for whom a healthy lifestyle was important, but who were uncertain about how to best adjust to a new environment as they started their first year of college, having just left home. They wondered: *What routes are safe to run in the morning? What gym is the cleanest? Do the dining halls have healthy options?* Despite the demands a new place can bring, students who found that their new neighborhoods contained some of the same visual cues—the same sparks—as their old ones better sustained their exercise routine than those who didn't have familiar visual cues to trigger their old habits.

The power of visual sparks is evident in our brains. Dopamine is a neurotransmitter released in the brain by neurons when we are doing things that we really enjoy—when we eat delicious food, have sex, play video games, or even do cocaine. When researchers study dopamine, they often choose to involve monkeys as the test cases. This isn't such a bad deal for the monkeys, because they get to do pleasurable things, like drinking juice. Think happy hour with a corporate credit card. Researchers know that when monkeys drink juice, their brains experience a rush of dopamine. The monkeys learn that if they press a lever, they get a sip of juice. And—though at first it doesn't seem like such an important detail—when the monkey bellies up to the juice bar, a red light comes on. It doesn't change any part of what happens. The monkey still presses the lever. He still gets a shot of juice. But over time, he mentally cuts out the middleman and associates the light with the juice. What researchers have found is that eventually just being in a red-lit room produces a dopamine rush—without the sip of juice. For the monkeys, the red light is a visual spark, and this spark triggers a response in the most basic brain circuitry, just as seeing a neighborhood gym can elicit an urge to hit the treadmill in some people who enjoy exercising.

Furthermore, motivational sparks can have an impact when they are unleashed on not just one or two monkeys or a handful of college students, but on organizations as a whole. A telecom company in the Netherlands worked with psychologist Rob Holland and his team to test the large-scale influence of visual sparks. The company aimed to reduce its impact on the environment. Its managers decided that for the first few months, they would focus on having employees recycle paper and plastic cups.

They installed recycling boxes in common areas to collect the items. A special team repeatedly instructed employees about these recycling boxes and underscored the ease as well as the importance of using them. Despite setting the goal, the amount of paper and plastic cups in the personal wastebaskets did not decrease.

The researchers then asked employees to explicitly write down their intention (hopefully on a piece of scrap paper they would eventually recycle). Employees wrote things like "If I finish my coffee, then I will put the cup in the recycling bin *next to the water cooler.*" This simple statement, paired with the visual spark, made a world of difference. Before the researchers intervened, employees had been tossing well over 1,200 plastic cups into their personal wastebaskets each week. But, in the week after employees set intentions that could be visually sparked, employees threw away far fewer than 200. This strategy reduced employees' bad habits by 85 percent and helped the company reach its overall goal.

In the Line of Sight

There was one room in our Connecticut home that realistically could and should house the drum kit. We didn't design the place but found ourselves with a room in the basement with no window onto the outside world. The walls were twelve-inch-thick concrete, reinforced with rebar, and the ceiling was able to support the weight of the disco ball Pete had given me for our first Christmas together. (We have a special kind of love and gifting style.) The drums sat directly underneath, and if you hit the bass drum hard enough, the mirrored ornament would start spinning, even when in its OFF position. We conjectured that the previous owners probably used this space as a workout room or a dance studio, and maybe they really wanted to get a good look at themselves on their way out because one wall was covered in mirrors—which doubled the sparkling effect of the disco ball. If you have vertigo, best to not visit during a rehearsal.

Besides its bunker-like properties, there was one other feature of this room that made it the perfect choice to lay down the set. You had to walk through this space to get to the garage. Every time I wanted to leave the house by any means other than on foot, I had to pass by the drums. Kick my shoes off at the door? See the kick drum staring me down. Jump into the car for a quick grocery run? Trip over a pair of drumsticks I no doubt threw across the room in frustration during my last practice.

Leaving the drums in the room that functioned as a major thoroughfare in the house meant that my visual frame included a frequent reminder of what I'd set my sights on mastering. My frame included the spark that fired up spontaneous practice sessions—even sometimes on my way back in from the store, milk and melting ice cream be damned.

We've all likely heard the phrase "out of sight, out of mind." This idiom sums up the effect that leaving sparks out of a visual frame can have on our choices and actions. We can intentionally design our environments, leaving out the things that prompt actions we want to tamp down. And we can include visible cues that will trigger better decisions. Leaving the drums in my perceptual line of fire ignited more practice sessions than I likely would have laid down without the spark. I can't tell you exactly how many, but I did keep track during one week around the holidays when I stayed up at the house longer than usual. I commandeered Mattie's Magna Doodle drawing board and ticked off each unintended practice session that was inspired by simply walking through the space. I am proud to say that I filled it with enough hash marks that it looked like a close-up of a football field.

Since what we see affects what we do, deciding what to put before our eyes can change the choices we make. Learning how to frame and what to frame shapes what makes its way into our mouths, into our trash cans, and onto our résumés, and what we can check off our own bucket lists.

6

Reading the Room Right

It was Christmas Eve and Mattie found himself toddling around in a red-and-white footed fleece onesie resembling a baby tuxedo, but festooned with a black belt and buckle the size of which might qualify him for rodeo riding. On his head occasionally sat (when he failed to realize we'd put it back on him) a crimson hat with plush white trim, fuzzy pom-pom, and glittering snowflakes. His dress coupled with his stature (he still only came up to my knee) and impish grin conveyed quite the elfish appearance, though I think his nana, who had dressed him, was going more for mini-Santa. If he'd been old enough and had caught sight of himself in a mirror, he might have divorced us and emancipated himself from this costumed absurdity.

That night, Mattie didn't seem to mind, though, because all of his family had collected themselves around the drums to hear him play. Pete stood him up on the snare and put two weighty drumsticks in his hands. We all put on headphones and waited for the show. Mattie started wailing on the rototoms, usually a few too many inches out of his reach. The splash symbol got a good workout too. His cacophony of sound stopped, though, when Pete tried to lay down a beat behind him on the bass drum and hi-hat. Mattie looked over his shoulder, as if questioning the right for his spotter to join the one (little) man band. He approved of what he heard, evidently, because he started swaying Stevie Wonder–style, followed by a few hip jazz-cat head bobs in time with Pete's tempo.

Freeze frame.

Roll camera again a week or so later. A blizzard had fallen and temperatures were too low to take a kid outside without getting visited by Child Protective Services. Mattie and I were cooped up inside for more hours than either of us could handle while maintaining mental stability. We needed something new to add to our activity repertoire after blowing through his toy box and library. So I thought I could try to replicate that festive holiday performance with my son and get in a little practice time myself. The two of us headed over to the drums. I sat down behind the set, picked Mattie up, plunked him onto the head of the floor tom, and gave us each a set of sticks. He started in on the crash cymbal while I cranked the sound system and cued up "Your Love."

I decided I was just going to focus on nailing the bass drum, snare, and ride. I was pretty sure that attempting to coordinate three limbs was still ambitious at this stage of my budding hobby. And indeed it must have been. Because again, like he did with his father, as soon as I started playing under and around him, Mattie stopped. But rather than busting out the spirit of "Superstition," there were no dance moves, no head bobs. He wasn't feeling it. There was no beat. Dare I say the way he looked at me may have been the first time I saw how disgust looked on my child's face? And he'd been known to play with the contents of his own diaper. I stunk.

This really shouldn't have come as any surprise, because sometime between when I'd started to write this book and that snowstorm, I'd fallen off the wagon. Progress was minimal. And even that was an overstatement. My resolve had dissolved. I'd spent less time on the kit than I had shaking my son's maracas as he paraded around singing a rendition of "The Itsy-Bitsy Spider" that only a mother could love or understand.

The reasons for my abdication of the drummer's throne were of course many, as they are for some major projects of mine that make it that far, and maybe some of yours. We're lost in the middle. The finish line is not nearly in sight, but we're far from having started the journey. It's at this point that interest fades and commitment wanes. I'd like to say that time was too short in supply. That I was called away on business to a foreign land that banned percussion. That someone had stolen our set. Or that I had broken precisely and surprisingly only the fingers I would need to properly hold the sticks. None of those things were true. (Shocking, I know.)

But I ascribe one reason for my failing progress to my husband's face.

The first time I sat down at the drums, he smiled wide and bright. Sincere encouragement, which in retrospect I may have confused with what was really shock at what my beginner's luck had produced. But by my second and third and fourth times behind the kit, that smile had flatlined, much like my potential for rock stardom. My husband, my parents, my friends. They were all asking to hear Mattie on drums, not me. I can't blame them, though. One recent afternoon I had sat down and recorded myself on the snare, bass drum, and ride. I appalled even myself.

In all honesty, I must confess, Pete's emotional palette wasn't to blame. It was not the absence of his smiles. It wasn't the presence of his grimaces. The problem was that from my first lesson to this point in time I wanted to limit his evaluative palette to only positive remarks. Tell me I'm fabulous, and hold the rest.

Avoiding a Floccinaucinihilipilification Nation

"Floccinaucinihilipilification" is the longest word in the English dictionary. And it's one Americans avoid at all cost. Not because it's hard to pronounce and challenging to spell, but because it goes against our core beliefs about how to promote success in ourselves. We want to focus on the positive and avoid the negative—but that doesn't work, just as it didn't for my percussive pursuits.

Erudite (and perhaps bored) students at Eton College in the mid-eighteenth century are said to have constructed the word "floccinaucinihilipilification" from bits of Latin roots that literally translate into "a trivial tuft of wool or hair, a trifle, a nothing."

Altogether, the word comes to mean an act or habit of describing or regarding something as worthless.

Besides being an archaic joke, floccinaucinihilipilification is almost a cultural taboo. We do everything we can to avoid thinking of ourselves as unimpressive, and instead work hard to maintain our own healthy self-view. We might concede when a challenge arises, lest failure threaten the good view of ourselves that we hold.

One reason we aspire toward positive self-regard is that we think it's the best way to stay motivated. My research team surveyed more than four hundred people from all around the United States and found that over 95 percent of respondents think that people with positive views of themselves accomplish more than people with negative views of themselves. And this translates into the types of feedback that we seek. We think employers should offer more praise than criticism, to encourage better performance. And friends should give their approval rather than a critical analysis when trying to motivate us. Parents think teachers should give positive feedback to children rather than negative feedback, to foster development.

But science says otherwise. When our efforts do not warrant positive feedback, much like my lackluster percussive performances as of late, receiving it can backfire. Roy Baumeister, a psychologist at

Florida State University, analyzed the results of more than two hundred studies of several thousand individuals and found that feedback, performance reviews, and praise designed to increase self-esteem don't work to help people better meet their goals. For example, positive regard for oneself does not improve the quality of job performance. Fostering high self-esteem in children does not improve grades in school. People with high self-esteem are no more likely to become leaders. They are not better liked. They act just as aggressively and no more generously than others, despite the fact that those with higher self-esteem *think* they're more popular and socially skilled.

Baumeister himself was surprised by the results. He was actually quoted as saying that his findings were the biggest disappointment of his career. The fact that positive feedback and favorable self-views didn't lead people to achieve more seemed to undermine our most basic belief about who accomplishes the most in life, and how we should motivate ourselves to do more.

So what if we don't find our inspiration by exclusively receiving positive feedback that makes us feel good? Where do we find it? Part of it comes from reading others right, even when what they have to tell us might not be all that positive. Sure, encouragement feels good. Praise can put a smile on our faces. But compliments do not always inspire us. Sometimes we're called to action by knowing where we've come up short. Charity fundraisers know this, and in at least one instance have partnered with academic researchers to show how highlighting missteps can motivate better than showcasing successes. The South Korean office of Compassion International partnered with social psychologist Ayelet Fishbach to raise funds for a new campaign benefiting AIDS orphans in Africa. The team solicited regular donors, giving feedback about current progress. Some regular donors received positive feedback as part of the solicitation. They read that the campaign *had already received* 50 percent of the funds they needed to meet the $10,000 goal. Others received the same information but in the form of negative feedback, indicating that the organization was *shy of its goal* by 50 percent. What motivated additional financial support among these people? The negative feedback. Knowing that the organization they were committed to was falling short inspired eight times as many people to make a donation. As this campaign demonstrated, sometimes we need to see what's really in front of us, even if that means getting floccinaucinihilipilificated every once in a while.

Learning to Read the Room

Reading others' emotional expressions for what they really are—even if that's negative—rather than what we want them to be can be the difference between landing the deal and losing it. Who gets the promotion and who stays in the cube. Who feels satisfied with what they're doing and who doesn't. In all fields of employment, and across the life span, people who read others' emotions better experience happier and more productive lives. Children as young as seven years of age who read others the best, even when what they see might not be a sign of encouragement, are also the ones who achieve the highest academic performance. Managers who can read emotions create psychologically healthier environments, and this practice shifts the way employees engage with customers, thereby boosting monthly sales figures. Doctors who can gauge the emotional state of their patients are less likely to get sued in medical malpractice cases. In one study, the business students in Singapore with better abilities to read emotions created more value for both themselves and the students playing the role of the buyer in a deal. Reading others right can be satisfying and lucrative, but it's not necessarily easy. And that's where we begin the next story.

One spring night I snagged a plus-one to the New York Academy of Art's Tribeca Ball. It's an annual charity event in a space where artists occupy one hundred or so studio stalls. For this one evening, they push aside their printing presses and saws. They turn down the kiln's scorching temperature and dry their brushes, though paint spattered on the floor just a few days before still teases the fancy stiletto heels of the party guests. Every available flat surface is covered in art you can admire, buy, eat, and kick if you aren't looking carefully.

I was the guest that night of a friend of the event's organizer, a guy who had Andy Warhol white-blond hair and was now busy circulating with his guests. I wandered into the basement, caught up in a stream of human movement that pulled me down a flight of stairs. Pin lights illuminated the buried recesses of the subterranean space, every inch of which was painted white. I caught the eye of another solo drifter as I passed him. I smiled, assuming—I'm not sure why—that we were both a little lost in this surreal scene.

"Hi," he said. "I'm Dennis. I'm sorry, but can I help you get that?" I was hoping he wasn't offering to pick spinach out of my teeth from the spanakopita I had snatched off the hors d'oeuvres tray on the way down. My anxiety bubbled up to the surface.

But before I could respond out loud, he reached behind my shoulder and brought back a lime. On the next beat, he had a deck of cards in his hands and the citrus had vanished.

"I'm a magician," he explained, though that was evident.

I came to learn that Dennis Kyriakos was working that night. He had been invited to dazzle guests with his tricks and illusions as he meandered through the galleries. An eight of spades I had written my name on and stuffed back into the deck appeared folded up and tucked inside his wallet a few minutes later, though his hands never left my sight, or so I thought. I opened my hand and watched as he placed one red ball on my palm before I clenched my fist tight. When I opened it later, there were two squishy crimson things, despite my never having felt anything change inside. I was hooked, and any semblance of high-society decorum I had been trying to cultivate earlier on had dissolved.

Since that night, I've had Kyriakos perform for my college

students many times. I teach them the science of visual gaze and attention; Kyriakos lets them experience it for themselves. His sleight-of-hand tricks catch us off guard every time, and leave us wondering how what we just saw was possible. Students love him, and I know it's for far more than just the break he offers from my lecturing.

Asked to explain what makes his audiences swoon, he said, "It's about knowing how to read people right." Kyriakos was a shy and awkward kid who had been picked on and bullied, he explained to me. He was in want of a different persona, and found it in magic.

"The books told me that I could be the life of the party. 'Want to be the center of attention? Learn magic.' So I did, and what I've realized is that we're all the same to a certain degree. No one wants to be made fun of. No one wants to be made a fool. I didn't then. And no one should feel that way now. That's why it's really important to me to know how people are feeling when I'm working a gig, and find the people who are in the right state of mind to have this experience with me."

How does he find the willing in his audience? I wondered.

"Some of it is obvious. I'm looking for people who are nodding their heads at me. Not the person with their arms folded with a look saying something like, 'Yeah, you aren't going to get me.' There's a smile on their face that's genuine. You can see that in their eyes, not their mouth. Then you've got to be on the lookout for the people who are jumping out of their seat, yelling 'I love magic!' That's too much. It's got to be the right kind of energy."

Reading other people's emotions correctly is a surprisingly tricky thing to accomplish, even for people like Kyriakos who quite literally have a trick up their sleeve. Results from the work of vision scientists Shichuan Du and Aleix Martinez bear this out plainly. Du and Martinez showed more than one hundred pictures to a group of university students and staff, and asked them to pick which of six possible expressions appeared on the faces in the photos. Each picture appeared for half a second. Long enough to see it, but not enough time to really study it in depth. The researchers were measuring first impressions and initial perceptions. In general, the group knew what happiness looked like. They were accurate 99 percent of the time. But fear was the hardest to read. Study participants recognized genuine fear only about half of the time. When they made a mistake, it was often because they thought those scared faces were actually surprised.

Beyond confusing these two, participants in this study struggled to identify other sets of emotions as well. The group was wrong about anger around 40 percent of the time. When an angry face appeared, the group was certain they saw sadness or disgust in about a quarter of the instances. The same with disgust; it was a challenge to recognize that emotion too. About half of the time, the group misidentified a look of disgust as one of anger.

Even the people we might suspect would be quite good at reading others' emotions struggle just as much as the rest of us. About thirty years ago, a social psychologist named Paul Ekman tested how good different groups of people were at reading the expressions of people who were lying or telling the truth. He tested college students, and also those he thought would be particularly adept at identifying deception: psychiatrists, criminal investigators and judges, federal agents at Quantico who conducted polygraph tests, and even U.S. Secret Service agents.

Ekman showed these various groups of would-be lie detectors videos of women being interviewed about their reactions to a movie each had just watched. All the reports were positive, but not all were truthful. Some of those women had just watched nature films and actually felt happy and content. But other women had just watched a gruesome film portraying amputations and burn victims. These women were lying when they said they felt good. Ekman's respondents knew of these two possibilities, but did not know which film each woman had watched. Their job was just to guess which women were trying to deceive their interviewers and which were telling the truth.

It might come as no surprise that the college students had a hard time telling the difference. On average, they were right at about the same rate that a statistician would expect among people who were just randomly guessing, without any real insight or ability to read emotions.

But some of those people had gone to school or been trained, or just seemed like they should have a natural ability to read people better than the rest of us, right? Psychiatrists are doctors of the human psyche. Polygraph technicians have machinery at their disposal, and their entire job is to pick out indicators of deception. But when tested by Ekman, all of these groups showed accuracy rates indistinguishable from that of the college students, or predicted by chance. In other words, all of these groups were essentially guessing. Guessing poorly.

Except for one.

Only one group of Ekman's lie detectors could separate truth tellers from liars at rates that exceeded chance. It was the Secret Service. On average, the Secret Service agents were right 64 percent of the time. And some of them were *very* good. Ten agents were right eight or more times out of ten.

This led Ekman to wonder what it was that distinguished the truth tellers from the liars. What was it that the Secret Service agents were picking up on that the psychiatrists, judges, and investigators were not? It turns out that the agents had been trained to pay close attention to certain facial movements in order to detect lies. When he reevaluated the videos of the women's emotional confessions, Ekman now found what the agents saw: subtle differences in the ways the women smiled revealed when they were being truthful and when they were lying about experiencing pleasant feelings.

Our corrugator muscles, which sit around the insides of our eyes, fire up when we are actually experiencing suffering. Think about when the sun is bright, and what happens to your eyes around your nose when you squint. That's the corrugator muscles pulling the tops of your eyelids down to keep out the glare. Or think about the frown lines we all get on our lower forehead—the ones produced by the muscles just on the insides of our eyebrows above our nose that some people treat with Botox. The women who were lying about feeling good gave themselves away with these muscles. They also gave themselves away with their lips. Some liars' upper lips curled up with disgust ever so slightly, and the corners of their mouths curled down just a bit. The words the women used were equally convincing, and they smiled just as much, but the disgust they'd felt earlier seeped into their expressions of positive regard.

Framing the Shot

We may never find ourselves sitting in front of Paul Ekman or surrounded by Secret Service agents, but we likely will find ourselves at some point wondering if someone we love is really upset. Or if our child is truly happy. Or whether our boss is actually pleased. So how do we know? The key to reading the "tells" of others' emotions is about framing the shot. If we know where to look, we can teach ourselves to read emotions better.

All smiles require that we flex muscles around the mouth, but to tell the difference between a real smile and a staged one, look to the eyes. The way we use the muscles at the outer corners of our eyes, called the orbiculares oculi, distinguishes a genuine from a stilted expression. In a real smile, we contract those muscles, pulling in the skin next to our eyes, and giving ourselves crow's feet that later on we might pay handsomely to erase. When smiling on command rather than when actually inspired, we use the risorii muscles in each cheek to pull our lips into the right shape, but the crow's feet don't emerge.

How you can you tell the difference between pleasant surprise and unwelcome fear? These expressions share raised eyebrows and wide eyes, and might look similar if we orient toward the baby blues alone. The difference in emotion can be read in the lips. Stretched lips, pulled back at the corners, are the only muscle movement that can reliably distinguish fear from surprise. A surprised mouth pulls down more than a fearful one.

Anger and sorrow actually have some similarities, and if we try to discern these expressions with a quick glance at another person's eyes, we might confuse them. Eyebrows lower and eyes close off when someone is either mad or sad. In the same vein, angry and grossed-out mouths can look quite similar. The tight lips that we might associate with pent-up rage could also be disgust. To read anger right, we should frame up the mouth and nose. The lip-depressor muscles that pull our lower lip down remain taut and flat-lined when we feel anger, but the corners of our lips turn toward the ground when we honestly feel sad. And when anger and disgust are strong, we can tell the difference between a cross expression and a repulsed one by looking at the nose. It scrunches up a bit when we're angry but bunches even more when we're grossed out.

It's a challenge, of course, to know what parts of the face to frame up when we're trying to read what another person is feeling. The expressions might live for just a brief moment. Or maybe we didn't get as good a look as we'd like. When we are gauging what someone else is feeling, we might get them wrong, or at minimum see something others may not.

Part of the reason for our visual idiosyncracies is that faces can be particularly expressive. As humans, we often feel multiple emotions simultaneously, and they can show up on our faces all at once. This makes it tricky to read or intuit what other people are feeling when we get mixed messages from what we see on their face.

Take the photograph on page 121, for example. It's of me. Not a particularly flattering depiction, I know, and, yes, those are in fact my natural wrinkles. It took a fair bit of humility and a lot of bravery to post it to a few social media sites. But I did, asking others to de- scribe the emotional expression they saw on my face upon first glance. You can play along too. What do you see?

About a hundred people responded with a single word each. Even though everyone was looking at the same photograph, the group saw thirty different emotions in that single snapshot. The word cloud below presents the most-often stated responses in larger size and the rare responses as smaller. A quick look will show you that, for the most part, the group saw some sort of negative feeling— "discomfort," "apprehension," and "awkwardness" being the three most commonly mentioned. But 15 percent of people saw something entirely different; they saw a positive expression—happiness, joy, and playfulness, for instance.

The unique visual interpretations we reach can have a big impact on some of the most important relationships we have. To prove the point, social psychologist William Brady and I created a more rigorous test of how people read faces. We gathered three dozen photographs of men and women smiling and frowning. Importantly, there were mixed messages in each photograph. Every single person displayed hints of both positive and negative expressions. In one photograph, for example, a man's eyes crinkled at the outer edges, which was a cue he felt happy. In that same photo, though, the man's lips curled up at the edges, suggesting disdain or disgust. We asked over three hundred adults in committed relationships to decide whether each person looked like they were feeling a positive or negative emotion. When we analyzed their decisions, we could tell which parts of the faces they had visually framed up. If they indicated that the majority of photographed people appeared to express positive emotions, we knew they had framed up those areas of the face that displayed happiness or amusement. If they reported that most expressed negative emotions, we knew they'd framed up those that evinced anger or sadness.

We thought that these predispositions for misperception might change the way people experienced conflict in their personal relationships when problems cropped up. We asked our participants to think about relationship issues that were troubling or irksome. They talked about imbalance in household chore distribution, financial strain, or differences in opinion about how to discipline the kids. Sure, these concerns made them feel frustrated, worked up, and angry, but some people experienced the disagreements as wounding battles while others chalked them up to minor blips. Perhaps surprisingly, those who more accurately identified expressions for what they were, reading both the positive and negative emotions equally well even when that meant recognizing the frustration or discontent on their partner's face, felt okay after conflict. Reading negative emotions right does not ensure despair, but instead might prompt a truer understanding of what dynamics of the situation can be repaired.

———

Sometimes the situation we are in does not require us to perceive a single person's reactions. Sometimes the situation we face requires that we read a crowd.

Even if you're not a New Yorker trying to cross the street at rush hour in Times Square, you might hate crowds. Regardless of where we live, there's one place in particular we all could find ourselves in that produces a particular source of dread—in front of a large room filled to capacity, delivering a speech. A national survey of more than eight thousand people found that public speaking was the most commonly held fear. In fact, many people said they feared it more than death. One reason that we loathe public speaking is that the public's reaction feels important but so uncertain. We care about other people's opinions of us, so whether they're giving us a thumbs-up or thumbs-down really matters. Billionaire investor Warren Buffett long suffered from these anxieties, even going so far as to drop out of college classes when they required speaking aloud in class. He now takes questions for five hours from the more than forty thousand attendees at each year's shareholders' meeting.

The fear of public speaking doesn't apply just to special occasions. It's not just about delivering a killer quarterly report at the team meeting. Or standing up at a wedding and giving a knockout toast. It's also everyday public speaking that gets our heart racing. It's just as scary to talk to a small group as to a large crowd when you haven't prepared your thoughts.

When we're trying to read a room, how do we decide whether we're about to get a standing ovation or the hook? It's about how we read the emotional expressions on the faces we see in the crowd. The way in which we look at the people in front of us, including where we direct our gaze as we scan the room, determines whether we believe the crowd is with us or against us. In situations like these, many of us find ourselves seeking encouragement from others looking back at us. We're hoping for praise, or at least reassurance, to get us through the dry mouth and anxiety. And this is exactly when knowing how to frame the shot might keep us from dying in front of the crowd.

Chris Anderson was born in a remote village in Pakistan to missionary parents. He studied philosophy at Oxford, started a world news service in the Seychelles islands, and was an editor at two of the UK's early computer magazines. But these are likely not the things we know Anderson for. Instead, we know Anderson because he started TED.

TED is a nonprofit organization dedicated to finding "ideas worth spreading." Each year, TED holds a conference replete with luminaries from technology, entertainment, design, the arts, and the sciences. Speakers have a maximum of eighteen minutes to share their most innovative and engaging contributions to society, and the topics are wildly varied, from the science of orgasm to education reform. Many have taken Anderson up on his offer to present, and the resulting infotainment has made TED Talks viewed well over a billion times.

To create the 2013 TED event, Anderson and the TED selection team tried something they never had before. They traveled the globe, visiting six continents and listening to the most unique stories every city they stopped in had to offer. In a piece for the *Harvard Business Review*, Anderson reflected on that scouting expedition.

After listening to about three hundred stories, they found one that was particularly incredible. While in Kenya, Anderson met Richard Turere, a Maasai boy who also happened to be Kenya's youngest patent holder. Since the age of six, he'd had the responsibility of protecting his family's animals from nighttime lion attacks in their village, Kitengela, on the edge of the Nairobi National Park. The lions were cunning, and they weren't deterred by the tactics that members of Turere's tribe had taught Turere. The livestock continued to be killed—sometimes as many as nine cows a week—and sometimes the lions were, too.

Through trial and error, Turere learned that the lions kept their distance if he walked through the fields holding a torch. However, the fields were big and Turere was still quite small. To scale up his solution, he took apart his parents' radios to teach himself the basics of electronics and engineering. He pieced together solar panels, a car battery, and a motorcycle's turn signals to create a blinking light display. The visual illusion of movement in the fields at night stopped the lions from attacking. Villages across Kenya took his idea and started installing "Richard's lion lights."

Anderson thought this idea was worth sharing, so he invited Turere to tell his story at the TED2013 conference as one of the youngest speakers ever to take the main stage. Turere was thirteen years old by then, and his English was not very good. He'd be delivering his talk not where he lived in Kenya but in Long Beach, California, so he'd have to muster up the bravery to get on a plane for the first time. In practice sessions, his sentences came out in a jumbled, stilted manner, and with a live audience of 1,400 people it was likely to be no better.

The TED staff worked with Turere to help him frame his story and practice his delivery.

If you watch Turere's talk, you can see that he was nervous, but he charmed the audience nonetheless (they gave him an instant standing ovation at the end). So, what was it that Anderson and the TED staff advised to help Turere deal with his nerves? *Find five or six friendly-looking people in different parts of the audience, and look them in the eye as you speak.*

The work of a group of researchers from the University of Texas at Dallas, led by Jonathan Shasteen, helps explain why the TED advice is so sound. The researchers used sophisticated technology that tracked the movements of people's eyes without them knowing it as they scanned a crowd of faces. Sensors embedded within a computer monitor's frame recorded where people directed their gaze. The researchers found that the way we scan a crowd can be partly responsible for our thinking that it is against us, and thus for the fear we have when we stand in front of others. As we scan faces, our eyes naturally land on angry faces faster than on happy ones. If left to our own devices, we gravitate toward signs of hostility and miss signs of inspiration. So, Anderson's advice to frame up the face of a friend or six in the crowd is like a counteractive agent, helping us to align our overall impression of the group with what might actually be the truth.

Other research suggests that this strategy may be something that comes more naturally with age. Elderly people are more inclined than younger ones to regard their social environment in the way the TED staff taught Turere to before his TED debut. For older adults, this pattern of eye gaze contributes to their feeling a greater sense of emotional satisfaction. But even among people for whom it does not come as second nature, practicing framing up happiness when reading the crowd can bring about benefits. Children who make this style of looking a habit reap the benefits well into their adult years. Clinicians found that kids as young as age seven who experienced social anxiety but learned to look for smiles rather than frowns showed less severe symptoms weeks later. In fact, half of them no longer met the criteria for a diagnosis of anxiety—as compared to the baseline group, in which 92 percent of children still held the diagnosis. In a similar vein, college students who practiced directing their attention toward the smiling faces in a crowd during the week they were studying for their final exams reported feeling less stressed about how they would perform on the upcoming tests.

The same is true for salespeople. In one study, telemarketers practiced framing up friendly faces when scanning a crowd, and subsequently their *phone* sales—not in-person sales—skyrocketed, increasing by almost 70 percent. Before they practiced framing up the smiling faces in a crowd, telemarketers would, on average, have to contact thirteen people to make one sale. But after practicing, they made a sale after every seven contacts. How is that possible? Well, the researchers found that repeatedly practicing framing up the happy faces rather than the angry ones lowered the salespeople's cortisol, the neuroendocrine marker for how much stress people's bodies are registering. Practicing framing up the friendly faces instilled a calm confidence that contributed directly to their bottom line.

Framing Up Failures and Thinking About Them Differently

Research suggests that frames that help us see the world accurately work best when we believe there is a chance to learn and grow. Carol Dweck is a psychologist at Stanford University who studies motivation and achievement. She has found that the mindset people adopt as they are working toward their goals reliably predicts who is likely to succeed and who is likely to fail in the long run. According to fifty years of her own work, people who approach new experiences with a belief that valuable skills can be learned through effort and investment find inspiration in knowing where they really stand, even if that news might seem disappointing to some. These individuals hold what she calls a "growth mindset." They see novel experiences as opportunities for improvement, which nurtures a healthy passion to learn. Finding out what you don't know is just as important as—if not more important than—showing people what you do know. In this way, failures don't define a person, but are instead part of a normal process of development.

She found that there are other people, though, who approach uncharted territory with trepidation because a possible failure, to them, seems like a pretty damning experience. These people have what she calls a "fixed mindset": they believe that disposition and personal characteristics are unchangeable—that people are born with a set amount of intelligence or capacity. Poor performance, to these individuals, implies a lack of ability that can't be overcome. Winning rather than learning is the goal, because failure defines who they are overall. Those with a fixed mindset view taking risks as a potential way of exposing their shortcomings, faults, and weaknesses. So rather than risk others finding out they are not capable of performing, they avoid even trying—which ultimately proves destructive, as they avoid opportunities to learn more.

The thing about these two different types of mindsets is that they change how our brains respond to mistakes we make. There's a test based on Dweck's work that researchers give that assesses people's mindset. You can take it here. Using this scale, how much do you agree or disagree with the three statements below? When you've answered them all, sum up your answers, and divide by three.

MINDSET TEST

1	2	3	4	5	6
Strongly Agree	Agree	Mostly Agree	Mostly Disagree	Disagree	Strongly Disagree

1. You have a certain amount of intelligence, and you really can't do much to change it.

2. Your intelligence is something about you that you can't change very much.

3. You can learn new things, but you can't really change your basic intelligence.

Now, there's no score that diagnoses you as having a growth or fixed mindset—in fact, your score could change if your beliefs about ability do. But people with higher average scores (think four and higher) tend to think people can learn new skills. On the other hand, people with lower average scores (like three and lower) tend to believe that you can't really change something like your basic intelligence—that you have a certain amount of it, and really can't do much to increase it.

Psychologist Jason Moser and his colleagues at Michigan State

University administered this mindset test to research participants. They also created another interesting test, a visual search game in which participants had to quickly and accurately identify whether there was a mismatch in an image they saw. They asked participants if the images in the periphery were the same as the ones in the middle. Moser had the students take this test while wearing an EEG cap measuring brain activity across sixty-four points. Moser was interested specifically in the "Pe signal." This is a brain wave that peaks when a person is consciously aware of having made a mistake; it can detect an individual's awareness of that mistake in as little as one fifth of a second. Faster than the snap of a finger.

Moser knew which students held a stronger growth versus fixed mindset as they thought about whether intelligence is something you are born with or develop. From these differences in mindset, Moser could predict whose brains would pick up on their mistakes and whose brains would, in a sense, deny that they ever made any. Individuals with a growth mindset showed enhanced Pe amplitude. Neurologically, they were acknowledging whenever they'd made an error. Compare this to individuals who held a fixed mindset. Their neurological profiles were muted, as if they were not recognizing when they made a mistake. Importantly, recognition of error was key to improving performance on the test later on. Individuals with greater Pe responses performed better at the task almost immediately. A growth mindset allowed for faster recognition of mistakes, which helped the students learn, rebound, and improve.

When we pay attention to our mistakes and believe that they don't mark us as incapable but instead give us an opportunity to grow, we also experience healthier mental lives and positive well-being. Researchers trained NCAA Division I athletes to adopt a growth mindset. Having learned to approach the possibility of failure as an opportunity for advancement, these athletes were less stressed, handled their own feelings of disappointment better, and had more energy to throw into their respective sports. Another study trained college rowers to use a growth mindset. These athletes developed mental toughness. They showed stronger belief in their own ability to achieve, which is a key component of success.

And success is defined by more than just shaving a few seconds off the timer or nailing another three-pointer. Success can take the form of rebirth. Bethany Hamilton is a professional surfer who experienced a horrific accident that changed the course of her life. She was winning competitions when she was only eight years old. In 2003, at the age of thirteen, she went out for a surf at Tunnels Beach in Kauai with her best friend, Alana Blanchard, and her family. It was 7:30 a.m. The light was perfect. The sand was golden and the cliffs were shrouded in green at the mouth of the bay. The turtles were swimming all around them. As Hamilton lay on her board, with her left arm dangling in the water, a fourteen-foot tiger shark swam up and bit her.

Her friends paddled her back to shore. Blanchard's father created a tourniquet from a surfboard strap. They rushed her to the hospital. She was in shock, having lost 60 percent of the blood in her body. Her left arm was nearly entirely gone. But three weeks after the attack, Bethany Hamilton left the hospital. One week after that, she was back on her board surfing again. Within a year, she would go on to win first place in the Australian National Scholastic Surfing Association competition, and she is now ranked as one of the top fifty female surfers in the world.

For most people, losing an arm would have been a career ender, and for Hamilton it could have meant stopping her career nearly as soon as it began. Paddling out over waves with one arm could have been much more difficult, and balance nearly impossible to achieve. But not for Hamilton. She has a growth mindset. Hamilton described her mental state: "Whatever your situation might be, set your mind to whatever you want to do and put a good attitude in it, and I believe you can succeed." She took this as an opportunity to show both herself and the world that she could relearn her sport.

We may not find ourselves surfing with sharks in Hawaii or

working toward national-champion status, but a growth mindset is just as important when working toward our own health goals. Like any pursuit that really matters, our search for success might first or often be marked by failure. We mustn't shy away from them, and should avoid fixating on showcasing perfection. Dweck coaches us to adopt the mantra "Becoming is better than being." Embrace the missteps. Look for the places where we can improve, acknowledging the shortcomings they imply. Frame up the constructive criticisms. They are the stepping stones to success.

I'm not a good surfer. I've gotten about a half dozen private lessons from an excellent teacher who, because of her excessive patience and friendship, continued to offer instruction despite my inability to reciprocate with anything even as simple as getting my feet on the deck during a wave. Neither am I a particularly skilled skier. I needed six months of rehabilitation and reconstructive surgery on my knee after I tried hitting the slopes out west for the very first time. But I don't define myself by these athletic gaffes. I tried. It didn't work out, but, at least for surfing, where the falls hurt far less, I'll keep on trying again.

When it came to writing this book, the missteps I experienced shared some of the same sting as those athletic exploits. In brainstorming the content of each chapter and the messages I would share, I reworked my plan a total of nine times, scrapping about 80 percent of my ideas from one take to the next. It felt like a herculean effort to land on something I was proud of, much as it does when I try to get the board underfoot in the surf. From one iteration of the manuscript to the next, I could have focused on the content that had landed on the cutting-room floor, seeing that scrap as an indication of my inability. *Maybe I don't have the chops to become a writer,* I could have wondered. But that mindset would have ensured a failed final product, as it would for any skill we deem ourselves fundamentally and fatally incapable of improving enough to meet our mark.

Those eight versions of the book's plan that now sit in a folder as rough cuts won't ever have an audience. But they still have a starring role in this story. With each version, I pushed to think differently and try again with a new tack. I think of these eight iterations as mile markers in my intellectual marathon. I see them as flags representing important moments in this adventure. Crossing over the Queensboro Bridge into Manhattan and later entering Central Park for the final leg of the New York City Marathon are points of note for those who run the race. They mark evolutionary phases of the challenge. And so do the versions of this book you won't ever see.

I also have cloistered evidence of my evolution as a drummer, and that too won't see the light of day. A few recording sessions were videotaped before I had showered for the day, and my bed head was on point. Some came during the first few weeks of my training, when my style was reminiscent of a baby giraffe trying to run. I don't think of these clips as evidence of inability, and I didn't at the time of filming. They were markers in my musical marathon. They were stages in my personal evolution, not verification of inability.

A mindset of *becoming*, not *being*, shapes a culture within us and outside us. Edward Deci is an expert in motivation science and a professor at the University of Rochester. He's taken his insights and applied them to improving employees' lives at some of the biggest companies in the world. One example from his work showcases the motivating power of framing up the positive. At one point in Deci's career, a Fortune 500 company specializing in office machines called him in for a consult. It was a tough time in the industry—competition was steep, profits slim. Employees were worried about job security, and rightly so: layoffs and pay freezes were not uncommon. Morale was low.

Deci was brought in to help. He started by conducting interviews and discovered that, on the whole, managers gave far more negative feedback than positive. Managers structured their comments in ways that commented on employees' worth as individuals rather than the value of their actions. This needed to change.

He created a program that trained fifteen thousand employees. Managers learned how to take the employees' perspective, soliciting, listening to, and understanding their ideas, reactions, and experiences. Employees learned how to take initiative and were offered opportunities to do so.

Most important, managers received guidance on how to structure feedback to praise their employees' efforts when it was warranted. Over the course of three days, at an off-site location, managers learned how to deliver constructive, positive, and even flattering comments in response to employees' ideas and decisions—and to do it more often.

The results? The managers' new positivity spread to their employees, who reported seeing more possibilities for career advancement, feeling more satisfied with their jobs, and having more trust in management—including trust in those at the highest levels in the organizational hierarchy, with whom employees would not previously have had any contact.

Years later, Jacques Forest, a professor of management science at the Université du Québec à Montréal, and his team analyzed the financial impact of this shift. Did the decision to train managers in delivering effective positive feedback pay off? Yes. They calculated the cost in current dollars incurred by rolling out the training, and the mental-health-care savings the organization had accrued. Forest discovered that the return on investment for the company was more than three to one. A sound investment indeed.

The Right Tool for the Job

It might seem like a mixed message, what I've offered for how to approach feedback. I suggested ways to frame up others so we can read their emotions right, even if that means finding out they aren't so happy with us. I've also suggested framing up the faces of people expressing encouragement, selectively tuning in to aspects of our social environment that might make us feel good. We can frame up our world in ways that highlight some of our best contributions to it, and we can also frame it up to see it as it truly is.

When we're looking to enter into a new venture, we find motivation in accentuating the positives. We can also frame up our visual surroundings in ways that promote a complete and true reflection of what the world really holds. Sometimes that way of framing might reveal something about ourselves that could seem like a vulnerability or shortcoming. But this inspires progress—as long as we approach the opportunity with a growth mindset. When we believe in our potential to change, adopting a frame that exposes where our efforts might best be placed can improve the odds of success. Just as the visual strategies for seeing our way to success act as different tools that might serve unique purposes, so too might the options for framing up our visual surroundings to see the world as it is or as we'd like it to be.

7

Forgoing the Forbidden Fruit and Perceiving Patterns

Pete left me.

For a business trip. Not divorce. But it was for a week. And there were enough time zones separating us, and unreliable enough cell service, that I got a taste of what life as a solo working parent is like. It was rough. Our bedroom smelled like poop. Not from me, not directly. But somehow when Pete empties the diaper pail he also manages to take out the smell too, an elusive skill that I don't seem to have. Mattie was sick with the flu, and because of that I am certain more food came out of him than went into him. The bed didn't get made. My sheets felt wet (how?). We broke a lamp. And the vacuum that tried to clean it up.

And I kicked off the first day of my adventures in single parenting with a medical emergency. Mattie and I were playing. He was crawling over me like those goats some people bring with them to hot yoga. Things got weird—weirder even than sweaty zoo animals in exercise class—and Mattie head-butted me. On purpose. In the mouth. My lip split open and swelled to twice its size faster than the speed of sound. I know because I felt it expand even before I recognized the sound of my own yelp. Mattie and I both cried because of all the blood. The day hadn't started off well.

By the middle of the afternoon, I was so beat that I did something I had never done before. While Mattie napped, I napped too. But not with the feeling of luxury that this rare moment warranted. No. I just sort of listed over, falling onto my side in the living room. I ended up in the fetal position on the hardwood floor. And I decided I'd stay. No pillow. A blanket had fallen on my face and felt like it belonged there. I didn't have the energy to move to the couch that was close enough to kick if there was reason to. As quickly and easily as I'd toppled over, I also fell asleep. Baby-induced concussion, maybe?

I woke up when Mattie beckoned for my services, crib-side. He used me as a mommy ladder, climbed out, and headed straight for the iPad. I'd wondered what he did with his days when I was away writing this book, and I think I figured it out then. If the Apple Store down the street had a punch-card loyalty program for visits to the Genius Bar, Mattie would have gotten his tenth cup of coffee for free a long while ago. He looked like he'd had lessons, knew what he was doing. Without losing a beat, he woke up his electronic friend, took that chubby little pointer finger he usually reserves for wagging at me when he's telling me *no*, and started playing a song. Of the thousands on the menu and with the ability to start the song wherever he wanted, he cued up Frank Sinatra belting out Hoagy Carmichael's line "I get along without you very well . . ."

As this day has made very clear to me, no Pete, I do not.

By the end of the week, after schlepping myself and Mattie out of the city and to the country, I collapsed into bed as the night set in. My mind was organizing the ever-growing to-do list. What I had forgotten to do that day kept me awake. What I needed to do far exceeded what I did do each day. Coupled with that, Mattie had made friends with the sunrise and decided that this week of all weeks he wanted to greet each and every one of them personally. So I confess, I didn't practice drums. I didn't even see the sticks. I was so tired. I wanted a break.

I knew I wasn't alone in wanting something other than what I had. And I recognized the problem that this posed for the goals I was working toward—other than keeping Mattie and me alive, healthy, and happy. I went back to read a study I remembered about the struggles of temptation and wanting something else. Researchers found more than two hundred adults from the city of Würzburg, Germany, who agreed to report on the things they wanted during their day. They all received a prototype smartphone. It wasn't really all that smart, but it could randomly beep and ask some personal questions about every two hours for a week. The main question this intrusive little device posed was whether its owner wanted something at the moment. That something could be anything. If the answer to the question was yes, the device asked for a description of what that something was. And people seemed unabashed about offering that insight into their inner lives. Now, respondents weren't hooked up to any machines that could document every single want and every shifting desire—despite what the movies might lead us to believe, these kinds of machines don't yet exist. But because the devices were set up to randomly ask their owner what was going on in their mind so frequently throughout the day, and because people were not shy in answering, the researchers collected a lot of data. In fact, they had more than ten thousand answers to read through, and from this haul they could do a very good job of approximating how often we want things.

And the results were clear. By even the most conservative estimates, people feel like they want something about half the time they are awake. One out of every four times their devices asked them what they wanted, people said food. Followed in frequency by a nap and a drink. People wanted coffee more often than they wanted to watch television, check their Instagram feed, or have sex—though those were still pretty popular cravings.

It's not bad to want something. Wanting to eat, sleep, and have sex keeps us, as a species, alive, quite literally. But sometimes those things we want right now don't resonate with the things we want later on. And, in fact, about half of the time people wanted something, they simultaneously said they didn't want to want it. They said their desires right then conflicted at least somewhat with something else they were working toward. Altogether, these findings imply that during one-quarter of our waking lives we find ourselves pulled toward something we wish, at least in part, wasn't luring us in that direction.

Temptations can catch our eye and occupy our mental bandwidth. When we see them in front of us or notice them nearby, it can be hard to think about anything else. For example, if we realize that a tray of cookies is sitting against the back wall in a boring meeting, our minds may begin to formulate a plan to excuse ourselves and snag a treat on the way out the door.

In other words, there are times when, if we look myopically, we might act narrow-mindedly. Like chocolates to a dieter, a gin and tonic to an attempted teetotaler, or the splurge to a saver, focus sometimes has us acting like a moth around a flame. The things that capture our attention can lead us to make decisions that seem ideal in the moment but sit at odds with our long-range plans. One candy bar today won't expand our belly, but one candy bar every afternoon likely could send us shopping for a new pair of pants down the road. Buying an iced cappuccino on the morning commute in and the evening commute out on the same day, once, won't break the bank, but it could make a significant dent in our net income and savings goals if we kept this up throughout the whole month.

Expanding Our Focus

Remember the pantry attendants stocking the snack areas at Google? Their work demonstrated how a narrow focus might lead us to make the wrong choices based on what's close at hand. Knowing that employees visit snack stations to get a drink but happen to see the snacks nearby and grab a handful, the scientists decided to separate the food from the beverages. One beverage station was placed six feet from the snacks. Another beverage station was set up seventeen feet away. The scientists recorded all of the drink and snack choices that four hundred employees made over seven workdays.

That difference of eleven feet mattered. When the snacks were close by the beverage station, 20 percent of employees stopped for a treat. But when the snacks were farther away, only 12 percent of employees indulged. Consider the typical male Google employee. He's 180 pounds, leaves his desk for a water or coffee about three times a day, but otherwise lives a fairly sedentary lifestyle at the office—because all those perks keep him there longer than most other jobs would. For him, these percentages might mean he's throwing back another 180 snacks each year. If we conservatively estimate that each snack costs him 150 calories, his impulsive selections could translate into about two to three pounds of weight gain every twelve months—simply because the snack cart happened to be in view when he went to get a drink of water.

We don't have to work at Google to design a space for ourselves that can encourage choices to make us healthier, happier, and more satisfied. Along with Shana Cole and Janna Dominick, I found that some people know how to do this intuitively. People who successfully navigate the dieting scene tend to look at their surroundings in ways that mimic the healthier experience Google's pantry-stockers were trying to create. We asked a few hundred people to tell us whether they set goals to curb their consumption of unhealthy foods. They also told us how successful they were at watching their weight or losing a few pounds. Next, they estimated how far away different types of foods appeared to them. To do this, we had staged a sort of cafeteria, covering a table in chips and cookies but also carrots and bananas. We found that dieters who struggled the most to avoid succumbing to temptation saw the unhealthy foods as closer to them than dieters who were more successful at choosing healthy options. Of course, the distance separating the dieters from the foods was always the same. Struggling dieters simply saw the distance to bad choices as being shorter, and as a result held weaker intentions to eat healthy in the near future. Why does this misperception occur? It seems to be because of narrow focus. The things that look close at hand are the things that we can't pull our eyes away from.

Take, for instance, the case of the cupcake. Mia and Jason Bauer together opened Crumbs Bake Shop on the Upper West Side of Manhattan. The establishment acquired its notoriety for the enormous heights its confections—slathered in frosting and adorned with gooey embellishments—could attain. The "colossal cupcake" towered six and a half inches over the plate it was served on. Everyone loved their cupcakes. The Bauers started as a mom-and-pop shop, but within ten years they had seventy stores, twenty-two of which were less than a year old, which earned them a place on *Inc.*'s "500 fastest-growing companies" list. The Bauers joke that the first word out of their kids' mouths was "cupcakes."

But, like they were for many of us, the teenage years were rough. The stock was trading at thirteen dollars per share, but the year Crumbs turned thirteen, the stock fell to three cents a share. Then less than one cent a share. Nasdaq had already planned to delist the company from the exchange well before Crumbs closed all of its doors forever.

What happened? Of course, hindsight is 20/20, but industry analysts surmise that one key factor in Crumbs's initial success was also the reason for its fall from glory: a narrow-sighted focus on the sale of a single product—those cupcakes.

The Norm of Narrow Focus

We may find ourselves adopting a narrow focus, and making choices we wish we hadn't, when it comes to how we think about time. We wake up and think about what we want to get done today. We *don't* wake up and think about what we want to get done this *month*, or at least few of us do. When presented with the restaurant menu, we contemplate whether we can calorically afford to get dessert tonight. We don't look at that menu and factor into our decision our rate of dessert consumption for the past two weeks and our anticipated rate of indulging for the two weeks to come. When our child is scream-ing the word "phone," which he's just learned to say with enough clarity for nonparents to comprehend, we might quickly cue up Thomas the Tank Engine videos to calm that very, very loud child right now. (Or, at least I have.) We aren't thinking about the inten-tions we have for a screen-free childhood. Some of the decisions we make in our daily lives might not align with our goals because we make them with a focus on the here and now, rather than tomorrow and beyond.

I wondered whether a narrow focus might be impacting me, and I thought I'd take a turn at being my own research guinea pig. I enlisted a group of students I was teaching to test themselves as well. We put on our figurative lab coats and, Jane Goodall–style, con-ducted a naturalistic observation study of ourselves in the wild. I could envision a few different ways that a narrow focus might impact me, and the students agreed that these were facets of life worth exploring. So, all twenty-five of us kept track of our unintended expenses—those impulse purchases—for two weeks.

Max tracked his tuna-sandwich splurges. Hartej wondered how often he buys e-cigarettes. Others asked themselves how much they spent on food deliveries, taxis, and clothes. I had very little sense of where my money went but knew I seemed almost out of it all the time. So I set an alert on my phone to ask me every four hours what purchases I'd made since it last asked me.

What we found out about ourselves surprised nearly all of us.

I discovered that about 25 percent of the times that my phone asked me, I had made a purchase I did not set out to make when I woke up that morning. All of my unintended expenses during this two-week period were for food. Half the time, I wanted to bring my lunch to work but didn't get it packed before I went out the door. Then I walked past a pastry shop that beckoned my taste buds; nearly all do. Someone makes my coffee most mornings (thanks, Pete), but I still racked up quite the bill with the barista next door to my office.

I also recorded how I felt afterward, and found that my reactions fell distinctly into three categories. A handful of my own reactions were blatant rationalizations after the fact: "I have to eat. At least it's healthy." A third of the time, I blamed the expense on fatigue: "Third coffee just this morning. Must have forgotten to count." A third of the time, I felt guilty: "Bought this almond croissant to share with Mattie and Pete . . . didn't share it at all . . . bad Mommy," or "Ugh, damn that fig-and-pecan bar. Three bites in, and I already feel like I shouldn't have spent my calories or dollars this way."

My students seemed to share my experience. Through the process of tracking and then compiling to see the big picture, Yuqing realized she spent almost twice as much money in a week on lunch than she budgeted for. That $35 soup and salad definitely didn't help the bottom line. Likewise, Anna computed that 35 percent of her spending was on what she labeled "irrationally expensive" food, and that the vast majority of the $280 she spent on splurges went toward coffee and bagels. Gabrielle learned she was a very loyal Juno customer who spent as much on the ride-sharing service as she did on one month's cable bill. Aleksander computed that exactly 62 percent of his splurges are on chicken-and-avocado-salad sandwiches.

We weren't fortune-tellers, but at some level we'd known something like this would happen. Before we started tracking, we'd thought we might succumb to unanticipated temptations. We estimated that our unintended expenses would come in, collectively, at just under $1,600. But in reality, our tracking proved that we spent far more. Our group spent about $2,400 mindlessly in this two-week period, which was amazing because only half of us in the group had a regular job.

That $800 separating expectation from reality had real impact. For me personally, in the twelve days I was really keeping track, I spent $75.30 that I hadn't planned to. That's more than pocket change for sure, though not a sum that would be a real financial strain. But when I converted it into currency that was even more meaningful, the expense was painful. At New York City rates, I'd spent the equivalent of five babysitting hours without thinking about it. That's like two date nights I just tossed away. Or four Zumba classes I could have attended, which could have burned about four thousand calories that I could have reallocated toward many more fig-and-pecan bars—without the guilt. Each of those thoughtless choices tallied up to something tangible.

My students, too, felt the impact of their splurges only when they took a step back and looked at the total bill. One woman tallied up how much she felt she'd tossed away. "I could have put that money toward saving up for something nice," she told me, "or, more realistically, spent it on makeup." One caffeine junkie realized how much cheaper sleeping would have been, and another was disappointed in himself for spending so much on something that just kept him up later than he wanted; he could have instead bought a lot of nachos at the movies. One man realized that his impulsive purchases in this two-week period could have translated into three tickets to see the New York Rangers hockey team, two and a half tickets to *The Lion King* at the student discount rate, or two nights in a hotel room in the Financial District in Lower Manhattan. He would even have had enough money left over for room service.

The process of tracking expenses and stepping back was, for some, like reconciliation for a Catholic over Lent. For those plagued with guilt, the experience illuminated the financial misgivings that were easy to ignore day-to-day. For others, though, the experience was satisfying. Two students felt more in control and less stressed now that they knew the source of their bad habits. Another was happy to learn that her actual expenditures confirmed her suspicions about her own spending and aligned well with her budget. A fourth was certain she was a secret chocolate binger, but was delighted to discover that she ate far less than she thought.

The pleasant aspects of tracking my own expenses were lost on me, though. From one day to the next, none of those feelings changed what I did or the choices that my students were making. Despite my remorse, I still ate the whole pastry. And I went on to buy another the day after.

There are many reasons for our unintended purchases. For one, we're good at rationalizing these minor acts of transgression against our wallet. One woman realized that she had six go-to justifications she gave herself as she dialed up the car service rather than stepping down into a subway station—including the small price of luxury and an irrational fear of catching bedbugs underground. Perhaps an even bigger explanation, though, is that the consequences of any single decision tend to be too small to compel different behavior the next time around. Each of the choices I made felt like momentary blips or errors, but not major failures.

Of course, scientists have documented that the process of observing can change the behavior of the observed. Employees work more efficiently when they know employers are watching. Kids as young as five are less likely to steal stickers from a friend when observed by others their same age. Museum patrons move through galleries slower when people are watching them. But eventually the feeling of being in the spotlight fades and people revert to their usual way of being.

It was not enough to just log what went out of my wallet or into my mouth. Though all of those fiscal and caloric expenditures were memorialized, bearing witness to them did little to change what I or my students did one day to the next. When I looked back at the numbers, I saw that I spent 60 percent more money in the second half of my own case study than I did in the first half. Why? Taking note of behaviors does little to change them because that act alone keeps the reporter narrowly focused. Recording how much money I spent on that sushi snack from the corner convenience store (a risky choice of venue to patronize for raw fish, I am aware) led me to think only about that expenditure, not the total spent that week.

This was the moment when I wondered if the ineffectiveness of annotating my expenditures was unique to my fiscal health. Might annotating be more helpful in another area of my life? Say, my aspirations for single-song stardom on the drums?

I turned my sights on how I spent my time instead of my money. I set my phone to ask me once, twice, or three times a day—as it wished, over the course of a month—whether I had practiced the drums since the last time it had asked me. My phone also asked me how I felt about myself after each session concluded, if I had indeed practiced in the elapsed time span. I filed away each of my reports in the same way that I save our tax documents after April 15—all in one big file without much thought and with very little organizing; I generally know where they are, but I'm glad the IRS hasn't asked to see anything specific. As soon as I've sent off the returns, I am definitely not looking for them again.

Until the day that I actually did go hunting for those daily practice reports. After my one-month period of data collection had expired, I headed off to my office, opened my door, and sat down at my desk. I had my phone export the reports to my computer so I could crunch the numbers and compile the results. I saw that I had responded to my phone's questions on average twice a day, though some days I left no notes to self. I'm sure on those days my musical development was back-burnered. Had I practiced, I'm certain I would have given myself credit for it. Nonetheless, I discovered that I had in fact gotten in ten practice sessions in that thirty-day span. That's the equivalent of two or three times each weekend! This shocked me, and I literally patted myself on the back. Which is of course the exact instant that one of my students walked past my open door and caught me in this moment of self-congratulatory exuberance. We had a brief chat about self-esteem versus hubris.

I settled back in to examine the trajectory of my emotional states. That analysis started off easily, because the first three times my phone asked me how I felt after I practiced, I pled the Fifth. I left the response box blank. I'm guessing that my reactions, had I annotated them, would have involved a word not fit to print here. After my fourth practice session, I noted, I had cried. I'm surmising that this reaction stemmed from some mix of anxiety and pride, because I also noted that Pete told me during that practice period, "You're great! And I'm not [expletive]ing bull[expletive]ing you."

The choice of words shocked me, because he had previously reserved this kind of language for only the most maddening days at the office—the kind that lead to broken screens on cells when you forget that slamming the phone down when you hang up on someone in contemporary times is far more likely to lead to permanent device damage, and doesn't have the same oomph it did when we all used landlines. So maybe I cried from confusion. Or maybe from the powerful nature of his compliment. I'm not sure now. But, I can see from my reports that, following his enthusiastic praise, my own satisfaction with my improvements increased dramatically. The session after, I felt *better*, then *kinda proud*, followed by *definitely better*. An upward trajectory if ever I've seen one. I capped off this progress with one of the proudest moments of my drumming life to date. The data on my phone stamped the moment— 9:35 p.m. on February 10—but I think I will remember it even without the notes: Mattie, for the first time, danced to the sounds he heard me make! After I got over the initial guilt inspired by being reminded I had let my infant child stay up that late just to hear me practice, the unfalsifiable evidence that I was now making music really lifted my spirits. After that, I felt *inspired* to try for the next level. In my next practice session, I attempted coordinating three limbs to enact separate and unique movements simultaneously. I told my phone that I felt *like I was at the edges of my brain*—but not enough that it shut down or anything of that nature, because over the course of the next two sessions I was *happy* that I felt *quite a bit less awkward*. As the thirty-day period came to an end, I closed out my reporting feeling *proud*. I think I rocked pretty hard. And though it didn't happen while I personally was sitting behind the kit, three sticks were broken in one night. *Maybe I loosened up the wood grain for Pete.*

I'd like to say that I have introspective powers of deduction and could feel the progress I was making in the moment. I don't. And I couldn't. In some sense, the process of logging my time seems remarkably similar to tracking my expenses. On any given day, I had no idea whether I was doing better or worse at saving money, or spending my practice time well. The narrow focus on the day-to-day was not giving me insight, nor was it motivating me.

However, after having stitched together the trajectory of my experiences over the course of this month, I felt encouraged in ways that I hadn't before. Stepping back and looking at the change in my experience across a longer swath of time was inspiring. From one day to the next, with incremental progress or the few steps back anyone can experience after a few steps forward, it can be challenging to detect forward momentum. But when we take a step back, patterns become clearer. The arc of the experience takes form when we look more broadly at the choices we make. And at least for me, when I looked holistically, and opened up my focus to reflect on my progress over the course of one month rather than one day, I could see that I wasn't still scrambling to get my footing. I had real traction and was well on my way up the mountain. It's only by stepping back to view a wide expanse of actions, and considering our choices juxtaposed against one another, that patterns emerge and we feel the motivational impact.

Turning Film on Its Head

I'm not the first to realize the impact of a wide bracket; and the idea of it, arguably, was not invented by psychologists. In fact, the idea of a wide bracket might date back to 1928, and might be attributable to nineteen-year-old Robert Burks. Back then, Burks was starting his first job inside the special-effects department at Warner Bros. Pictures. He joined the team at an interesting time. Rightfully situated among its brethren, Warner Bros. resided on Poverty Row in Hollywood, a section of town populated by studios near financial ruin, dotted with tough-guy extras and silver-screen cowboys languishing on street corners, awaiting casting calls for westerns that might not ever make it to the theater.

But, the studio was at the precipice of a transformation. Sam Warner had just convinced his brothers to think beyond silent pictures and produce *The Jazz Singer,* the first film in the industry to include speaking actors and synchronized singing. Though Sam Warner died the night before the opening and his brothers couldn't attend the premiere, it was with this film that Warner Bros. left Poverty Row. Now flush with cash, the studio grew quickly from there on out. Its prospects were on the rise—as was Burks's career trajectory. Within his first year on the job, he was promoted to assistant cameraman. And by ten years, he had honed his craft and was leading the special-effects cinematography team. At the age of forty, Burks was promoted to director of photography—the youngest fully accredited person in this position within the industry to date.

In his late forties and fifties, Burks became the darling of Alfred Hitchcock, leading the director's cinematography team for twelve productions. It was with *To Catch a Thief* that Burks became a legend. This film was the first of five that Burks shot using VistaVision, a brand-new form of cinematography that literally turned film on its head. Burks put the film into his cameras horizontally rather than vertically, and shot with a wide-angle lens. By doing this, he could capture far more on the film's negative than any cameraman had before. The effect was a crisp image that could portray the entire field of vision—including the foreground, the middle distance, and the far background—all at once, with sharp focus. Before, camera-men for movies like *Casablanca* struggled to clearly depict the fez on the head of the patron at the back of the bar as well as Humphrey Bogart up front, next to the piano. But with the wide bracket, audi-ences for *To Catch a Thief* could clearly make out the sunbathers on the beaches of the French Riviera in the background, even as the camera placed Grace Kelly and Cary Grant speeding along the cliffs by the Mediterranean Sea in the foreground. For his use of this rev-olutionary technological advance and cinematographic effect, Burks won his first Academy Award.

Even though we don't load film into our minds literally, our eyes and brains have the capacity to create the experience of VistaVision figuratively—to see the world through a wide bracket when it serves us well. To do this, we need to give as much weight to what lies in the periphery of our field of vision as we do to the things that fall right in the center. We can look at the world as if through a wide-angle lens, composing an image that includes all the elements of the surrounding scene. As it was for Robert Burks when shooting a film for Hitchcock, a wide bracket is all about taking note of everything that surrounds you.

Here's an example of what I mean. Think of paintings created by the artist Chuck Close. He lives with a neurological disorder, called prosopagnosia, that leaves him unable to recognize people based on how they look; nonetheless, Close achieved international acclaim by painting portraits of people's faces.

Close found a unique way to work around his prosopagnosia. He deconstructs his canvas into a grid. Each square on the canvas coin-cides with a square cell on the photograph of the person he uses as a referent for the work. He taught himself to narrow his visual atten-tion onto the shadows, contours, and colors that reside within each tiny square on the referent. He looks intently at the skin between a nose and an eye, for example. This may take up six adjacent cells on the referent photograph, and inside each appear several rings of concentric squares of alternating shades of pink and tan. Or, when narrowly focusing his gaze on an upturned corner of a mouth, he might see small circles, triangles, bean-shaped areas of light and dark, color and the absence of it. He reproduces what he sees in these referent cells onto the canvas in larger form. What he paints is a patchwork quilt of tiny shapes and figures. But the image comes together for us the audience only when we take a step back and look at the big picture, and see with a wide bracket.

The Right Tool for the Job

It's not meant as a contradiction to have earlier explained the benefits of a narrow focus, only to say now that this might prove problematic. It's not meant to confuse you to have first suggested you zoom in on what you want, only to now suggest you should expand your breadth of attention. We need diversity in the tools we use, because there are situations when one will work better than another, as I have mentioned before. An artist's palette includes more than one color. A chef's knife block includes more than just cleavers. A good wine cellar is stocked with more than just rosé from the South of France. Narrowed attention, like all of the strategies in this book, may be more effective some of the time, and a wide bracket at other times. The key is knowing when the right time to use either may be. Indeed, a narrow focus can inspire us when we are nearing the end of our journey, but a wide bracket may motivate us better when we're just starting out.

Take the following study, for example. Dutch students played a boring word game, but they could win money for pushing through the monotony. The more questions they got right, the more money they could make. I remember my college days, living hand to mouth; I would have happily jumped on this gravy train. It seems these students felt the same, since they all played along to some degree or another. But what the researchers actually measured in this study (though the students didn't know it) was how quickly the students moved through the different stages of the game. The researchers knew from their previous studies that players took shorter breaks when they were motivated. Here, the researchers tested to see if focusing the students' attention on how much they had left to go before the game was over would foster greater motivation and encourage them to work faster.

This wasn't a footrace, and the players didn't have a finish line to cross. So, to approximate the kind of visual experience runners have as they get close to the end, the researchers made a progress bar that was filled with dots. With each word game the students finished, a dot disappeared. This visually tracked what remained to be completed; when all the dots were gone, the game was over.

Did this type of narrowed visual focus on the end motivate the students? Remember, it pushed the Zenith Velocity runners and Joan Benoit Samuelson to be the first to cross the finish line. The same happened with the word-game players. Nearing the end, they worked faster and better, and as a result made more money, when they focused their attention on what they had left to accomplish. But this tactic backfired when the students were just starting out. If they narrowly focused on the end state too early, their pace slowed, they made more mistakes, and they left with their wallet a little thinner than it otherwise could have been.

In my own research with my student Matt Riccio, we surveyed dozens and dozens of people competing in three different New York Road Runners races. The youngest runner was twenty, and the oldest seventy. On average, these runners held steady at an eight-and-a-half-minute mile and logged about eighteen miles per week in training, so they were capable of finishing the four-, six-, or nine-mile race they were about to compete in. They told us about the different ways that they focus their attention at different points of a race. We found that these seasoned athletes changed their strategies depending on whether they were just starting out or nearing the end. In the last half-mile, almost 60 percent narrowed the focus of their attention more often than they expanded it. But at the beginning, over 80 percent widened their focus more often than they narrowed it. Both tactics are useful, and both are needed to get the job done. It's about knowing when to use one and when to use the other.

A wide bracket leads us to make decisions that better align with our long-term objectives, and helps us avoid temptations that seem great now but that we'll regret later on. In fact, some of the most successful diet programs—ones that help people avoid temptation, lose weight, and keep it off—rely on a system that encourages clients to assume a wide bracket. Based on their caloric and nutritional values, the foods that clients eat cost points, and each day clients can spend a specified number of points. The daily allotment encourages clients to consider each meal with respect to others eaten that day, and to divvy up the daily allocation of points across time. Rather than narrowly focusing on the meal on the table, clients assume a wider frame by thinking about meals over the course of a day. Even more, some programs encourage clients to bank unused points and roll them over to another day. The rollover points that become available at the end of a day have a shelf life of one week. In this scenario, a full day's worth of choices is considered with respect to those made across the week.

Wide brackets that encourage consideration of larger swaths of time help individuals, even those outside of supervised programs, to make choices that better align with their longer-term goals. It was a cheeky test, but two researchers from the University of Chicago tempted passersby with a food giveaway of either chocolates or carrots. A poster near the stand advertised the giveaway, though the researchers used two different phrases to describe the promotion. Some of the time, the poster read that this was the Spring Food Stand. Other times, the poster read that this was the April 12 Food Stand. Though the setups appeared identical, the words on the poster changed the type of mental frame that passersby held.

Considering a specific day in April created a narrow focus, while considering the season induced a wider one. And that mindset impacted choices. People took more carrots and fewer chocolates when the poster advertised the SPRING FOOD STAND, but they took more chocolates and fewer carrots when the sign announced the APRIL 12 FOOD STAND. Pointing out the date kept people narrowly focused on the choice they made that day, and as a result they picked what tempted them in the here and now. However, mentioning the season induced a wide bracket and encouraged them to consider their present choice along with future opportunities. The wide bracket aligned the choice they made now with the health goal they hoped to achieve later.

Wide Brackets and Finding Patterns

A wide bracket can also reveal broader patterns that are less apparent when we consider decisions or events in isolation. This fact is quite evident if we return to financial decisions and planning for our retirement needs.

When we save for retirement, we are investing in a future that usually is fairly far off. The goal is to find long-term gains over and above any short-term losses our portfolio might suffer, and market analysts have found that the best way to accomplish this is to invest in stocks rather than bonds. Equities have a much higher rate of return than fixed-income securities, in the long run.

Take for example, the Standard & Poor's index, which tracks large capital U.S. stocks. In 1926, S&P tracked ninety stocks, and by 1957 it had expanded to its current list of five hundred. Each dollar invested in 1925 in large stocks tracked by this index is now worth almost $450 after accounting for inflation. Compare this to long-term U.S. Treasury bonds that you might hold on to for twenty years. One dollar invested in bonds in 1925 would be worth just under ten dollars today. In other words, S&P stocks have outperformed bonds to a staggering degree—in spite of two stock crashes in the 2000s and even the Great Depression. The other (less risky, but decidedly less lucrative) options? If your relative in the Roaring Twenties had decided to use that dollar to buy gold, you could sell that nugget for a little over four dollars today. Not a great return for all those years of safekeeping. Say that same relative had put that dollar under a mattress and somehow it took you all these years to find it. Of course, it is still a dollar bill, even if a little weathered. But it would only buy you what seven cents does today.

Most people know that investing in equities is a good gamble over the long term, yet many of us struggle to keep our money in them.

One reason analysts find for the reticence to hold on to stocks or buy them at all is that novice investors peek too often at their portfolio and are scared by what they find. They narrowly focus on the changes in daily stock valuation, or the one-month historical trend graph. But stocks naturally rise and fall throughout the course of a day or week or month. It's the rare winner that maintains a steady upward trajectory without any dips in its line of growth. When we think about how many hours we toiled away at work, and the vacations we opted out of, to earn the money we invested in the markets, those dips in the valuation of our stocks hurt. And rises of the same magnitude feel only slightly enjoyable. This is a common reaction, and scientists refer to this human tendency as "loss aversion."

We may come to dislike stocks when we (prudently) evaluate the status of our retirement portfolio if we check in on it too often, and consider a stock's performance in the short run. But if we could resist looking at our portfolio for longer periods of time, checking on it only once a year, say, the hedonic impact of any one or two dips would lessen, and we would be in a better position to evaluate each stock's performance for the long run. By adopting a wide bracket to evaluate the contents of our portfolio more broadly, we may find our affinity for equities growing and our retirement wallets a bit thicker.

Wide Brackets and Time Management

One semester, I found myself mentoring an eclectic group of college students on principles of motivation. Some of these students planned to use the strategies we discussed with clients in therapy later on. Some would repackage them for education, to help children struggling through school. And others wanted to take them to the corporate world to improve group dynamics in industry. Across the board, my students thought they and their future clients had one thing in common—that they could all benefit from better time management. The group decided to test their own reactions to narrow frames and wide brackets, and to assess their progress with a personal project. Before we talked about any of the science, each person set a goal for one week. Something that could feasibly be accomplished within a seven-day period, something that mattered to them, but something that would also feel like a stretch at the outset. One student said she wanted to get a film production she was involved in off the ground. One said she needed to firm up plans for a university-wide event she was hosting. Another wanted to finalize the contents of his portfolio for graduate-school applications. Another aimed to lose three pounds.

They all employed the strategy of materialization, writing down a sort of contract with themselves, stating the goal they hoped to achieve. Then the group added a narrow focus to their materializing. They all kept their notes by their bedside so that every morning they could make a plan for the day, and every night they could reflect on their progress. When they woke up, they made themselves a list of assignments for the day, things they could do to advance their project. The event planner said she would make a phone call to confirm the space reservation. The filmmaker said she would reach out to a producer to discuss budget. The grad-school applicant said he would revise his personal statement. And the dieter said she would hit up an exercise class after work. They all thought about their overall schedule for the day and took note of when they could work on their assignment. Right before turning the lights out at the end of the day, each student reflected on how well they'd followed through with their plan. They thought back on how their day had unfolded and estimated the time they'd spent working on their project. When the next day came around, they did it all again, until the week was over.

In the second week, the group started off in the same vein as before. They established their goal on the very first morning. But we switched up how they approached thinking about their project, and how they would allocate their time. This time, they adopted a wide bracket. Rather than highlighting one or two items they might complete in a day, in this initial session they generated a list of all of the tasks the goal would require for the week. Each student's assignment list topped out at eight or nine entries. Next, they considered their schedule for the whole week, thinking in detail about each of the next seven days, considering what was already set for the hours between waking up and falling asleep. They scheduled in time for each of their new project's assignments. A phone call to the film producer was set for Tuesday at 9:00 a.m. That two-hour block of time after school and before dinner was earmarked for the grad-school application's revision. Time for the gym was fitted in over lunch on the five weekdays. Like before, each night as they flopped down into bed, each student reported on how much time they'd spent working on their tasks that day.

At the end of the two weeks, the students turned in their notes. When I tallied up their progress and compared their success from one week to the next, the results were striking. Using the wide bracket to approach their to-do list led two out of three students in the group to find more time in their week to work on their goals. When I looked at the group as a whole, the average student spent an additional two and a half hours on their project that week when they planned it using a wide bracket, compared to when they'd used a narrow focus to think day-to-day about what they wanted to accomplish.

My students' experience was not unusual. Over thirty-five years ago, a team of academic advisers met with college students every week for almost three months during the first few semesters to teach study skills. Together, they created flowcharts of what they would need to accomplish, where and when they would work on their tasks, what they would need to achieve to feel good about themselves, and how they would reward themselves. But only some of the students assumed a wide bracket. These students broke their flowchart down into weekly blocks and set milestones for each month. Other students assumed a narrow focus. They set milestones, but the deadline for accomplishing these targets was the end of each day. Now, planning and tracking—or materializing—with either wide or narrow focus helped these students academically. Both groups were less likely to have dropped out of college a year later than students who had not participated in the program. But students who learned to plan using a wide bracket earned much better grades than students who learned to plan using a narrow focus. In fact, assuming a wide bracket led to nearly a full-letter-grade advantage: the monthly planners had on average a 3.3 grade point average while daily planners had a 2.4, which was essentially the same as for students who had not made plans at all.

Wide brackets improve outcomes primarily because they help us to overcome our tendency to underestimate what it will take to get a job done. Face it: we are notoriously bad at planning how much time our projects will actually take. The Sydney Opera House took ten years longer to build than architects anticipated. The completion of Boston's Big Dig project—to bury a major interstate underground—took over nine years more than expected. And Jean Drapeau, the mayor of Montreal, announced that his city would create a state-of-the-art coliseum, covered by the first retractable roof ever made, in time for the 1976 Olympic Games, but it wasn't until thirteen years after the torch was passed on to the next host that the roof and the project finally closed. Of course, you might say, projects of this scale are never going to come in on time. Political changes and economic downfalls might be impossible to foreshadow and accommodate. But for projects that we manage for ourselves, for which we are the sole agents responsible for completing, these issues don't apply. Sadly, people are no better than companies or governments at meeting deadlines. Students trying to complete their research projects in time to graduate take three weeks longer than their best guess when planning out their schedule. Wide brackets help us to unpack our bigger jobs into their constituent parts and see how each of these parts can be worked into our already busy lives.

Becoming a Self-Psychologist

"It was nuts. There were five Oscars sitting on the table at the diner. We were all still in our tuxes. I'm not a hundred percent sure what I ate, but I'm banking on an egg sandwich of some sort. Then, we just went in to work."

This was not my Monday.

I was having dinner with Patrick Osborne, an animator, who won an Academy Award for Best Animated Short Film with his directorial debut, *Feast*. Osborne was indulging my inquisition into the juicy details of how Los Angeles parties on its most glamorous night of the year.

I told Osborne that I cried when I saw *Feast* for the first time. And each of the next four times I saw it, too. I loved the film! I felt like the six-minute-and-forty-nine-second depiction of a man named James at the peak of his bachelorhood and his formerly orphaned Boston terrier named Winston bingeing on movie-theater popcorn, pepperoni, and nachos in varied shades of neon yellow really spoke to me. I don't know why. I admitted to Osborne that I sneak my own snacks into movie theaters, I don't like pepperoni, I've never been a bachelor, and I prefer my food to come in colors found in nature rather than crayon boxes. On the surface, I don't have much in common with his protagonist, but I still felt like this was *my* story. He said, "I know. I made it to have that effect."

Osborne drew the scene from Winston's perspective, less than a foot off the ground. From that perch, we see the legs of the tables, the bottom of the door as it swings open, and the shoes on the waitress, Kirby, with whom James falls in love. There are few scenes that show the face of any person, the houses in the neighborhood, the clothes on the characters, or anything else that could lead us to feel like this was someone else's story. It could be our story. And the brilliance of Osborne's work is that, very quickly, we *want* it to be our story.

And how he does it is through food. For most of the piece, we watch Winston eat. It starts just as kibble, when James adopts Winston. The culinary experience of these "home-cooked" meals far exceeds that of the street scraps he'd been scavenging. But it's Winston's reaction to his first taste of bacon that breaks down the barriers separating our species. Yes, Winston, that is what heaven tastes like. I agree. And there's no going back to dried dog food after that. Spaghetti and meatballs. Gooey peanut-butter-and-jelly-sandwich midnight snacks. A rare burger at the bar. Easter ham. Chips and dip with the big game.

All that feasting, though, changes when James meets Kirby. Now it's peas with vegetable puree and parsley garnish while dining over linen. Celery sticks and spinach. Just as their caloric intake declines, so too does Winston's morale, until the night when James goes on a junk-food bender. Strawberry ice cream. Freezer waffles. Sugar donuts. Microwaveable mac and cheese. Though the grounds for the menu change may seem obvious to us, it takes Winston much longer to realize that James and Kirby have broken up.

It is the parsley, though, that eventually brings Winston great wisdom. Kirby would top off each meal with a fresh sprig. Even as she scaled back Winston's allotment of fried eggs and cheese curds, she continued to add the herb on top of each bowl of kibble. So now, when a plate of pasta comes Winston's way topped with parsley that moves James to tears, Winston puts it all together. He snatches the greenery from James's forlorn fingers, hops out the window, and hightails it to Kirby's restaurant. James in his robe and boxers, looking the worse for wear, rekindles his connection with his lost love. Cut to the next scene: Winston in a tuxedo bow awaiting his fair share of the wedding cake. A new house and shiny new bowl filled with kibble without the trimmings. It brings a smile to Winston's face as he falls to sleep. He awakes to find a meatball rolling his way. Sopping with tomato sauce. Dripping with deliciousness. He looks up to see a baby in a high chair, who in slow motion takes another plump and dripping morsel and drops it straight down into Winston's agape mouth. And that, people, is love at first sight.

Osborne set out to tell a story through food. It's a classic tale of love and loss and love again, told from the ground up, with meals marking the passage of time and the monumental moments. "There's the single-guy dinner, the trying-to-impress-someone-on-the-first-date dinner, simple everyday stuff, the breakup meal, the romantic meal. You can see so much about someone's life by watching it unfold through food," Osborne told me.

Osborne went on to explain that the premise for *Feast* came from a one-second moment in time. I wish any one of my many seconds at work were half as valuable.

"I was beta testing this app that makes one-second videos and strings them together to make a movie. I thought that if I turned the camera around, I might learn something about myself. So, I snapped a clip of one of the meals I ate that day. Every day. For a year. And when I watched that six-minute production of my life in food, I couldn't believe it. I ate like shit."

Pause here. Osborne is a healthy guy. Fit. In shape, from what I could tell. He told me he'd sent away for a profile of his DNA. He found out he is genetically predisposed for sprint racing but defies his genetic composition by running an eight-mile loop through the Hollywood Hills, metaphorically high-fiving the iconic sign along the way, as part of his normal routine. He didn't look like the kind of person who'd lick the saffron aioli off his fingers or the plate like

I was doing at that moment. So, when Osborne told me he didn't indulge in the light-fare menu, I questioned his self-assessment.

"I joke that documenting every dinner for nearly a year led me mostly to a better understanding of why I'd been steadily gaining a few pounds a year since college. In reality it gives me a pretty wonderful appreciation of my quality of life. Not just because I'm grateful to be eating well, but also the kaleidoscope of locations, environments, and people that surround those meals. They represented a full life and it made me feel grateful to watch. When you take a step back, and see something like your choices from a wider perspective, the patterns are so much clearer."

Wide Brackets Improve
Our Memory and Decision Quality

The app that inspired Osborne to see the patterns in his life is called 1 Second Everyday and was created by a Japanese-American artist born in Peru named Cesar Kuriyama. 1 Second Everyday selects a moment from each day's video. From one week to the next, the collection of clips grows, reflecting the diversity of your experiences. It strings them together to make a moving montage of memories. When you hit PLAY, you can watch your life unfold before your eyes.

Kuriyama, in turn, was inspired to create this technology on the day he turned thirty. "I hate that I can't remember what I've done with my life," Kuriyama told me over dinner one night. "I knew I was going to quit my job. I saved up enough money to get by for a year and I was going to travel, but I didn't want to forget that adventure, like I had most of my twenties. I tried writing journals in the past. That didn't work. I couldn't stick with it. So I had to design my own way to remember."

And he did. Kuriyama started with no knowledge of computer programming or design. Literally none. He studied film and graphic art in college. To get his project started, he asked the Internet to teach him how to make an app. Kuriyama knew that he needed some seed money to get the project off his laptop and into the world. He thought $20,000 would do it. Within only one week, a Kickstarter campaign gave him that financial injection. And over the next three weeks that the project was posted on the crowdfunding site, he received another $40,000 from more than eleven thousand people who saw its potential. Within a year, Kuriyama had created a platform that Osborne and I and two million others around the world have downloaded and found inspiration in.

As of this writing, Kuriyama is into his eighth year of capturing one second every day. I asked him how he chooses what snippet gets added to his montage and he said, "Everything and anything. People are really good at selecting the best aspects of their lives and sharing them. But we don't record our bad days. Our moments of disappointment, sadness, anger, or guilt. When we've embarrassed ourselves. When we let ourselves down. Those are important parts of our life too, though. These are our everyday. That's why the name of the app is 'Everyday.' So we can remember every day."

I haven't had the app as long as Kuriyama has, but I can assure you that I have not used it like he was describing. I've cried sitting at the drums, trying to get the roll off the toms to sync up with the beat, frustrated at my clumsiness. I didn't think to turn my camera on at that moment. Yes, my phone is waterproof now, since I bought the updated model after I toppled into a pool at a party with an older version in my pants pocket. But I didn't want to test whether this new model could sustain the deluge streaming down my face when I put sticks in my hands. I've used the practice pad as a coaster for my morning coffee plenty of times, blatantly ignoring the reminder I set out for myself to work out the beat. I didn't want to capture a memory of how easy it was to blow off my commitment.

I asked Kuriyama why he wanted to remember all the dirty bits of his life. I sure didn't. And he said, "Life is so short. Reliving all parts of my life helps me to appreciate every moment I have." He told me about one of his single seconds in life. He captured the clip in the first year of his project. And it was a one-second video of a wall. Nothing on it. Nothing moving. No people. No sound. Just a wall. That meant absolutely nothing to me, but everything to him. That wall was what he saw in the first second after he walked out of a hospital room having learned that his sister-in-law's intestines had strangulated. The blood supply became cut off and the pain was overwhelming. In the emergency room, she came close to death. Several times. "We don't want to remember the bad stuff, but when we do it helps us appreciate what is so good about our life too. And reminds me that time is short. When I watch the video of my life I'm making, and see the years pass by, I remember that every day is important. Every day is an opportunity to do something that matters."

I asked him why not shoot *two* seconds of every day, then. Kuriyama replied, "Watching a year of my life would take twelve minutes. That's like half an episode of *Seinfeld*, and that's way too long."

There are plenty of other social media platforms that try to do what 1 Second Everyday has done. Despite their differences, they all provide a platform for people to present curated versions of their lives. We stitch together footage depicting some aspects of what each day was like, what we did, who we were with, and how we felt. Other footage falls on the cutting-room floor. It's usually not a random choice of what stays rather than goes, but a carefully crafted selection, which more often than not highlights the happy, fun, interesting, and impressive aspects of our experience.

For example, computer scientists from the University of Southern California and Indiana University analyzed the content of almost twenty million tweets produced by more than eight million individual Twitter users. The researchers tagged the emotional content conveyed in each post. They found that while most of Twitter's content is neutral, there is 60 percent more positive content than negative content. They also found that positive tweets were favorited five times more, and were retweeted four times more, than negative or neutral tweets. People post, like, and spread positive stuff more than negative stuff.

By design, 1 Second Everyday encourages a more representative collection of memories. It tries to cultivate a habit that counteracts the positivity bias in our selection process. By compelling users to memorialize some part of every single day—even their worst days—it becomes harder to select only the most positive aspects of their lives to commit to memory.

To find out whether this strategy for finding motivation would work for more people than just Kuriyama—whether a juxtaposition of good and bad can help us better meet our goals and find happiness—I reached out to Nick Powdthavee, a scientist at Warwick Business School who studies the economics of happiness. He focuses his investigation on how technology motivates individuals to do what makes them happy.

"Nick, you're an expert on happiness," I started off. "Aren't people happier and more energized when they relive the best moments of their most exciting days, rather than the mixed bag of memories that a video of everyday life creates? Isn't that exactly why puppy videos exist, and why we take pictures of our babies when they're smiling and not when they are screaming?"

"Yeah, absolutely. Go check out the video of Putney that my wife made.* When people reflect on just the best parts of an experience, in that very moment people are happier, but in the long run they may not be," Powdthavee responded. "When we flip through pictures where everyone is laughing and smiling, we do feel good. Right

---

* I did. Putney is their golden retriever. In two minutes and forty seconds, I, along with the nearly nineteen million other viewers, watched Putney grow from a round-bellied floppy fluffball to a six-month-old precocious and gangly adolescent, paws still disproportionately large for her body. I watched Putney face her fears, standing off against a plastic water bottle, the baby gate, and bumpy concrete. I shared her intrigue over meeting sheep for the first time. I cheered when Putney won at tug-of-war with her friends in her backyard. I chuckled when she fell asleep while standing, head landing in her water dish. Putney's video was amazing.

then. It feels good to remember having gone to that party and talked to that girl who then took a selfie with our phone. It might make us happy to watch a video of our new puppy when he's sleeping. But when we're trying to decide what we should do in the future, all those incomplete memories might lead us to make the wrong decisions. Knowledge is power in this context too."

Powdthavee went on to explain that if we are actively engaged in trying to make ourselves forget about the restaurant that gave us food poisoning, the job we didn't get, or the person's feelings we hurt when we said the wrong thing, we might make the same mistakes again. Remembering the bad alongside the good can help us make better choices in the future. And that will make us happier in the long run.

I was inspired. And in an effort to make a change moving forward, I snapped a one-second video of the disgusting chicken wrap I'd bought off the flight attendant earlier that day—insides and outsides the same color of oxidized mayo flecked with green that was either tarragon or mold—to remind me not to rely on airlines to feed me anymore.

The Neuroscience of How Remembering the Past Improves Planning for the Future

Neuroscientists wrote books about him. They talked about him at their conferences. They traveled far to meet him. But his true identity remained a mystery to most everyone until his death a few years ago. They referred to him as simply K.C. in order to protect his identity back then. K.C. was not a fugitive, not an informant, not a celebrity trying to blend in at the grocery store, nor any other character trying to keep his name and likeness out of the papers. Instead, due to a serious accident that left him with a traumatic injury, K.C. had a remarkable brain that helped researchers uncover some of the most groundbreaking facts about how memory works and why we have it. K.C.'s brain was one of the first to suggest the connection between thinking about the past and planning for the future.

When he was only thirty years old, K.C. ran his motorcycle off the road and suffered serious brain damage of a very unusual kind. Though I never met him, everyone says that both before and after his accident, K.C. was a charming and sociable man. Well-spoken and knowledgeable. He knew that 007 and James Bond are one and the same person. He could describe the tallest tower in Toronto vividly with his eyes closed. And he could explain the difference between stalactites and stalagmites, facts that I have seen be useful in conversation with New Yorkers far more often than seems reasonable. Despite the seriousness of his accident, his mind seemed sharp, his recollection of black-and-white facts accurate, and his ability to contribute to Team Trivia Night spot-on.

K.C.'s major problem was that he could not remember anything that happened to him personally. He had problems making new memories of any kind, but there was a specific type of old memory that he could not pull up. Facts, like statements from Trivial Pursuit, were there; but personal experiences were not. K.C. could not recall anything that he had witnessed, done, or felt himself. For instance, two years before his accident, he surprised his family the night before his brother's wedding by having his hair permed. For the rest of his life, he knew his brother had married. But he could not remember himself being at the wedding, or how his family reacted to his curly hair. He also knew that he and his family along with 100,000 other people had evacuated their home for ten days to escape a chemical spill in his neighborhood, but couldn't remember if he was scared or anxious. He knew of the accidental death of his brother, with whom he was very close, but he had no recollection of where he was when he heard about it, who told him, or what it was like for him at the funeral.

K.C. also couldn't plan for the future. When doctors asked him what he thought he might do in the next fifteen minutes, later that day, the next week, or with the rest of his life, he said he didn't know. He described his mind as being blank, the same kind of blank as when he tried to think back on his past. K.C. suffered an inability to mentally time travel into his own past and his own future.

Many neuropsychologists have studied K.C.'s brain, and those of other patients who have experienced similar accidents and memory impairments. These scientists also use neuroimaging technology to measure the activity in different regions of the brains of individuals who have not suffered any injuries. The results converge, and the evidence is clear. The neural circuitry involved in remembering episodes from our past is nearly identical to the circuitry involved in planning for the future. Regardless of whether we are using our minds to travel back in time or predict the future, the prefrontal cortex and parts of the medial temporal lobe, including the hippocampus, are active.

Interestingly, these brain regions happen to be the same ones that respond when people watch their videos from the 1 Second Everyday app. I heard about a remarkable neuroscientist, Wilma Bainbridge, who has been studying users of the app. Bainbridge is smart, of course. She got her PhD in brain and cognitive science from the Massachusetts Institute of Technology. She's also incredibly busy. She worked on a team to make robots act more like humans. She taught computer programming to high school students in Jerusalem. She can speak English, Korean, Arabic, and Japanese. And Bainbridge created the subtitles to a television show called *Reset*, a psychological drama about how people would change their lives if they got a do-over. Now she conducts research at the National Institute of Mental Health in Maryland, and she is discovering what makes certain things easier to remember and others easier to forget. That she had time to chat with me about her work must have meant that I caught her while she was waiting in line for a coffee or something.

When I asked Bainbridge what got her interested in studying people who use 1 Second Everyday, she told me that she herself had been using it for about six years. She went on to explain that she had scanned her brain while watching her montage. The result? "I found where I process time." When she looked over the movies she'd made of where and when different regions of her brain were active while looking at the videos, Bainbridge could tell from the silhouetted and ghostly X-ray-like images whether she had been watching footage of her life from long ago or one that was relatively more recent. That got her interested in the idea of mental time travel and what thinking about the past does for us in the present.

Bainbridge told me that she gathered a group of people who had been using the 1 Second Everyday app for a few years or more. Some of them hadn't missed a day in six years—like her, in fact. She had them watch five minutes' worth of their own videos as they lay still in the bed of the fMRI machine. As she watched the different parts of their brain respond on the monitor, Bainbridge saw what neuroscientists might expect. The part of the brain that specializes in making sense of faces lit up when the clips portrayed people. The part of the brain that specializes in processing houses and places lit up when the clips included those kinds of images.

But what Bainbridge was particularly interested in was whether there was something special that happened when people watched *their own* videos. So she had her participants also watch five minutes of someone else's daily videos. Participants saw people and houses and places in these videos too. The people were strangers and most of the settings were unfamiliar, but brain activity was generally the same. The face parts lit up, and so did the building parts. But a few regions of the brain were particularly active in response to personal videos, but not to others' videos. When people watched their own 1 Second Everyday videos, a specific part of the hippocampus and a specific part (the frontal pole) of the prefrontal cortex were uniquely sensitive. These areas are the same brain regions that were damaged during K.C.'s motorcycle accident.

When you put all the evidence together, Bainbridge's work tells us that when people review their personal cinematographic creation, they are remembering their own unique past that no one else could possibly re-create. But, even more interesting, when they watch their own 1 Second Everyday videos, people are also engaging the same brain systems that are necessary to plan for the future.

I dedicated a month to the 1 Second Everyday app and gave it the chance to inspire me. Each time I played, I nabbed a clip of my solo gigging. Toward the beginning of the month I caught the first part of the tune on film. Toward the middle, I turned the camera on partway through the song. And as the month closed out, I waited to hit RECORD until I felt the song nearing its end. At the end of the month I compiled my one-second clips and reviewed my camera-work. If I'm being perfectly honest, the 1 Second Everyday app did not do for my percussive practice what I thought it might. I had hoped that it would show me how I'd changed, whether for better or worse, but after the fact I realized that a one-second moment in time would not be enough to really showcase any change in my abilities. I did happen to memorialize the time that I caught the crash from below rather than via the more conventional placement of stick-meets-topside-of-cymbal. I saw myself fall off the chair after a hasty attempt to hit RECORD on the camera and make it back in time to catch the snare hits that open the song. And I was reminded of my tendency to sit on the front end of the beat when I practiced on Saturday, followed by a swift transition to my love of the backbeat on Sunday, a stylistic choice that I can assure you was not intentional. But with only a musical beat or two recorded for each day's single second, it was easy enough to explain away the rhythmic imprecision as anomalous. The thin slice the app captured wasn't enough to clue me in to any meaningful developments in my abilities. Even when I let it memorialize my worst practice sessions alongside some of my more glorious riffs, a one-second snippet didn't show enough for me to really chart the course of my waxing or waning aptitude.

But those one-second moments *did* correct my faulty memory, just as Powdthavee said they would. I'd thought that I had fallen into a consistent practice routine. A review of my clips assured me I had not. I'd believed myself to have been practicing each weekend that month. That wasn't true. The blank days on the app's calendar marking where I should have practiced, and thought I had, served as evidence of that. And I shared the experience that Bainbridge's participants had when she was scanning their brains. As I watched my own footage, as minimal in length as it was, I too was planning for the future. I didn't feel proud of what I heard myself doing yet. It wasn't good—though it was certainly better than when I'd started. But the reason for the stagnated progress was a lack of consistent or frequent attempts to better myself. Using a wide bracket to review the time I spent at the kit over the previous month led me to redouble my intentions and efforts. Back to the kit I went.

8

Getting Unstuck

About the same time that Mattie learned nouns, he also developed preferences, penchants that at times conflicted with my well-laid plans for us both. I described this stage of child-rearing as a combination of "taming a lion" and "negotiating with terrorists." But I'm a parent and a psychologist. As a result, I was fully anticipating using reverse psychology on my little beast at some point in his life, and felt pretty confident in my ability to employ this tactic effectively. I was right on only one of those counts.

As the sun started to set one weekday night, I corralled my sticky toddler, mustachioed with the remnants of his dinner, and tried to get him ready for night-night time. We had a bedtime routine, of course. He wasn't going straight from meal to mattress. My goal was to get him stripped down and in the tub. But he knew that, post-bath, confinement in his crib was imminent. So out came his stalling tactics. He was well aware by now that asking to play with his trucks or blocks wouldn't buy him any time. He tried instead to ask for stories.

That is when I found myself in a stalemate against my child. We were looking at each other eye to eye, him standing now atop the small mountain of pillows he had created. Mattie asked for "Books!" as dogmatically as can any child who has just learned how to say the word and understands what it means.

I responded, "Bath," as hopefully as would any mother who desperately wants to get a dirty and tired child clean and into bed.

To which Mattie replied, "Books," which was obviously followed by my "Bath."

"Books."

"Bath."

"Books."

"Bath."

"Books."

I decided to employ my psychological powers. As my child stared me down, awaiting my "Bath" (or, he hoped, my surrender), I turned the tables in this call-and-response. "Books," I said.

And I almost won! As if in slow motion, I saw him draw his lips back. I watched as his little mouth start to form the syllable *Baaa*. He caught himself, though, just before the sounds came out. He cocked his head to one side, chuckled, and then said with renewed confidence and gusto, "BOOKS!" I settled in for a few good reads, and cuddled up next to my satisfied if slightly grimy baby boy.

Throughout the course of my life, I have found myself throwing in the towel on more than just my choice persuasion tactics. Learning how to disengage from even the most well-formulated plans has been not only par for the course but also a good move at some points in time. But, of course, one of the hardest parts of setting goals can be realizing that you might have to let them go or shift the course you've charted.

We humans struggle to disengage from accomplishing things we set our sights on, because we get stuck thinking about a single interpretation of how to feel successful and happy. Many of us believe that once we set a goal, we have succeeded only when we make good on that exact promise to ourselves. But victory does not have to look like what we thought it might at the outset. When we free ourselves from a linear pursuit of a single objective, we might find success disguised in other forms.

So when do we know it's time to try a new approach to meeting our aspirations? What are the signs that the pursuit of a particular goal will likely bring us up against a dead end? Sometimes the world tells us and we just have to listen.

That's exactly what happened for Steve Sims. He grew up in East London and came from a construction family. He was a bricklayer, but he wanted more. He saw where money came from and went for it. Sims transitioned careers and landed a gig as a stockbroker. After six months, he talked his way into a transfer to a branch in Hong Kong.

But talking your way into something doesn't mean you're really ready for it. Sims flew in to Hong Kong on a Saturday, and was fired by Tuesday.

With no plan B, but a fair bit of brawn, he started working as a nightclub doorman. Standing at the door, he got to know Hong Kong's famous and elite, and became the linchpin in the middle of a prestigious social circle. He knew who the best partyers were, and where the best parties were happening. He started throwing events himself, and the people came. Still with his sights set on a career in banking, he took his Rolodex of heavy hitters to the bank. He thought that his many established relationships with wealthy clients would fast-track him through the interview and land him the gig in finance he'd wanted for quite some time.

But that just didn't happen. That's not to say the banks weren't impressed with his client list. They were. They just didn't want to sign him on to manage investments. However, they did want to finance his events, since they understood that he could make money *and* give them recurring access to people who had it to spend. And with this, the parties grew. They grew so large, in fact, that he had to limit attendance. Those on the list received the password for entry a few hours before the party, then whispered odd phrases to the bouncers. That was about when Sims's aspiration to achieve success in banking died, but Bluefish, an exclusive luxury concierge service (named after one of the first open-sesames) was born.

Sims now arranges deep-sea tours of the *Titanic* and high-flying expeditions through outer space. He arranged for a client to walk the runway at New York Fashion Week. He turned another into James Bond for a day, entertained by sexy vixens and chased by spies through the streets of Monaco before being kidnapped and held for ransom by pirates in the Mediterranean. He assembled a team of professional race car drivers so that two Harvard lecturers could crash stock cars. Steve makes billionaires' most outrageous dreams become reality. And he started it all by first giving up on his own.

Giving Up to Really Grow

Theodor Geisel had hundreds of hats stashed away in a closet behind a bookcase in his La Jolla home. They were plumed, fluffed, be-ribboned, and spiked. He had a Baroque Czech helmet, a plastic toy Viking cap, a white leather marching-band busby, a black-and-white convict cap, a teeny-tiny sombrero, a fierce pickelhaube, and a floppy felt chapeau festooned with plumage.

Geisel, better known as Dr. Seuss, loved his hat collection and used it to his personal and professional advantage. He would unveil his stash at just the right moment when entertaining visitors, and place a different one on each guest's head. The hats broke the ice at dinner parties that seemed too cold and aloof.

But they also took on another role—that of literary muse. At times in the late 1960s, Dr. Seuss would be up against a project deadline and working head-to-head with Michael Frith, the editor in chief of Beginner Books at Random House. Into the early hours of the morning, the two would be perfecting the cadence of his next poetic masterpiece. At times, they would find themselves stumped by a turn of phrase. The word they had was just not right, but what to replace it with was up in the air. Dr. Seuss would bound to his closet and grab hats for himself and his compatriot. He would use the fez, the sombrero, or the military helmet as inspiration. The hats helped them to let go of the word they had once committed to, so that they could blaze a new linguistic course.

As with Dr. Seuss, there are times when our best interests are better served by putting away one hat and putting on another, by disengaging from one course of action and trying something else.

Researcher Carsten Wrosch, at Concordia University in Montreal, has spent his career investigating whether disengagement from ineffectual pursuits proves more advantageous for individuals than the continued chase of unattainable outcomes. Most recently, he applied this question to understanding how people recover from separation or divorce.

His scientific conclusions were surprisingly aligned with Neil Sedaka's most famous line. *Breaking up is hard to do,* particularly because it's not always clear what we can do to make ourselves happy after it happens. Should we move on to a new romantic conquest? Seek out a new social scene? Double down on raising our children or reinvest in our career?

To answer these questions, Wrosch surveyed younger adults in their twenties to mid-thirties, and (relatively) older adults in their forties and fifties. About half were committed to a romantic relationship, while the other half had found themselves separated or divorced in the last few years. As is no surprise, those who were recently separated reported poorer emotional well-being than did people currently in relationships. They had lower self-esteem and higher levels of depression when thinking about their relationship status. And this was true of both the younger and the older respondents.

As anyone who has felt the initial sting of rejection knows, those

feelings didn't last. When Wrosch followed up with all of the respondents fifteen months later, those who had separated or
divorced—both younger and older—reported feeling better.

But *how* they found happiness depended on their age. The difference between those who were happy fifteen months later and those
who were not had to do with how they structured the new goals they
formed as soon as their relationship had dissolved. To figure this out,
Wrosch had asked all respondents at the outset to list five goals they
were working to attain in the next five to ten years. He read their
lists and put each entry into one of two categories. Was the goal
about finding a new relationship partner? Or was it about forming a
social connection in some other way—like joining an archery club
(something we've all dreamed of doing after bingeing on some television series)?

Among those in their twenties and thirties, the happiest were
those who had recommitted to finding love despite the previous setback. For younger adults, the sea is teeming with fish, so to speak.
The supply is well stocked. And the opportunities for finding someone else to cozy up to are plentiful.

For those in their forties and fifties, romantic prospects are relatively bleaker. There are fewer fish in the sea, since many in this de-
mographic are already partnered up, and others may have chosen to
prioritize a career over commitment. Wrosch found that when older
adults had recognized this reality constraint and shifted their social
priorities away from finding a mate, and instead toward strengthen-
ing bonds with family or making new friends, they reported having
more satisfying and stable emotional lives at the fifteen-month
follow-up compared to those who had doubled down on finding Mr.
or Mrs. Right. Connecting with other people still mattered, but ad-
justing the way in which companionship was sought out separated
those who were happy from those who were not. The venture that
yielded the biggest return was the one that had them moving fur-
thest from their original plan for happiness.

Though disengagement can be a useful tool for ultimately achieving what really matters most, we don't try it all that much. Why not? The answer to this question has something in common with a visual illusion that is just as hard to shake as our commitment to a hard-wearing goal.

Below is a photograph, albeit of slightly degraded quality, of a person. You likely recognized it as a depiction of Albert Einstein, right? But if you squint, perhaps quite hard, hold the book at arm's length, or both, you might eventually notice that another face appears. Another icon, this one platinum-haired. Can you see Marilyn Monroe?

Aude Oliva, executive director of the MIT-IBM Watson AI Lab, created this visual experience by filtering photographs of the two twentieth-century titans and overlaying them. Einstein and Monroe are both very much present in the same visual image, but when we look at the composite, we have a strong predisposition to visually favor one over the other. We can force ourselves, by changing how we look at the page, to perceive another interpretation. But as soon as we revert back to a more natural way of reading, our initial perceptual experience takes hold once more.

We have a hard time disengaging from a goal that matters to us for the same reason we have a hard time letting go of Einstein and instead seeing Monroe in this image. Just as we get stuck on seeing that single interpretation, we get stuck thinking that there's only one way to be successful. And that's just not true. At times, we may need to consider alternative paths to accomplishing our goals. The course we are currently on may be taking us down a dead-end road.

How do we know when our failures reflect an insurmountable inability rather than a mild glitch to troubleshoot on our journey? How do we know when it's time to disengage?

The ingredients in our own mental stew might give us some insight. When we find ourselves thinking far more often than we usually do about both the costs and benefits of persevering, we may have reached a decision point. This mental juggling of pros and cons occurs when we have invested time, effort, and energy into the pursuit of something important but have stumbled along the way. Is this the time to double down or cut our losses?

This question is one that marathon runners often ask themselves around the eighteen-mile mark. With just over eight miles to go, physical and psychological resources have been heavily taxed but are still drawing down. Runners' bodies shift from burning glucose to burning fat, which depletes energy reserves at even greater rates. Some people can't feel their feet. Others say it feels like their legs have filled up with lead bullets. Dick Beardsley, who tied for first place in the inaugural London Marathon, described it like this: "It felt like an elephant had jumped out of a tree onto my shoulders and was making me carry it the rest of the way in." Here, runners have hit "the wall." Given this phenomenon, you might think that at each mile marker in the race, the percentage of people exiting to the sidelines would increase. As fatigue worsens and sore muscles feel the burn even more, it seems logical to assume that more and more people would turn in their bib and be done with it all. But no.

In 2009, the New York Road Runners released data on the people who hadn't finished the New York City Marathon the year before. It turns out that dropout rates creep higher from about the six-mile mark and are the highest between the fifteen- and eighteen-mile checkpoints. From the eighteen-mile mark on to the finish line, just past the twenty-six-mile mark, the dropout rate falls sharply. If you can make it past the eighteen-mile mark, the odds of finishing tip back in your favor.

The wall is a real thing, and it's at this point where people start weighing the costs of continuing against the rewards of finishing. It's also the point at which disengagement becomes a serious consideration, like no other time in the race. Researchers from the University of Zurich and the University of Bern studied the thoughts that pass through marathoners' minds before, during, and after hitting the wall. These runners in their study were, for the most part, experienced. Though some had taken up running only a year earlier, others had been running for thirty years. Every week, this group ran more than thirty miles each. After training for and competing in a marathon, these runners reflected on their experience at four points during the race.

As you might imagine, as the race progressed, runners thought more and more often about the benefits of giving up. At a steadily increasing rate, the lure of a cold compress on aching muscles and a stiff massage became temptations too appealing to deny. But as the runners neared the wall, their minds started racing, if you will, with other considerations. Thoughts turned more often to the benefits of continuing, like how good that finisher's medal would feel hanging from their neck. They also thought more and more about the costs of giving up, like how disappointing it would be to see others wearing that medal when their own necks were naked the day after. In fact, the frequency of consideration of all such pros and cons peaked at the eighteen-mile wall and fell sharply thereafter. The mental juggling of costs and benefits was most active *at* the wall, the point in a marathon when dropout rates are the greatest.

If you're a marathon runner and are physically up to the challenge, disengagement probably may not be the appropriate response. You can reasonably be assured that there is a second wind on the other side of the proverbial wall. But in other realms, it could be the healthy choice.

Carsten Wrosch, studying the experience of disengaging from relationship goals, created a way to index his participants' usual experience when presented with the challenge of changing course. He asked: How easy is it to cut back on the effort you put into working on a goal that matters? How committed do you feel even after quitting? How hard is it to let go? His team aggregated all these answers to create an index reflecting how easy or difficult it was for each individual to disengage.

The researchers then sent the participants home with a bag full of small test tubes. Over the next four days, participants spit into these test tubes four times a day and put each tube in their fridge until they went back to the lab to turn them in. From these samples, the researchers could measure cortisol, a hormone our body creates that helps us to deal with stress.

When the researchers combined the results of the disengagement index and the cortisol samples, they found an important connection between the two measures. All participants exhibited their highest levels of cortisol within the first hour of getting out of bed. This is normal and expected. When we first wake up, our body produces cortisol to help us get moving. In healthy people the cortisol levels drop off over the course of the day, until we go to sleep. And in this study, participants who had a notably easy time disengaging saw their cortisol levels drop dramatically over the course of the day—by half in the first four hours, then by half again in the next four, and then slightly more right before bed.

However, people who had a harder time disengaging than the average person did not show the same drop in cortisol levels over the course of the day. Instead, their cortisol levels stayed about 30 percent higher at every checkpoint after waking up. This is dangerous, because sustained levels of cortisol can increase our vulnerability to illness and wear our body down. It appeared that those who struggled the most to cut themselves off from working on a goal they couldn't accomplish were living chronically with more stress than people who found ways to disengage when the timing was right.

Wide Bracketing to Disengage

Vera Wang is one of the most sought-after contemporary female fashion designers. According to market sources, the retail value of goods bearing her name is estimated to exceed $1 billion per year. She dressed not only herself but also Jennifer Lopez, Chelsea Clinton, Ivanka Trump, and Chrissy Teigen on their wedding days. First Lady Michelle Obama chose Wang's designs when hosting a state dinner at the White House to honor Chinese president Xi Jinping and his wife, Peng Liyuan. She has amassed a personal fortune of over $630 million.

But design is not where she started.

Wang was seven years old when she put on her first pair of figure skates. Although she grew up on the Upper East Side of Manhattan, the rink at Central Park wasn't where she wanted her blades to touch ice; her sights were set on the competitive arena. Wang trained hard for a decade, and always intended her career to be one she would dress for in spandex and sparkles. In college, she hitched a ride to the North Atlantic Figure Skating Championships in West Orange, New Jersey. Her nearly perfect performance earned her the senior ladies' title and a mention in *Sports Illustrated*.

After that, though, titles weren't recurrent. As a teenager, Wang and her partner, James Stuart, competed at the U.S. national championships. They didn't win. Wang wanted a spot on the Olympic skating team, but Peggy Fleming, the reigning ice queen, beat out Wang for a spot. After their pairs loss, Stuart decided to skate solo. And Wang decided to hang up her skates for good.

She regrouped at the Sorbonne in Paris, and realized that what she wanted out of her life didn't need to come from the rink. In an interview with Style.com, Wang described her passions as "that love of beauty, that love of line, and that love of telling a story of some sort and reaching people emotionally." She first thought she could find her passions in figure skating. When she reached a plateau and accepted that younger skaters were quickly closing in on her tenure on top, which had seen its term, she turned toward design instead. From one perspective, Wang was naturally widening the bracket of her life's lens, and in so doing, the passions that had inspired early morning lace-ups now found their application in the world of fashion. We don't know Wang for her fifth-place junior doubles performance at the nationals in Philadelphia, but we do know her for the empire of tulle and mousseline she built. Disengagement meant the opportunity for redirection, reinvention, and rediscovery. Knowingly or not, by adopting a wide bracket, Wang saw how all the little pieces could come together, and how other paths and choices might lead to the same outcome.

Indeed, when we assume a wide bracket, we see relationships across different activities and pursuits. If we're considering a healthy diet, a wide bracket helps us see the connection between how much we're eating and how much we're moving. If we're trying to reduce our anxiety, a wide bracket leads us to realize that the number of hours we spend in elective overtime at work comes at the expense of opportunities for self-care.

Wide bracketing also lets us pool outcomes on our to-do list, and can shield us against the risk of falling short of the goal despite our best efforts. Say we're fresh off a lively extended-family reunion with cousins, aunts, and uncles. Our desire to maintain positive connections with these kindred relations has never been urgent. Whatever interest we might have felt may have been stymied by a second cousin who has yet to return an email, or a nephew who screens every call and doesn't return them. If we were to focus exclusively on these missed connections, our enthusiasm to cultivate companionship within our newfound (or newly rekindled) family could easily wither away. With too many failure experiences, motivation to persevere deteriorates. But a wide bracket can put these failures into context alongside the successes.

A wide bracket can help us find a different and perhaps even better way to achieve what we want. In New York, cab drivers choose their own hours. Some drivers rent cabs from a fleet for twelve-hour shifts. In one study by a group of economists, drivers were paying the fleet owners $76 to take a car for a day shift and $86 to take it overnight. They had to return the cab with a full gas tank at the end of the shift, which cost them about $15. Other drivers leased their cabs from an owner by the week or month. A third type of driver owned his or her own medallion (costing about $130,000), a requirement of the city to drive a cab legally. Drivers could keep all the fares, including tips, and could take on fares as long as they wanted up until the contracted period of time expired. If they returned the cab late, they'd be assessed a fine. Then—like now—in New York, drivers got most of their fares by "cruising" and looking for passengers. Fares were set and regulated by the city's Taxi and Limousine Commission. So cabbies' revenue depended both on the demand for rides and the number of hours they kept their car out.

The economists wondered whether drivers made the best decisions about how many hours to work on a given day. They knew that the optimal strategy would be to work more hours on days when demand was high, and fewer hours on days when fewer people were standing around looking to hail a cab. Weather has an impact—pedestrians rethink their idea to walk to their destination when it's icy cold or raining; rush and lunch hours also see spikes in the need for a ride. This strategy would maximize both the average daily wage and leisure time. Work when demand is high. Take a day off when demand is low.

To test whether drivers in fact chose their hours optimally, the economists analyzed almost two thousand trip sheets from fleet companies. Drivers were required to keep lists of the time a fare was picked up and dropped off, and the dollar amount of the fare (excluding tip). The researchers knew how many hours the drivers worked during each shift, which could be verified against the meter in their cab, and could compute the average daily wage the driver earned.

What they found was that in fact some cabbies did not use the strategy that would maximize profit and leisure time. When they were making a smaller hourly wage, drivers worked more hours. These drivers were reluctant to work shorter days when revenue streams were running shallow. Cabdrivers who paid daily for the use of their car made decisions using a narrow focus. They took it "one day at a time," setting a loose daily income target and quitting for the day once they had that much cash in hand.

Other drivers, though, made decisions that better balanced work and time off. Drivers who were paid weekly or monthly, and those who owned their own cab, worked fewer hours on days when their average hourly wage dipped, and more on days that held the most potential for fares. Because they chunked their expenses and revenue with a wider frame, they found themselves choosing a more efficient labor schedule.

Assuming a wide bracket, and setting goals for the week or the month, they could minimize labor and maximize profit in addition to leisure. They could make more money, working fewer hours. The wide bracket turned off the ignition when their efforts weren't paying off.

In 1982, the first female editor in chief of *Cosmopolitan* magazine, Helen Gurley Brown, sparked a conversation around the phrase with which she had titled her book: *Having It All.* The idiom quickly and ferociously established a foothold in common discourse and left most people—especially her female readers—feeling overwhelmed and deflated. The incantation led people to believe not only that it was possible to both balance and excel at meeting the demands of competing roles like *parent* and *professional* but also that real success in life required it. We felt pressured to do more, and to do it all well.

As the decades have passed, the definition of "having it all" has evolved, but what has remained constant is the feeling that the maxim places many impossible demands on all of us. In her book *Off the Sidelines,* Senator Kirsten Gillibrand urged her readers, "Please, let's stop talking about *having it all* and start talking about the real challenges of *doing it all.*" In a similar spirit, Anne-Marie Slaughter, the first woman to serve as director of policy planning for the U.S. State Department, wrote a piece for *The Atlantic* titled "Why Women Still Can't Have It All." She wrote it, in part, because other women told her she shouldn't. *That is not a message that should be sent to other women,* she was admonished. But she wrote it anyway because, despite all of the doors that her life had opened for her, she still felt she couldn't get where she wanted to be.

The ubiquity of the phrase "having it all" contributes to our assumption that most people aspire to wear many hats (perhaps not as literally as Dr. Seuss did), and to wear them all fabulously. It also leads us to believe that we should want this. Our understanding of these social norms and societal expectations, even if they are wrong, might be one reason that people find it difficult to give up on a goal they've been working toward. Even if we want to quit, we might not think it's okay if we do.

When Mattie was about a year old, I had lots of balls in the air. I was juggling my own research career as a scientist, teaching, moving my just-retired parents halfway across the country, writing this book, and trying to learn one song on the drums well enough to not embarrass myself publicly. I was experiencing my own struggle with having it all, and getting really annoyed that the phrase existed. About that same time, a major brand approached me and asked whether I wanted to serve as a scientific consultant for a study on how women define their ideal life. Do women really hold the multitude of goals that the phrase "having it all" implies, we would ask, and does that lead to happiness? I jumped at the opportunity, which was a surefire way to feel spread even thinner. I knew I had only myself and my tendency to say yes to blame. But this question was one I personally wanted to answer.

We chose to tell the stories of a dozen and a half women whose lives were different from one another's but not all that uncommon. These were strong and confident women who had already accomplished some pretty amazing things—like receiving graduate and professional degrees, earning salaries that allowed them to live a comfortable life in the city of their choosing, and managing deep and meaningful relationships. But they were all at a choice point in their lives, and were not living exactly the dream they'd hoped they would. Their journey wasn't over but instead in progress.

We designed a survey that these women completed at home, in private. They considered what "having it all" meant to them personally, and defined what their ideal life would entail. We asked what aspects of their life were most important to bringing a sense of fulfillment and happiness. Did it mean carving out time for mental health and exercise? Was it managing a team of accomplished employees at a top-performing firm? Or was it dedicating one's life to philanthropy? Did it allow for spending time caring for others? They also told us about the women in their lives whom they rely on when making some of their biggest decisions, like whom to date, when or if to have kids, or how to finish school and land the right job. These were their support networks.

A few weeks later, we sent a cryptic invitation to these women and their support networks, inviting them to an address in a posh neighborhood in New York City. The invite wasn't as creepy as that might sound, but it wasn't all that informative either. We told them we wanted a chance to learn more about what they wanted in life, and hoped they could bring their mom, their sister, best friend, law school study partners, or whoever else they had indicated were the women they relied on the most. They didn't know it, but it was a social experiment. Not one that would stand up to the rigors of the peer-review process that scientists undergo when publishing their academic work in professional journals, but one that would adhere to the same principles. We had a hypothesis about the process by which women define their ideal lives, but we were going to let the data tell us whether or not we were right.

Before the date on the invitation, I had some prep work to do. I met with the film production crew who would be capturing the experience and creating a video to share the results. The crew and I talked about who the women were, the challenges they were facing in their lives at the moment, and the questions I would ask that could uncover what was holding these women back from living the lives they really wanted. We talked about the psychological reasons people get stuck making the same decisions, again and again, that don't bring them happiness in the long run. And we batted around ideas on what inspires people to change.

Then the conversation turned to clothing. Particularly mine. No one has ever accused me of being fashion-forward, and that was especially the case after Mattie joined our family. Time was a precious resource, and I didn't go shopping for much more than diapers on the Internet in those days. When the production team began asking me about the contents of my wardrobe and evaluating whether any of it would work for the shoot—a day and a half away—I panicked. The filmmaker leading this project was Lucy Walker, and she had tight prescriptions for what would work on camera. My closet was certain to disappoint. She was out of my league both professionally and personally. She was schooling me on some recent report on psychological research she'd just read in the news, results I hadn't heard about yet, while looking like she was fresh off a visit to Donatella Versace's personal closet. Two of her films had been nominated for Academy Awards, and several more had been named best picture at film festivals in pretty much every country that holds them. Coincidentally, on one of our first dates Pete and I had ended up at the Museum of Modern Art for a world premiere of one of her films, and sat next to the musician Moby, who did the film's music and who used to DJ with Walker in New York City. Also, she wears velour without looking ironic.

Walker specified that my outfit should have sleeves. No tight patterns. Saturated colors. No logos. Professional but interesting. Contemporary but enduring. After the list came in, all that I had left that would fit the bill was shoes, and those likely wouldn't appear on camera. My schedule was tight and I had only a two-hour window to flesh out my staid and outmoded wardrobe. I whipped through every store in SoHo that fell along and within a three-block radius of my route from the production team's office to my apartment. I bought everything that met her specifications and hoped that the return policies would be generous when Walker turned down my selections. I snapped some extremely unflattering selfies as I tried on the clothes in the dressing rooms. I sent them on to Walker's production team. All my choices failed. They decided to call in a specialist to take over.

A fashion consultant called me within the hour and asked a few questions about sizes and style. I gave numbers for the first and reported having none for the second. She was on the case. By the next day, she promised, she would procure the contents of a new closet that blended Walker's requirements and my partialities. "Trust me," she said. "I know what you're after. Check out my website. You'll look great and the camera will love it." As soon as we hung up, I pulled up her site. It read like a Pinterest page, full of pictures; featured prominently were photographs of people dressed exclusively in body art and tattoos. I went to bed scared.

In the end, there was no need for my fear. The dress the consultant picked out was perfect. But even more important, the social experiment we conducted that day went off without a hitch and the results were particularly enlightening.

When the women and their social-support networks showed up to the address on the invitation, my fashion consultant was prepared to freshen any of their outfits too, should they need it. And sound engineers were tucking away microphones in the most unusual places on each participant. I wore mine in a belt around my upper thigh, like a scientific superhero with secret powers of amplification.

After all the prep work, I met the women next door. The production team had transformed an empty storefront into a one-day pop-up "shop."

When these women walked in, they were surprised. This wasn't a usual store or a normal shopping experience. But that was the point. I explained that today they would be shopping for their ideal life. I encouraged each woman to think about what she really wanted to accomplish in every facet of her life. Each section of the store offered selections, and she should fill her basket with choices that reflected her biggest aspirations that could be realistically achieved. The women saw jars, bottles, bags, canisters, and tubes. Each one was labeled with something like 40–60 HOUR WORK WEEK, NANNIES, DONATING TO CHARITY, and COOKING HEALTHY MEALS. I handed a basket to each woman and sent them off into the store to shop.

After a while, they brought their shopping baskets up to me at the checkout counter. They didn't know it, but I had the survey responses that they had completed weeks earlier at home, and I knew what areas of life were most important to each woman. At checkout, I combed through the products they'd selected and compared these choices to what they had said in the survey.

I found that these women were determined and motivated. Compared to what they'd said on their survey form, when they shopped for their ideal life in the store, 89 percent of the women formed more ambitious goals. Even more interesting, what I found countered the stereotype that all women are striving to "have it all." Instead, I found that these women all wanted a special life that was unique and different from what the other women in the store wanted, and that's where they intended to focus their efforts. Seventy-seven percent of the women who set more ambitious goals in the store made these choices in the domains they had said were the most important aspects of their lives. They weren't trying to achieve the highest standards in all facets of life. They aimed for the top in those areas that they personally found most satisfying, and those areas varied from one person to the next.

I knew that that one woman, Melanie, had graduated from one of the most prestigious law schools in the country and taken a position with a high-powered firm in New York City right after passing the bar. Her professional schedule robbed her of personal time, and she wanted some of it back. Her ideal life included more hours for personal growth and family time, and she was finding ways to get them. In fact, soon she would be leaving her firm and moving to Atlanta to start her career over again in a less stressful area of law. A bold move, for sure.

I learned that Cristina didn't have kids, but in her world she had a hard time admitting to anyone that she actually wanted them. In our first conversation I'd asked if children were a part of her ideal life and she said, "God no!" But in her basket, when she shopped the store, she had hidden away the THREE+ KIDS bag. When I asked about it, she replied, "If I'm being honest, that's always what I sort of pictured for myself."

Amanda had told me she has a lot of siblings and spends her time helping them, but the contents of her ideal life included more personal time. She told me she felt guilty about that, but wondered, "Why do you have to think as a woman that you have to sacrifice yourself?"

What was it about the shopping experience that affected what these women hoped to achieve in their lives?

In our conversations these women had told me that in everyday contexts, they tended to think with a narrow focus. They made life decisions in isolation, as one-off choices, without consideration of what trade-offs would necessarily follow. They were thinking about what they would do to meet the current demands on their time and talent. They were trying to solve today's problems with today's resources. Kaylan was in seminary school, so she thought her next job would be as a minister; that's what comes next. Kirsty said her doctor had told her it was time to have kids; she was considering it even though she wasn't ready yet. These women tended to think about what they could and should do with their life the way it was currently structured. As a result, their narrow focus left them feeling unfulfilled and trapped.

In contrast, this shopping experience had induced a wide bracket. The women were designing their ideal life holistically. They were finding ways to feasibly piece together their greatest aspirations. In the store, they saw all life's options before their eyes. The challenge was deciding which ones would fit in their basket. The size of the basket and the number of products that could actually fit into it were metaphors for the constraints imposed by reality. When Melanie picked up the plastic bottle that said she wanted a twenty- to forty-hour workweek, she had to wedge it in between the canister embellished with the $200,000 SALARY sticker and alongside the bag saying she wanted to go back to school to earn a doctorate degree in the future. Tasha tried to work a GRADUATE DEGREE bag into her basket, along with a can pronouncing that she wanted to feel constantly challenged at work, the tube indicating that she planned to retire before the age of sixty, and a jar saying that she would travel multiple times a year. I overheard Tasha ask her friend Kayon how she could possibly take on all that she wanted: "I'm starting grad school, and then you have work, you have all these things, but then how do you fit in, like, a family?" Kayon replied, "You fit in a family just the same way you fit in, like, all the new things you do. You gotta adjust, 'cause you want it."

The store pushed these women to see life options from a different perspective. They explained that in the store they thought aspirationally about what they really wanted. They were better aware of what was less important in their lives when they saw these unsatisfying choices nestled up alongside the ones that brought joy. This experience encouraged each woman not only to dream big about what she wanted across *every* aspect of her life but also to consider how these aspirations would feasibly work together. Some women felt emboldened to admit that they did not want to experience a traditional marriage, and felt content to foster connections with others through meaningful friendships or solo parenting. Others could now say they planned to leave careers that came with cachet for less glamorous ones, realizing this was how they would feel satisfied. Assuming a wider perspective by considering how all parts of their identity might coalesce helped them to realize what mattered most to them, and what could be sacrificed. As Tasha said, the experience helped her realize that "I need to upgrade my perspective on life and what I want."

The wide bracket gave these women the strength to recommit to a set of goals that was personally gratifying, and to push back against others' expectations. They were more likely to break from the social norm.

I knew the women I worked with were unique, but I wondered whether there was evidence of wide brackets affecting resistance to conformity outside this context. I turned to the work of a social psychologist named Dominic Packer, who had asked a similar question in his research. In Packer's study, a group of young adults considered what aspects of their community could benefit from improvement. And they all had thoughts to share on what needed to be changed in their neighborhoods and at school. Then the researchers gave them information about what the social norms were for expressing their beliefs. In particular, they learned that their peers disapproved of the expression of critical opinions. The researchers also manipulated the focus of participants' attention. Some considered whether to share their criticisms while assuming a narrow focus, whereas others made that consideration while assuming a wide bracket. Though all the participants wanted to see certain things about their community changed for the better, the question was whether they would conform to the social norm that their peers had established. Would they remain silent because they knew their peers thought that was right, or would they voice their concerns?

Just as the women shopping in my store were more ambitious and less conventional once they had assumed a wide bracket, the young adults Packer studied were more likely to defy societal expectations when they assumed a wide bracket. Those who wanted to make change happen but knew that sharing dissenting opinions was a social taboo were more likely to speak openly when they assumed a wide bracket, compared to those who took a narrow focus. A wide bracket encouraged them to see beyond the immediate social pressures to say silent. It gave them the strength to push back against expectations and to do what they thought was best for themselves and society.

Thinking about changing course can be intimidating. A good bit of trepidation might come from what we consider that change to represent. If we conceptualize change as failure, then it comes as no surprise that we might try to avoid it. But if we think of it as simply finding another route to a goal we already had, then it might be something we more readily accept.

College students aspiring to become doctors regularly cite the extremely challenging nature of their biology course as the reason they leave the premed track. Leaving science, though, does not have to mean that they have failed in their attempt to join the medical profession. In fact, according to the Association of American Medical Colleges, 45 percent of people accepted to medical school in 2018 held degrees in other fields, such as math or the humanities. Changing majors does not necessarily mean changing career possibilities. It might just mean finding another route to get there.

Actor Will Smith started out at the age of sixteen wanting to be a rapper. He and his friend dubbed themselves DJ Jazzy Jeff and the Fresh Prince. He won four Grammys, even. But the IRS came knocking and opened the door on some financial irregularities. Smith lost much of that newly found wealth. That setback didn't mark tragedy and it didn't mean the end. He pivoted to acting and took the Fresh Prince to Bel-Air, with the success of a television show based on that same name. His film career took off soon thereafter. He's won two People's Choice Awards and has been nominated for two Academy Awards and dozens of others. *Time* magazine has named him one of the one hundred most influential people whose power, talent, and moral example are transforming the world.

Kendra Scott is the CEO of a fashion and accessory company that bears her name. She employs two thousand individuals, 98 percent of whom are women. She was named Ernst & Young's Entrepreneur of the Year in 2017. But Scott didn't start with the stars aligned. She had only five hundred dollars, a spare bedroom to work from, and a mom who took calls on her company's behalf. She threw her infant son into a baby carrier and went door-to-door at local boutiques trying to find stores that would sell her pieces on her behalf. Small orders were placed that offered enough cash to buy supplies to make the next round of product. When her oldest son was three and the other just one year old, she divorced, and now her family's livelihood depended on her taking her business to the next level. She had to find a new way forward. Though a college dropout, she opened her first retail business, and it worked. Within three years, Oscar de la Renta chose her pieces to accessorize his line at a spring runway show. Scott now sits on *Forbes*'s list of America's richest self-made women, positioned higher than Taylor Swift, Beyoncé, Donna Karan, and Diane von Furstenberg. Her brand is valued at over $1 billion.

Setbacks might come in education, business, or personal life. They might come early or they might come later on. Regardless, they need not be thought of as failures to meet a goal; they can instead be embraced as opportunities to seek a new path forward.

9

Doing More by Doing Less, and How to Think Beyond Today

Looking to find time in my day to get more practice sessions in, I was doubling and tripling up. I found a fifteen-minute window when Pete was getting Mattie dressed for bed, before family story time. If I put the four-minute recording of "Your Love" on repeat, I could lay down three and a half repetitions in between warming the bottle of milk and tracking down Mattie's nighttime stuffed animal friends. There were a few ten-minute pockets here and there, when I was waiting for someone to return a call, where I could try to remember the sequence of licks in the B-section. I could listen to the tune while writing this book, to try to figure out how the bass drum and snare came together. If I air-drummed in the shower I could log a semblance of additional rehearsals.

All of the ways in which I was fitting more practice into my regular day involved trying to add stick-time on top of what I was already doing. They were multitasking solutions. While they felt like the right course of action for getting more done, I knew they weren't working. I recorded myself and listened back to what each session produced. Sure, I was improving. Yes, no longer did I look like an ostrich that was trying to fly but had yet to accept she couldn't. But I was still quite far from talented.

Multitasking is a common enough practice. Well over half of the five hundred people I once surveyed reported that they preferred multitasking to single-tasking in order to accomplish the goals they cared most about. But scientists have discovered that preferences don't match up with our real choices.

To get a baseline understanding of just how prevalent multitasking is in the workplace, a team of scientists led by Laura Dabbish from Carnegie Mellon University observed the minute-by-minute choices made by employees at one financial-services firm and at a medical-device company. They shadowed thirty-six managers, financial analysts, software developers, engineers, and project leaders for three days, following them around every minute of the day. With their stopwatch at the ready, the researchers timed how long each employee spent in continuous uninterrupted thought or activity before moving on to something else. They found that the average amount of time that employees spent on any single event before switching was just three minutes. Those breaks happened even more frequently when employees were working on computers, cell phones, or other electronics. Then, switching happened every two minutes or so. Of course, sometimes we have no choice but to pull ourselves away from what we're working on—a boss stops by or a colleague has a question. But the researchers found that, just shy of half the time, the employees interrupted themselves. It was their choice to switch from one task to the next. These employees rarely granted themselves the opportunity to focus their mental resources on just one project for an extended length of time. Instead, the ping of a text lured some away from the spreadsheets they were working through. A notification flag popping up in the corner of a computer screen would tempt some to click for the update.

Beyond the Brink

There is a problem with this kind of divided attention. Pushed past a certain point, our cognitive resources become spread too thin to be effective. We have less mental bandwidth available to make good decisions that advance the multitude of goals we are working toward simultaneously.

Andrew Ward and Traci Mann, social psychologists at the time at Swarthmore College and UCLA, respectively, found out just how damaging multitasking can be for our long-term goals. They focused their investigation on the effects of multitasking among individuals who were dieting. In their experiment, participants enjoyed a movie depicting works by well-known artists. The show created the experience of visiting a museum virtually, without requiring viewers to battle the crowds or worry about knocking their head into one of Alexander Calder's mobiles. This was pretty enjoyable. The other half was randomly tasked with an additional responsibility. During the movie, they were required to tap their feet as soon as they heard a beep in the room. They also had to memorize which specific artworks they saw, so they could pass a memory test later on. Was Monet's *Water Lilies* featured? What about Rothko's *Black on Maroon*?

In addition, everyone was invited to sample snacks like nacho chips, chocolate candies, and cookies as they visited the virtual museum. The researchers knew that this invitation to snack conflicted with the dieters' important long-term goal. The question was whether multitasking would make it more difficult for the dieters to refrain from succumbing to the temptation. Could they make choices that would align with their health goal even when their cognitive resources were spread thin?

The answer was a resounding no. When dieters multitasked, they were more likely to make choices about what and how much to eat that they would later regret. In fact, compared to when they were simply enjoying the art, multitaskers consumed about 40 percent more calories from the unhealthy snacks, despite the fact that they were trying to watch their weight. The optional nosh became an almost automatic act that they couldn't resist.

The Illusion of Multitasking

Despite the fact that multitasking impairs our judgment, many people hold on to the idea that it is a valuable ability to master in many contexts. Employers, especially, think it's an enviable and needed "skill." Indeed, consider that in the first month of 2019 alone, Monster.com, the global leader in online recruiting, posted more than three hundred thousand job descriptions that sought someone who could effectively multitask.

We think it's a talent worth cultivating perhaps in part because multitasking just *feels* right. Researchers asked a group of volunteers in Columbus, Ohio, three times a day for one full month what they were doing and how they felt. The more the workers multitasked, the more they reported having fun. But multitasking is not the right course of action in all situations. Though they reportedly felt better, the more they multitasked, the less productive these workers were.

We multitask to try to get more done in a day, but the more often we do it, the less effective we are. Besides its feeling fun, why do we continue to do something that works so poorly?

To gain some traction on this question, let's look to children. Back when I taught Introduction to Psychology, every year I would show a video clip of an experiment to my students. In it, you see a smiling adult sitting on a chair designed for hips half her size, at a table barely higher than a tall stair. Next to her sits a towheaded four-year-old boy in a puffy hoodie with bright, curious eyes, cheeks still plump from a love of whole milk at snack time. On a tray in front of the child, the adult counts out five candies wrapped in colorful cellophane and arranges them in an evenly spaced single row. She takes another five candies and places each below one already on the tray, forming a second identical, evenly spaced row. The adult asks the boy if the first row has more candies than the second row, if the first row has fewer candies than the second, or if they have the same number. The boy sits through this whole preparation with his head propped up on his fist, elbow on the table, his eyes darting from her face to the candies, keeping a careful eye out for a goodie that might be ripe for his plucking. He answers correctly that the two rows have the same number. But then, as the boy watches quite keenly, the adult increases the spacing between the candies in the second row. She asks her question again, and this time the boy says that there are more candies in the second row.

Though any adult watching this knows the number has not changed, the little boy equates the visual experience of greater length with greater quantity. Confusing space and number is almost an inherent part of our experience as people. Clever developmental psychologists have discovered ways of testing infants' expectations about how the world works. They know that babies enter this life with the understanding of what *more* is, and that *more* can describe what we see and what we hear. French scientists tested about one hundred infants, some no more than eight hours old. The researchers played a recording of adults babbling syllables to the infants, and at the same time showed them a colorful line. Not high art, but a visual image that babies this young could actually see and enjoy. Some of the babies heard many syllables in a row and saw a long line. Other babies heard just a few syllables and saw a short line.

The researchers hypothesized that these babies would pick up on the patterns they'd just been exposed to. To test their predictions, the researchers paid particular attention to how the babies reacted next.

In the next two tests, the experimenter made some changes. Babies who had heard many babbles now only heard a few. Babies who had heard just a few now heard many. Like before, a line appeared on the screen at the same time as they heard the sounds. One time, this line was long; another time, it was short. The question was whether the infants would react differently to the test pairing that changed for them relative to "the pairing rules" they learned in the earlier session. Researchers who study babies know that newborns look at things that they find new and surprising, so if they looked longer at the screen, these scientists knew that the pairing of sounds and visuals was unexpected.

What this team found was that the babies looked longer when the auditory and visual pairings changed. Greater length went with greater number, in these babies' brand-new brains. And these tiny humans were surprised when they experienced a mismatch.

Even with many years of life experience under our belts, we continue to confuse physical magnitude with numerical value, and this illusion is something that companies have used to their advantage to grab hold of our wallet. In 2011, Kraft made a dramatic change to its packaging of Nabisco Premium saltines to curb snackers' experience of staleness. In place of four sleeves of crackers, Kraft introduced its "Fresh Stacks" packages: eight (smaller) sleeves instead of the usual four. The saltines held constant at the same price point, but an astute consumer might have noticed that the entire Fresh Stacks box contained 15 percent fewer crackers than the original. You might think that value-conscious consumers would be up in arms, or at least less interested in buying the item, which now cost more per unit. But no. Two years before the packaging switch, Kraft earned $208 million from cracker sales; in the year after the switch, Kraft earned a whopping $272 million. Of course, inflation happens and marketing strategies change, but the new packaging was one of the most radical changes Kraft had ever made, simultaneous with one of the largest gains. And that trend continued. For the fifty-two weeks ending May 17, 2015, Nabisco Premium was the leading saltine cracker brand in the United States.

Choosing more even when it means actually getting less is a

common experience, and one that might explain why we believe that multitasking increases productivity. The reason for our overreliance on a generally ineffective tactic might be the same reason that marketers were able to rejuvenate consumers' interest in repackaged saltine crackers. Just as the visual illusion of more *seems* better, doing more with our time just *feels* right—though in reality it isn't always the right decision.

Stuck in the Illusion

We have trouble surmounting our impulse to capitalize on the illusory appeal of multitasking for the same reasons that children believe a row of five candies spread wide contains more than the row of five candies tightly bunched. We struggle to override our instincts.

Children fall for the experimenter's trick of changing the spacing between candies despite being capable of doing math. In fact, well after most kids can count to one hundred and are able to add and subtract, they will confuse greater length for greater quantity when the experimenter spreads one row of candies out wider. They have difficulty overcoming the visual illusion they experience *in the present moment*.

The same is true of adults. And, in fact, it's something you can experience right now. On page 202, you'll see a diagram of a home. On two of the corners is a bold black line. Which is longer? Which is shorter? You may have seen a version of this figure before. I have—and yet it still manages to deceive me, as it might you. The lines are in fact the same length, but that's not how we see it. Time and time again, the line on the right appears longer than the one on the left. That's because the outlines of the walls and windows act as flankers that distort our perception of distance. The edges of the wall on the right create a context that tricks our eyes into seeing it as longer than it really is. The edges of the window on the left contract our experience of that line's length. Despite knowing in our brains that they are the same, we see with our eyes two lines that are different from each other.

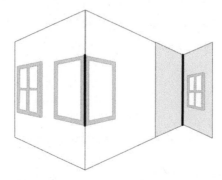

The visual illusion of greater length leads us to the wrong conclusion, in this example and elsewhere. We make the wrong choice, over and over again, even though we know the truth of the matter.

Neuroscientists wanted to understand the connection between our perceptual experience and our inability to inhibit our impulses. To do this, they put kids and adults in an fMRI scanner to determine what areas of the brain contributed to their decisions about whether two rows of objects contained the same number of items. The kids reported that the longer line had more items in it, even though it did not. Adults correctly said the two lines contained the same number. Though their responses were different, both the kids' and the adults' brain scans showed some remarkably similar patterns. Adults showed brain activity in the posterior parietal and frontal regions, areas of the brain that help us detect shapes and make sense of their spatial relationships with one another. When adults experienced the visual illusion, these brain regions kicked into overdrive, suggesting that they were experiencing the same visual illusion as the children were.

Adult brains also showed activity in the anterior cingulate cortex, a brain area that helps us stop ourselves from doing something we believe is wrong. Adults did not confuse the length of the row with greater quantity because their brains recognized that the illusion was happening and stopped what would have otherwise been a spontaneous and mistaken judgment.

In general, the brain areas that curb knee-jerk reactions, as does the anterior cingulate cortex, are not really mature until we reach our mid-twenties. It was surprising, then, that some of the kids' brains *did* seem to register the error, suggesting engagement of their impulse-control regions. These children were less likely to mistake greater length for greater number.

Even though, as adults, our neurological capacity to surmount our natural and reflexive tendencies has matured, we don't always exert our powers of control. We multitask beyond our cognitive breaking point even after knowing the behavior's detriments. As a study of credit card debt makes clear, it is hard to override our in-the-moment impulses.

Researchers from Columbia Business School and the University of San Diego's economics department worked with clients in Boston who were seeking assistance with tax preparation. Luckily for some of these clients, the day they walked in looking for help, the researchers had instructed the tax preparers to offer them a cash bonus. Just for coming in, they had the choice of receiving thirty dollars now or waiting one month to receive eighty dollars. Could you hold off for thirty days to get an extra fifty bucks? But some of the clients considered tougher decisions, like choosing between seventy dollars today or eighty dollars a month from now. Now the question was whether they would want to hold off for thirty days for a mere ten-dollar bonus. The clients saw the tax preparer's checkbook out on the desk and knew this choice was a real one.

The clients' preferences when considering the cash bonuses revealed something meaningful about how they approached financial decision-making. The researchers used these preferences to determine whether they were more focused on the present or the future. The present-focused clients were the ones tempted by the smaller sums they could take home right now, even though it meant they would be taking home less in the long run. The future-focused clients were interested in holding out longer for a fuller wallet.

After the clients left with their tax documents squared away, the researchers combed through their financial documents and noted the balance on revolving credit accounts each client held. What the researchers found was that present-focused clients were saddled with more credit card debt. In fact, they had almost 30 percent higher credit card balances than clients who weren't as tempted by the quicker but smaller cash offer. Focus on the present appeared to have played a substantial role in suboptimal financial decisions those clients had made in the past—as well as affecting their decisions in the year to come. Twelve months later, when they returned to the office for assistance with filing their taxes, they still carried much more debt than the future-focused clients.

Overriding the Present-Bias with a Wide Bracket

This general tendency to make a quick decision reflecting thoughts and preferences in the present undermines many of our best intentions to chart a course of action that benefits us in the long run, whether in terms of how we manage our credit cards or how we spend our time and cognitive resources to accomplish tasks. We continue to choose the immediately tempting solutions to problems, like the cash reward *today* or the multitasking option, because they seem like the right solutions to demands on our wallet and resources. How do we overcome that present-focus and make decisions that will benefit us more later? The wide-bracket mindset can help.

A wide bracket expands our focus and encourages us to consider options that lie at the fringes of what is possible. The decisions we make when considering this expanded range of possibilities may yield outcomes that are more lucrative and that better advance our more important goals.

Consider the 2009 Credit Card Accountability, Responsibility, and Disclosure Act, or CARD Act for short. With this bill, credit card companies were required to inform customers about the financial consequences of the amount they elected to pay toward their balance. The goal was to assist consumers in making wise financial decisions, and to encourage people to pay more each month toward their revolving balance. The CARD Act required that each statement include two components. First, statements must disclose the total time required to pay off their balance, and total fees customers would spend if they paid just the minimum each month. Second, statements must include the monthly amount needed to pay off the full balance in three years.

Do these regulations improve people's decisions about how to handle debt? Professors at the business schools of UCLA and Northwestern University sought the answer. They presented individuals with credit card statements that included the information the CARD Act now required. The participants imagined that the total balances and financial information provided on the bill reflected their own. Upon seeing the financial forecasts, individuals reported how they believed they would respond; they said they intended to pay five times the minimum, a sum that amounted to about 10 percent of the revolving balance. This might seem like a strong contribution to paying down the debt. But had that CARD Act information not been present, individuals would have paid more—in fact, the study showed that under some circumstances people would have paid almost *twenty* times the minimum if that financial forecast were absent. Of course, the minimum required payment fluctuates as the total balance of our account waxes and wanes, and as a result so too would the magnitude of the effect I just described. But even as the researchers changed these values, time and time again they saw that the CARD Act information actually reduced the amount paid to the account. The regulations seemed to have backfired.

The problem with the CARD Act requirements is that the financial forecast acted as a strong reference. Individuals interpreted it as a savvy suggestion for the responsible course of action. The payment amount contained within that forecast functioned as a compass, strongly guiding people's decisions about how much to pay that month. But it was actually much lower than what many individuals would have chosen to pay had it not been included. People's decisions reflected present considerations—paying less *now*—at the expense of long-term benefits for their fiscal health.

Was there anything that could counteract the detrimental impact of the three-year financial forecast that now appears on statements by law? The researchers created a wide bracket as a possibility. They presented a credit card statement that included the forecast, but added an additional note. Individuals saw a simple statement that they could pay any amount between zero dollars and the full balance. This simple addition had a big impact. It opened people up to considering the entire range of possible contributions. Those presented with the wide bracket of options intended to pay over *twenty* times the minimum, amounting to just shy of half of their revolving debt.

Wide-bracket framing pulls us out of focusing on the present. We think bigger-picture and with greater regard for our long-term plans, including how we spend our money. But it also influences how we spend our time. The impulse to save time *now* is why we continue to choose multitasking solutions even when they don't fit the situation. But wide brackets can break that pull, orienting us toward rewards that might require we wait for them to arrive, nudging us to choose quality over quantity, doing less in any one moment but doing it better. When the set of choices we consider expands beyond those that lie right in front of our eyes, we plan better for the future.

The Dilemma of Doubling Up

But there's a caveat. It is not always a mistake to succumb to our in-the-moment wants. There are circumstances where the choices that we feel pulled toward *right now* also align with our long-term interests. The key is knowing how to recognize these moments.

Diwas KC is a statistics guru at Emory University. He investigated the impact of multitasking on the productivity of emergency room doctors who must choose how best to juggle the care of multiple patients. For three years, he and his team gathered all kinds of data on the amount of time these physicians spent with patients, how they diagnosed their maladies, and whether the patients returned to the hospital with further complications. KC wondered whether physicians are more or less effective as their patient load grows larger. Does multitasking improve the quality of care and the efficiency of ER visits for these patients?

To understand how and when emergency room doctors multitask, consider the usual chain of events after you or I arrive at the hospital. A triage nurse evaluates our condition. The nurse enters our patient information into a virtual queue, and our electronic record is color coded to indicate how serious our symptoms are. Someone makes a physical folder documenting all of our medical information. An emergency room physician monitors the electronic queue to pick up new patients. The most severe cases are seen first. The physician also reviews the electronic and paper records, triage notes, and medical history reports. He or she orders diagnostic tests like X-rays or blood work, and seeks expert opinions from others, such as neurosurgeons or cardiologists. The doctor examines us and questions the family or friends who are present, in addition to reviewing test results as they come in from the lab. In the window of time when he or she is waiting for a specialist to weigh in or lab work to be done, the doctor could multitask. The discharge status of the last patient is in limbo as the diagnosis and course of treatment are being determined. Should the physician move on to the next patient during this time, or focus on the last patient fresh without muddying the cognitive waters with a new case? Would the patients be better off if the doctor multitasked?

Professor KC followed the experiences of more than 145,000 patients that physicians in this emergency room processed during a three-year period. He found that multitasking during the waiting window was both good and bad.

First off, multitasking when the patient load was minimal was linked to faster rates of patient discharge. Physicians used the idle time they had while waiting for test results to see new patients or attend to ones already in the queue. Multitasking sped up the process of evaluation and diagnosis for the entire caseload. When the demands on their time and mental resources increased, physicians doubled down on the job and worked faster.

To make this concrete: On average, KC's data showed, it took about one hour and forty minutes for any one patient to be released from the emergency room. Say a physician in the hospital was seeing three patients at once. Now, imagine that another patient arrived and the physician was suddenly handling four patients at the same time. You might think that the wait time would increase substantially for everyone. You might do the math like this: An hour and forty minutes divided by three people is about thirty-three minutes of face time per person with the doctor. So adding another patient to the mix would add another thirty-three minutes to everyone's wait time. Not so. Because multitasking can be beneficial, adding another person to the rotation actually led the doctors to work more efficiently. In fact, emergency room physicians increased their pace of discharging patients by about 25 percent when their load went from three patients to four. When that fourth person showed up, it added only about seven minutes to the discharge time for any one patient despite the doctor now simultaneously attending to more individuals.

Adding to our workload when things are relatively easy improves performance because low levels of stress actually assist in cognitive functioning. When we experience something new, unpredictable, or out of our control, our bodies respond by producing hormones—including cortisol, adrenaline, and noradrenaline—that prepare us to deal with that stress. These hormones impact the functioning of our hippocampus, amygdala, and frontal lobes—our most important brain structures for learning and memory. Multitasking, by indirectly engaging these parts of our cognitive system, helps us do our jobs better.

The problem is that the benefits of multitasking have a limit. At some point the mental cost of switching between tasks exceeds the benefits that low levels of stress offer us. For the emergency room doctors, as their patient load grew, there was a point—between patients five and six—at which the strain of multitasking among numerous patients became counterproductive. Whereas adding one more patient when the load was pretty small motivated the physicians to work more efficiently, adding one when the load was high crippled their efficiency. Because it took time to review the case files, remember the pending diagnoses, and recall what tests had been ordered for whom, the ability to move quickly through a patient load slowed down drastically as their caseload increased beyond five patients. The physicians' mental bandwidth wasn't able to keep up with the demands placed upon them. In fact, their pace per patient slowed down by 6 percent. To put that in perspective, when the doctors handled five patients at a time, any one patient sat in the ER for a little over two hours. When a sixth patient came in, that jumped to two hours and forty minutes.

The same pattern of effects emerged when KC examined the quality of the physicians' performance. With a small patient load, new admits increased the number of diagnoses per patient made by the physicians. This is a good thing, because a diagnosis ensures that symptoms are being addressed and the patient's problems are being solved. Multitasking when the caseload was small improved the quality of care for each patient. However, when the patient load increased beyond a tipping point, the physicians couldn't keep up. Once the number of patients exceeded four, physicians made fewer diagnoses per patient. Some patients even left without a diagnosis. When the caseload was high, patients were also more likely to revisit the emergency room within twenty-four hours, suggesting they were more likely to be discharged without their symptoms being fully remedied.

To sum up: When the physicians multitasked beyond the point where the stress was motivating, they kept their patients in the hospital longer than they would have otherwise, and were less effective at treating their problems.

Multitasking puts a strain on our cognitive resources. Sometimes this pressure inspires us to think more, think faster, and switch our mental focus more often. As is the case in quiet emergency rooms, when we are understimulated our minds operate at a slower, less efficient pace. Increasing cognitive demands invigorates us, and we are capable of rising to meet moderate challenges when we ask ourselves to tackle more than just the minimal. But there is a tipping point. When we try to tackle too much simultaneously, multitasking backfires.

How to Free Up Brain Space

Excessive multitasking can place a heavy burden on our cognitive system that we may be ill-equipped to manage. But even if we try to craft a lifestyle where we live in that sweet spot, balancing cognitive interest against ability, we will find ourselves in situations that demand we do more in less time. How do we optimize our performance when pushed beyond the brink? The work of a team of Spanish neuroscientists found a way to beat the burnout.

They tested Brazilian soccer player Neymar da Silva Santos Júnior when he was practicing some elementary footwork. In case you don't know him, Neymar is one of the world's best soccer players. He's been recognized as player of the year—more than once in fact—in every league he's played for. In 2017, he transferred from Barcelona to Paris Saint-Germain. His new team paid the equivalent of $262 million to simply buy him out of his last contract, more than doubling the previous record for a contract buyout. And the deal set Neymar's salary at just shy of one million dollars. Per week.

To test whether Neymar's brain behaves differently from the brains of athletes with less experience, they looked at what was going on when he moved his feet. They compared the patterns of his brain activity with those of four other professional soccer players who played for the Second Division in the Spanish soccer league (La Liga); two Spanish national-level swimmers about the same age; and one amateur soccer player.

Each athlete took a turn lying in an fMRI scanner and moving their feet in time with a metronome, as if they were running. The researchers also made a video measuring how much the athletes were moving their feet. In watching those films later, they ensured that any differences in brain activity they saw among the athletes could not have been the result of differences in what the athletes were doing with their bodies; regardless of their experience, their feet moved in the same ways in these testing conditions.

Despite these similarities below their ankles, the researchers found that Neymar's brain was less active than everyone else's. In particular, Neymar showed relatively little activity across a smaller surface area in motor-cortical regions that process foot movements. In other words, the amount of neurological real estate and processing power used to move his feet was far less than that of the other professional and amateur soccer players, and the swimmers (who don't train to use their feet in the same way). There is something special about what practice does—not only to Neymar's brain, but to all of our brains. If we practice, make habitual, or routinize parts of what we're doing, we free up mental resources that can then be spent elsewhere. In the end, we can handle more and experience fewer of the negative consequences of multitasking, because any one job doesn't require as much brainpower.

Despite how extraordinary he is on the field, the minimal computational power that Neymar's brain requires to move his feet is not unusual. In fact, experts in many professions show less activity in areas of their brain that seem to be specific to their craft. For example, when moving their fingers, professional concert pianists showed less brain activity in areas of their motor cortex than people who were not musicians. Professional Formula One drivers showed less brain activity in areas specific to vision and spatial relationships than amateur drivers while playing a video game that required they react quickly when something popped up on the screen in their peripheral field of vision. Expert air-pistol athletes showed less brain activity when shooting, particularly in areas that specialize in vision, attention, and motor movements compared to people who had never competed in the sport. Members of the Ladies Professional Golf Association showed less brain activity in these areas as well, compared to amateur golfers, just before taking a swing off the tee. And when envisioning themselves drumming, professional percussionists showed less activity in areas of their brain responsible for syncing up auditory and visual information, compared to people without much experience.

Over lunch one afternoon, I was asking Suzanne Dikker, a colleague of mine at New York University, what she thought the takeaway was from these studies. Not so subtly, I threw in a question out of personal curiosity.

"What's been happening to my brain over all the months I've been practicing?"

"I don't know," she laughed. "I'm not that kind of doctor."

I wasn't sitting on a chaise longue. We weren't talking about my childhood relationship with my mother (which was really quite lovely, except for a few teenage years that were admittedly my fault). But I was asking her to conjecture about me—someone she hadn't studied. Despite that, her actual expertise wasn't too far off. Dikker is a neuroscientist who investigates changes in brain rhythms as people live their lives outside of the usual stuffy, cloistered testing lab. Dikker explained to me that it's not that the brains of experts are smaller, or that there are real physical differences between their brains and those of novices. Instead, to perform as well as experts can at that moment, novices have to engage more of their brain and make those regions work harder than would those of a seasoned pro. With expertise comes neural efficiency, which frees up cognitive resources that can be spent elsewhere. Experts can multitask better than beginners because, in part, they have more brainpower available to handle what comes their way.

For me personally, these results were a call to hit the woodshed. If I worked hard to nail this one song, playing it would eventually be less taxing mentally and I could perform it even better with the extra cognitive resources I'd gain. But to acquire that expertise, I'd have to dive deep into a relatively shallow pool. The cliché applies here: *How do you get to Carnegie Hall? Practice, practice, practice.*

So, about two weeks out from the party at which I would debut my drumming chops, I finally came to accept that fitting practice around and on top of my existing workload wasn't going to work for me. Layering practice on top of an already full schedule wasn't bringing me the quality of improvement that I needed. I knew what the problem was, and I knew the solution. In all honesty, I didn't really like the drums—because I couldn't make my limbs do what I wanted them to. I was procrastinating, avoiding the concentrated effort I knew I needed to put in; but practice was the only solution.

I buckled up and focused. I sent Mattie off to Nana and Papa's with his stuffed bear, a lunchbox full of food, a bag full of washable paints, and a few extra sets of clothes. During my next practice session, I thought that I should have instead packed him a suitcase and a cooler, because he was going to be staying quite a while. I kept "Your Love" on repeat and listened to it so many times that the room started to spin, and it wasn't the disco ball kicking in. I had Cheerios and wine for dinner. More than once. Cooking held no status or priority here. It was go-time. And I needed to get this song learned.

What we were now calling the music room held constant through the summer at a dry and crisp seventy-two degrees. I didn't plan on breaking a sweat, but an hour into my first I've-got-to-do-this session I felt my face flush. I was sticky, and when I looked at the thermostat off to the side of the kit, I saw that my exertion (or perhaps the speakers I'd cranked for so long) had raised the temperature of the room by one degree! I was really doing something here! It took all afternoon to get it. My ears were ringing for a few hours after. But it felt so good. The progress was real. The lick that had flummoxed me and the three limbs I'd been trying to coordinate for so many months finally came out smoothly and not accidentally.

I couldn't get any neuroscientists interested in investigating what was happening inside my brain as I practiced my drums. Maybe they knew I wasn't yet show-ready. But I had a hunch that my brain had had quite the workout that day. I wasn't an expert and wouldn't be called in as a backup for the Outfield's reunion tour—yet—but I was certain that my brain could now take on a wee bit more than it could before, and that my multitasker quotient had just ticked up one notch.

10

Showtime

The day of my show, I woke up to a bed full of vomit. It was actually Mattie's bed. And it was his own, from his dinner the night before. I blame the half a watermelon he insisted on eating. Everything was in dire need of laundering, including Mattie himself. This morning surprise cost me ninety minutes and nearly all of the mental focus I had allocated for roadie work (since I had no staff, go figure). This setback is the reason, I believe, that it took until I was unpacking the boxes of T-shirts I had personally printed for my merch table to discover that the image was backward. It was my face and hands holding my own drumsticks, sure, in mottled hues of blue. But the show's slogan Pony Up: The One-Trick Tour, firmly affixed to the swag, required you to scan the printed words not as the English language usually commands, but instead in reverse, from right to left.

I rushed out to make some shirts using an at-home iron-on transfer paper system instead. The product was definitely second-rate, but legible to those both with and without the aid of a mirror. I piled up the cotton tops, still warm from my personal printing-press job, for ticket holders to peruse. I included the backward-texted ones too, thinking that the reversed imagery might appeal to those particularly interested in irony. This whole gig was a sort of through-the-looking-glass experience anyway. My face with drumsticks and transposed catchphrases was the concrete manifestation of just that.

I'd also printed up CD liners with the show's icon and motto. I intentionally left the disc-side of the plastic cases empty, except for a small placard indicating that purchasers should provide their own CD of preferred music. I was certain the cases would sell better if I didn't include a recording of myself. I filled a cooler with bottles of wine and beer clad in labels featuring my tour's logo. I had a few varieties of performance posters, announcing myself as the featured artist along with (previously) recorded artist the Outfield. I was playing along with a track off their studio album, after all. I took it upon myself to pre-autograph some of the posters in anticipation of a mad rush after the gig.

Just before showtime, I turned off all the lights in the music room and turned on the disco ball. I set up auxiliary globe lighting on the floor around the merch table. I checked my sticks to see if I had cracked them in my last rehearsal. Nope, I'm not that powerful. Yet.

The doors opened and in came the crowd. A dozen or so vied for a seat on the oversized couches.

I sat down on the throne. Mattie's friend Sarah checked and double-checked that her headphones worked, then settled in up front.

I turned on the stereo, cued up my tune, and hit PLAY.

I thought I had made a wise though cheeky choice in selecting a song that had the drummer wait out the first minute as the guitar and lead singer laid down the intro. Since the song was only four minutes long, that was 25 percent less for me to learn, I thought. In the end, it was awkward. Me sitting at the drums looking at them as they looked back at me. And my mom—an always loving but at times too honest critic—was keen to tell me later she thought I had frozen in panic. The stereo was cranked, so I couldn't tell jokes to cover my self-consciousness, though at this point I had better percussions skills than humor.

But then it was my turn to jump in. I nailed the snare on the pickup to the fourth beat before smashing the crash on the downbeat. Commence basic rock rhythm. *I'm off!*

As I opened and closed the hi-hat on the offbeats in between the eighth-note *chicks,* Pete smiled. I winked back, pretty proud of how all four limbs were doing their own thing and my brain didn't explode. I caught the fill and crash into and out of the interlude, and switched up the bass drum pedal action. I woke up the crowd with my first roll across the toms.

I live-streamed the event internationally. My sister lives across the continent and one country up, in Canada. She tuned in for the show. She's a professional musician and professor. Despite her having just flown back from Thailand a few hours before, still a little out of it because of the food poisoning she was fighting off, I knew she was listening closely and critically. She bobbed her head even more affirmatively when she caught the syncopation on the snare, which I had clocked probably four hours trying to perfect the week before.

I recorded the show too, and sent it off to a cousin who is a drummer. When he had heard what I was up to, he'd told me he routinely washes the family dinner dishes to that song. I'd like to think my performance inspired him to take on the breakfast ones too.

In the one or two moments when I wasn't counting the beat in my head like a bird in a cuckoo clock, I looked around the room. I saw my dad whip out a cell phone, light up the screen, and wave it over his head. Was he calling for an encore already, or lighting his way out? I saw Pete teaching Mattie how to give a thumbs-up sign. Mattie couldn't coordinate the necessary appendages. With his thumb and pointer finger both up and out, the product in Mattie's hand looked more like an imitation of a revolver. I wasn't sure of his intention. Maybe he meant to say, "Why don't you just shoot me?" But honestly, I doubt it, because I was doing pretty darn well!

In the third verse, my mounted-tom work was spot-on. I was rapid-firing alternating sixteenth and eighth notes on the floor tom and snare, then landing on the crash to kick off the final chorus. I was pulsing on the ride and driving it forward with crashes on every other beat. Yeah, I ended up too far on the backbeat on my last syncopation, but by then half the room was dancing, not taking notes. I was spanking the crash and rocking as hard as I ever had. I finished it off with the little splash for kicks, and threw the stick up in the air. It did a 360 and landed back in my hand. Rock-star style.

The applause was real, though I was ready to supplement it with a recorded track if necessary. Some of the audience popped up and headed over to the merch table. I set the mirror-printed tees apart from the rest, but left both versions available for the taking. To my great surprise, no one even noticed the aberrant print job. In fact, one fan, if I dare use that label, scooped up a first-edition version to take home as a souvenir. To her, the shirt looked contemporary and edgy, a visual experience that others who have not pledged allegiance to our friendship may be less likely to share.

The crowd called for an encore. But they must not have read the fine print on my concert posters. "One-trick tour" meant what every parent-friend with an only child has said to me when I've asked if they're having more: "Nope. One and done."

In this process of self-discovery, taking myself from a percussive nobody to a one-hit wonder, I've learned many valuable lessons. That I am not meant for a future in silk-screen printing is one of them. And, in fact, it may be the T-shirt fiasco that offers the biggest lesson of all. What we see might not be what someone else sees. Our perspectives are unique, and the malleability of our perspective is a source of opportunity. We can take advantage of the fact that our eyes may not see what is really printed on the page (or the shirt) in front of us, in order to see the world in a way that instead serves our aspirations best.

Using the Four Perceptual Tools
to Improve Our Mental Health

There's a part of our mental machinery that social psychologists call the "psychological immune system." Just as our bodies have ways of fighting off bacteria and viruses to improve our physical health, our minds have their own ways of maintaining and improving our mental health.

Consider this example: Researchers at Ghent University interviewed almost four hundred Belgian singers auditioning for a spot on a television program that would launch their professional career. A week before the audition, the researchers asked the contestants how they would feel if they lost the competition. On average, the group expected they would feel really unhappy. Unfortunately for most, their dreams of stardom were dashed when they were not selected to advance to the next round. But when the researchers followed up two days later to ask how they were doing, the same individuals who had expected to be heartbroken reported feeling something more like "meh." They didn't feel the pain they'd expected.

You can find the same discrepancy between anticipated disappointment and experienced positivity among three-, four-, and five-year-olds who receive only one sticker as a prize, rather than two; and people who lose their jobs, live through a traumatic personal injury, or witness a tragedy. We experience a resiliency we don't expect.

Reports of unlucky people's positive mental status flummox many of us looking at their lives from the outside. We think, *You tried so hard and lost. You gave up so much.* We expect them, as they did themselves, to feel disheartened. But they don't.

What we see is a result of the protective powers of the psychological immune system. Life's unfortunate circumstances pack a weaker punch than they seem like they should. Our cognitive system is capable of some impressive cookery. It can take the really

rather sour lemons in our lives and make some unexpectedly delicious lemonade.

I conducted a survey asking people whether they thought they'd
support a local organization raising funds for a national cancer-
research charity. The vast majority of individuals—eight out of ten,
in fact—said "absolutely" and explained that generosity is an important part of who they are as a person. But of course it's challenging
to foresee the hiccups of daily life that might stand in the way of
translating our theoretical plans into concrete behavior. When we
measured actual support after the event, among survey respondents
drawn from the same pool, we found that only three out of every ten
had opened their wallet and made a donation of any kind. Our best
of intentions do not always translate into real actions.

But this is a fact that we try to hide, perhaps most readily from
ourselves.

Our psychological immune system helps us in this regard. Consider the following nuance. In another survey, I asked people a few
days after a different high-profile charity event whether they had
supported the cause in some way. The time commitment had been
more, and the financial buy-in bigger, so rates of support were lower
than with the first event I tested. Here, only six out of every one
hundred people said they had helped out. And this percentage
tracked well with reports from local media. People were honest in
telling me that, despite the fact that they found the charity a deserv-
ing organization, they had not in fact done what they thought was
the right thing. But when I asked people a month later whether they
had supported the event, the levels of reported support somehow
climbed high. People were now misremembering their intentions,
and reporting having acted in a way they had only hoped they would.

It can hurt our sense of self to feel like we haven't lived up to our expectations of ourselves. One way we protect ourselves is by re-membering the past in more favorable ways. Our brains craft sum-maries of our past deeds that are like little white lies to help us feel better about what we did or didn't do. But that protective process can backfire in other ways. The problem is that accurately recalling not only our successes but also our shortcomings is essential for real growth and progress.

In this book, I offer four strategies intended to quite literally re-shape the way we see the world. *A narrow focus. Materializing. Fram-ing. A wide bracket.* Each of these strategies serves a different function. Knowing about each, we can better prepare ourselves for the multi-tude of difficulties that we stand to experience as we tackle life's biggest challenges.

Many of those challenges require that we surmount the unin-tended consequences of our brain's protective inclinations. We work hard to see ourselves, our surroundings, and our prospects in a posi-tive regard. And sometimes this focus on strengths rather than weaknesses is motivational; at other times it can be debilitating.

What we see predicts in large part the choices we make, which is why our decisions about what to focus our attention on have such a big impact on our daily actions. When we're looking for encourage-ment, we can find it through selective exposure to sources of inspira-tion. Orienting our visual frame around the people and things that support and represent our best intentions stacks the deck in our favor. We can inspire better decisions when we design the spaces we spend our time in to include visual sparks that align with our goals. But if we frame up the temptations, we threaten our prospects for achievement. If we leave the forbidden fruits in the bowl out on the countertop, we're bound to snag one on the way out and take far too big a bite.

A narrow focus, too, misrepresents reality—but it may inspire an energy that gives birth to real change. When we set our sights on a far-off destination, we induce an illusion of proximity, creating a sense that something challenging is actually nearer and more possible. What might otherwise appear insurmountable is now deemed achievable. And we try for it.

In other instances, drawing attention to wins rather than losses provides an inaccurate understanding of where we really stand, and discourages continued progress. There are times when we can find strength and purpose in knowing not just when we have succeeded but also when we've come up short. Materializing our progress, by tracking our choices and noting both our triumphs and our tribulations, fosters an honesty with ourselves that our psychological immune system might otherwise have killed off, and that can propel us forward toward our goals. Materializing can make us accountable for our missteps, but it also provides a forum for celebrating our victories perhaps more than we would otherwise. When we make a concrete and clear visual image of where we would like to be in the future, and couple this with a concrete plan of action, we set a goal in a responsible way. We can track our progress toward a definitive end with a clarity that we usually lack. Materializing rids us of biased memories that may lead us to believe we've made choices that better align with our goals than our actual choices do—as when my survey respondents honestly believed they had donated their time, talent, or treasury to a charity when they had not.

No one, at least no one I've met in my life, likes the symptoms that accompany the common cold. Sweating from a fever means more dirty laundry to clean. Drippy noses require repeat trips to the store to replenish the tissue supply. Coughs make you a challenging companion at the movies or the opera. We try to mask these symptoms with potions and lotions of all sorts. But all these physical ailments that we avoid when possible are markers of the recovery process.

In just the same way, our psychological immune system remedies the effects of choices or decisions that would otherwise make us feel bad. We have ways of overcoming the guilt of a caloric indulgence when dieting, or the stress of spending over our budget. But despite the discomfort of such negative reactions, if we allow ourselves to feel them they can have a motivating effect on our actions. Rather than trying to forget lapses in judgment we perhaps regret, remembering them can push us to do better in the future.

The wide bracket is a strategy that can help us do just that. Zooming out and capturing a broader swatch of our lived experience can better position us to find patterns in our behavior. When we see our choices for what they really are, rather than what we want them to be, we can piece together the puzzle of our lives in more optimal ways. We can find the triggers that consistently elicit the same choices, be they productive or disadvantageous. We can better see how our choices today affect tomorrow's outcomes, which reduces the temptation to make a decision that benefits us in the moment but that we'll regret later on.

Moreover, a wide bracket opens us up to the plentitude of options for how to get the job done. Knowing there are many rather than few paths that lead to a desired end offers a sense of possibility. It propels us off the starting block, but it also lessens the blow if and when the time comes for redirection and reinvention. A wide bracket offers a lens through which we can see other paths forward at points in time when having more options would be energizing.

When my song ended, I kept the lights dimmed and the disco ball spinning. I didn't want to induce vertigo in my fans, but if they left feeling a little worse for the wear, I wanted them to attribute it to the ambience and not the headlining act.

Eventually, the crowd started to thin. I noticed that some of the CD cases were gone, for what reason I have no idea, since no one listens to music off discs anymore. Lou took a poster but left it in our house on his way out the door. Several T-shirts had been taken, perhaps thanks in part to the five-dollar bills I had clipped to the sleeves.

I was proud of myself and what I had accomplished. It took far longer than I'd thought it would. I waxed and waned in my interest. I felt despondent periodically—until the practice paid off and the sound of myself grew less painful. On occasion, the annoyance I felt for taking on this challenge bubbled up. I wanted to be cool, sure. But the self-induced stress I incurred by choosing to work a full-time job, raise a baby (who was by now a toddler with all the usual charms and challenges), learn to play drums, and write a book about it was overwhelming at times.

But I didn't quit. I applied the tactics I've advised here to my own adventures in motivating myself, and found them effective. To be sure, what worked one day might have seemed less effective the next. There was no quick fix for the problems that stymied my progress, nor a simple one-shot solution. But that's the reality of life. Often, the things that bring us the greatest joy require real work.

At the end of all this, I accomplished my goal. I've got an act in my back pocket now that I can pull out should I find myself backstage with any Outfield cover band about to perform just one particular song at the very moment they realize their drummer isn't showing up. And next time I go hear Pete play with his band and someone in the crowd next to me realizes I'm his wife (probably because I'm wearing a shirt with his face on it—I made one of him, too) and asks what I do, I can now officially say I play drums too.

Acknowledgments

As I think about it now in hindsight, it's perfectly clear to me, as the idiom implies, that there are many people who hold great responsibility for this book and for whom my gratitude overflows. My agent, Richard Pine, and his team at Inkwell Management, took my fledgling idea for a book and gave it wings, patiently seeing through those awkward adolescent years of its development until it flew the coop. Marnie Cochran curated my collection of anecdotes with an editorial style sharper than a Japanese chef's knife and an emotional intelligence for how to deliver the feedback that tests at genius levels. She produced the voice I am glad to have found in this work. Thank you, also, to the team at Ballantine Books, particularly Lawrence Krauser, who made me sound clearer, brought the finish closer sooner, and made it all better than it would have been otherwise.

But before there was the way, there was the will. The nudge to write a book in the first place came from my friends. My colleague Adam Alter convinced me—in between his first and second books, when I presume he forgot what the stress of trying to meet publishing deadlines does to your sleep—that this journey would be fun.

On most days he was right. He kindly shared his knowledge, experience, and support every time I blindly stumbled into the next phase of this project. Fellow social psychologist Liz Dunn still offers surfing lessons despite my ineptitude at the sport, and advice on how to maximize happiness in writing and elsewhere.

As a scientist, I was trained to discover the causes of individuals' experienced lives. But despite the ace education I received, I chalk up so much of my own to sheer happenstance and luck in finding generous mentors. My PhD adviser, David Dunning, matched my excitement cheer for cheer when we together found the first evidence for the mind's influence on visual experience. My undergraduate adviser, Rick Miller, showed me early that there are opportunities for creativity and intellectual freedom in our profession that I wouldn't have known otherwise until much later. David Nabb, who chose Miles Davis's *Bitches Brew* as the soundtrack to his children's upbringing, taught me that music and parenting are more fun when done by breaking convention. My first PhD students and forever friends, Shana Cole and Yael Granot, were the yin to my yang as I cut my chops as a new professor. The 2016 TEDx New York team, including Thu-Huong Ha, Adam Kroopnick, and David Webber, were the first to help me find my public voice.

Some of the stories in this book are my own, but many more are not. Thank you to the many people who shared their fascinating tales with me so I could make my narrative richer. I am much appreciative of their gift. Thanks also to the many students who chose to include me in their college education. Without their collaboration in the scientific process, there would be many discoveries left waiting to be made.

One goal of this book was to increase awareness that our eyes may be an unknown source of strength and inspiration. But I'm not blind to the fact that my drive is perpetually fed by the support of my family. My mom, Nancy Balcetis, was a public school teacher. She dedicated her career to helping all children, regardless of their start in life, tell their own stories and find the ability to read others'. She cultivated a love of books in me that played a nontrivial role in my nearsightedness now; I spent many, many nights as a kid reading well past my bedtime by night-light. She helped me explore my writing style well before I could conjugate verbs properly. My dad, Mat Balcetis, was by profession a therapist but for me personally my first music teacher. He schlepped me to and from weekly lessons with others. And he spent loads of weekends traveling to my music competitions so he could be the loudest voice cheering me on in music, and all the other facets of my life. He still is. My sister, Allison Balcetis, gigged with me every week until college in different countries tore us apart, but only geographically. Her husband, Dustin Grue, coached me on how to rhetorically position a carefully selected quote when crafting prose, and on how to structurally position reinforcement rebar when pouring cement—one of those two lessons was particularly useful here.

Thank you to my husband, Peter Corrigan, for the trust and faith he has in me, and the carte blanche approval he gave to relay the stories of our daily life before either of us knew which I wanted to appear in print. But even more, and despite the perpetual bags under my eyes, I am glad for the adventure in parenting we are on together. Raising Matthew Corrigan and writing this book have been the two hardest things I've done in my life. Mattie was the first one I told that I was going to do this thing, and the first one I celebrated with over ice cream when it was done. He smiled his approval both times. I hope one day he's as proud to be my son (when he learns what that means and after he gets over all my references to the dirty bits of his infancy). I'm proud and grateful to be his mom now.

Notes

1   Seeing a New Way Forward

4   **He invited people with normal vision:** Pascual-Leone, A., and Hamilton, R. (2001). "The metamodal organization of the brain," *Progress in Brain Research* 134, 1–19.

5   **though the taste of salt:** Ohla, K., Busch, N. A., and Lundström, J. N. (2012). "Time for taste—A review of the early cerebral processing of gustatory perception," *Chemosensory Perception* 5, 87–99.

5   **distinguish the face:** Pizzagalli, D., Regard, M., and Lehmann, D. (1999). "Rapid emotional face processing in the human right and left brain hemispheres: An ERP study," *NeuroReport* 10, 2691–98.

6   **Most people see the head:** Fischer, G. H. (1968). "Ambiguity of form: Old and new," *Attention, Perception, & Psychophysics* 4, 189–92. For more great visual illusions, see Seckel, A. (2009). *Optical Illusions*. Buffalo, NY: Firefly Books.

11   **I had just read:** Trainor, L., Marie, C., Gerry, D., and Whiskin, E. (2012). "Becoming musically enculturated: Effects of music class for infants on brain and behavior," *Annals of the New York Academy of Sciences* 1251, 129–38.

13   **In fact, only four:** Kirschner, S., and Tomasello, M. (2010). "Joint music making promotes prosocial behavior in 4-year-old children," *Evolution and Human Behavior* 31, 354–64.

13   **Every December, Marist College polls:** NPR/PBS NewsHour/
      Marist poll, November through December 4, 2018, maristpoll
      .marist.edu/wp-content/uploads/2018/12/NPR_PBS-NewsHour
      _Marist-Poll_USA-NOS-and-Tables_New-Years-Resolutions
      _1812061019-1.pdf#page=3.

14   **Like so many other people do:** American Psychological Association
      (2012). "What Americans think of willpower: A survey of
      perception of willpower and its role in achieving lifestyle and
      behavior-change goals," www.apa.org/helpcenter/stress-willpower
      .pdf.

15   **And that's true for challenges:** For more on willpower, see
      Baumeister, R. F., and Tierney, J. (2012). *Willpower: Rediscovering
      the Greatest Human Strength.* New York: Penguin Books.

16   **Following the direction of experimenters:** Erskine, J. A. K. (2008).
      "Resistance can be futile: Investigating behavioural rebound,"
      Appetite 50, 415–21.

17   **To evaluate the importance:** Clarkson, J. J., Hirt, E. R., Jia, L.,
      and Alexander, M. B. (2010). "When perception is more than
      reality: The effects of perceived versus actual resource depletion on
      self-regulatory behavior," *Journal of Personality and Social Psychology*
      98, 29–46.

19   **But these shattering experiences:** Shea, A. (April 8, 2011). "Glass
      artist Dale Chihuly seduces eyes, and blows minds, at the MFA,"
      WBUR News, www.wbur.org/news/2011/04/08/chihuly-profile.

2   Finding the Right Kind of Challenge

22   **For instance, 3M holds:** For more on 3M's New Product Vitality
      Index, see www.cnbc.com/id/100801531.

24   **Marcel Just, a neuroscience:** Just, M. A., Keller, T. A., and
      Cynkar, J. (2008). "A decrease in brain activation associated with
      driving when listening to someone speak," *Brain Research* 1205,
      70–80.

25   **In 1840, Petzval crafted:** I had never before thought to look up a
      patent, but I did for Petzval's lens. The hand-drawn renderings are
      fascinating. You can find them here: US Grant US2500046 A,
      Willy Schade, "Petzval-type photographic objective," assigned to
      Eastman Kodak Co., published March 7, 1950.

26   **I started up a conversation:** Find out more about Provenzano's
      adventures as part of the Red Bull team here: www.redbull.com
      /us-en/athlete/jeffrey-provenzano.

27   **Provenzano and his skydiving teammates:** Bisharat, A. (July 29, 2016). "This man jumped out of a plane with no parachute," *National Geographic,* www.nationalgeographic.com/adventure /features/skydiver-luke-aikins-freefalls-without-parachute; Astor, M. (July 30, 2016). "Skydiver survives jump from 25,000 feet, and without a parachute," *The New York Times,* www.nytimes .com/2016/07/31/us/skydiver-luke-aikins-without-parachute.html.

31   **Joan Benoit Samuelson kept her shoes:** For more about Samuelson and other female athletes' stories, turn to Edelson, P. (2002). *A to Z of American Women in Sports.* New York: Facts on File.

31   **When she runs, Samuelson scans:** Longman, J. (October 9, 2010). "Samuelson is still finding the symmetry in 26.2 miles," *The New York Times,* www.nytimes.com/2010/10/10/sports/10marathon .html; Macur, J. (November 6, 2006). "In under three hours, Armstrong learns anew about pain and racing," *The New York Times,* www.nytimes.com/2006/11/06/sports/sportsspecial/06armstrong .html.

33   **Research, in fact, confirms:** Sugovic, M., Turk, P., and Witt, J. K. (2016). "Perceived distance and obesity: It's what you weigh, not what you think," *Acta Psychologica* 165, 1–8; Sugovic, M., and Witt, J. K. (2013). "An older view of distance perception: Older adults perceive walkable extents as farther," *Experimental Brain Research* 226, 383–91.

33   **In one University of Virginia study:** Proffitt, D. R., Bhalla, M., Gossweiler, R., and Midgett, J. (1995). "Perceiving geographical slant," *Psychonomic Bulletin & Review* 2, 409–28.

33   **In my own lab, I've found:** For similar results, see Cole, S., Balcetis, E., and Zhang, S. (2013). "Visual perception and regulatory conflict: Motivation and physiology influence distance perception," *Journal of Experimental Psychology: General,* 142, 18–22.

34   **Two of my students:** Cole, S., Riccio, M., and Balcetis, E. (2014). "Focused and fired up: Narrowed attention produces perceived proximity and increases goal-relevant action," *Motivation and Emotion,* 38, 815–22.

35   **Kenya's Eliud Kipchoge:** Robinson, R. (September 16, 2018). "Eliud Kipchoge crushes marathon world record at Berlin Marathon." *Runner's World,* www.runnersworld.com/news /a23244541/berlin-marathon-world-record.

36   **More than 60 percent of Americans:** Board of Governors of the Federal Reserve System (2018). "Report on the economic well-being of U.S. households in 2017–2018," www.federalreserve.gov

/publications/2018-economic-well-being-of-us-households-in-2017
-retirement.htm.

36 **In fact, an analysis released:** VanDerhai, J. (2019). "How
retirement readiness varies by gender and family status: A
retirement savings shortfall assessment of gen Xers," *Employee
Benefit Research Institute* 471, 1–19.

36 **Assuming a conservative:** Fontinelle, A. (October 3, 2018).
"Saving for retirement in your 20s: Doing the math." *Mass Mutual
Blog,* blog.massmutual.com/post/saving-for-retirement-in-your-20s
-doing-the-math.

38 **My class project was based:** Hershfield, H. E., Goldstein, D. G.,
Sharpe, W. F., Fox, J., Yeykelis, L., Carstensen, L. L., and
Bailenson, J. N. (2011). "Increasing saving behavior through age-
progressed renderings of the future self," *Journal of Marketing
Research* 48, 23–37.

40 **Again, psychologist Hal Hershfield:** Van Gelder, J-L., Luciano,
E. C., Kranenbarg, W. E., and Hershfield, H. E. (2015). "Friends
with my future self: Longitudinal vividness intervention reduces
delinquency," *Criminology* 53, 158–79.

41 **In another study, those connected:** Hershfield, H. E., Cohen,
T. R., and Thompson, L. (2012). "Short horizons and tempting
situations: Lack of continuity to our future selves leads to unethical
decision making and behavior," *Organizational Behavior and Human
Decision Processes* 117, 298–310.

41 **In another study, almost:** Ibid.

42 **That year also saw civil rights activist:** PBS produced a
documentary series on the civil rights movement that aired in 1987
called *Eyes on the Prize,* so named for Wine's song, which is used in
each episode as the opening theme.

3   Plating a Full Plan

45 **In fact, this is exactly what:** Byrne, R. (2006). *The Secret.* New York:
Atria Books/Beyond Words.

46 **"Ellen DeGeneres is":** *O, The Oprah Magazine* cover
(December 2009).

46 **In 2016, TD Bank conducted:** TD Bank (2016). "Visualizing goals
influences financial health and happiness, study finds," newscenter
.td.com/us/en/news/2016/visualizing-goals-influences-financial
-health-and-happiness-study-finds.

48 **A study led by a colleague:** Kappes, H. B., and Oettingen, G. (2011). "Positive fantasies about idealized futures sap energy," *Journal of Experimental Social Psychology* 47, 719–29.

53 **Shelley E. Taylor, a psychologist:** Pham, L. B., and Taylor, S. E. (1999). "From thought to action: Effects of process- versus outcome -based mental simulations on performance," *Personality and Social Psychology Bulletin* 25, 250.

54 **The Center for Responsive Politics:** Center for Responsive Politics (October 22, 2008). "U.S. election will cost $5.3 billion, Center for Responsive Politics predicts," OpenSecrets.org, www.opensecrets .org/news/2008/10/us-election-will-cost-53-billi.

54 **With the stakes so high, social scientists:** Rogers, T., and Nickerson, D. (2010). "Do you have a voting plan? Implementation intentions, voter turnout, and organic plan making," *Psychological Science* 21, 194–99.

55 **Accepting the possibility:** Morgan, J. (March 30, 2015). "Why failure is the best competitive advantage," *Forbes*, www.forbes.com /sites/jacobmorgan/2015/03/30/why-failure-is-the-best-competitive -advantage/#2e4f52e959df.

60 **And after presenting that first checklist:** Kaufman, P. D., ed. (2005). *Poor Charlie's Almanack: The Wit and Wisdom of Charles T. Munger.* Infinite Dreams Publishing.

61 **Back in Beijing in 2008:** Crouse, K. (August 16, 2008). "Phelps's epic journey ends in perfection," *The New York Times*, www.nytimes .com/2008/08/17/sports/olympics/17swim.html; Crumpacker, J. (August 13, 2008). "There he goes again: More gold for Phelps," *SFGate,* www.sfgate.com/sports/article/There-he-goes-again-more -gold-for-Phelps-3273623.php.

61 **A team of psychologists:** Fishbach, A., and Hofmann, W. (2015). "Nudging self-control: A smartphone intervention of temptation anticipation and goal resolution improves everyday goal progress," *Motivation Science* 1, 137–50.

62 **Inge Gallo, a researcher:** Gallo, I. S., Keil, A., McCulloch, K. C., Rockstroh, B., and Gollwitzer, P. M. (2009). "Strategic automation of emotion regulation," *Journal of Personality and Social Psychology* 96, 11–31.

63 **Traci Mann, a research psychologist:** Mann, T. J., Tomiyama, A. J., Westling, E., Lew, A.-M., Samuels, B., and Chatman, J. (2007). "Medicare's search for effective obesity treatments: Diets are not the answer," *American Psychologist* 62, 220–33.

64   **The three-step process:** For more information on how foreshadowing failure can assist in dieting, see Henneke, M., and Freund, A. M. (2014). "Identifying success on the process level reduces negative effects of prior weight loss on subsequent weight loss during a low-calorie diet," *Applied Psychology Health and Well Being* 6, 48–66.

4   Becoming Your Own Accountant

69   **For that album the band:** *Bird Songs,* the Grammy-nominated recording, is the twenty-second album by Joe Lovano, featuring Francisco Mela, Esperanza Spalding, James Weidman, and Otis Brown III, released by the Blue Note label in 2011.

72   **Perhaps this trainer had followed:** Hollis, J. F., et al., for the Weight Loss Maintenance Trial Research Group (2008). "Weight loss during the intensive intervention phase of the weight-loss maintenance trial," *American Journal of Preventive Medicine* 35, 118–26.

73   **Drawing from the largest nutrition database:** Olson, P. (February 4, 2015). "Under Armour buys health-tracking app MyFitnessPal for $475 Million," *Forbes,* www.forbes.com/sites /parmyolson/2015/02/04/myfitnesspal-acquisition-under-armour /#352145e46935.

75   **But within a year, running:** For more information on Nathan DeWall's running career, see his *New York Times* article "How to run across the country faster than anyone" (October 26, 2019), www.nytimes.com/2016/10/26/well/move/how-to-run-across-the -country-faster-than-anyone.html.

78   **In 2007, less than half a million:** U.S. Courts (March 7, 2018). "Just the facts: Consumer bankruptcy filings, 2006–2017," www .uscourts.gov/news/2018/03/07/just-facts-consumer-bankruptcy -filings-2006-2017#table1.

78   **As of September 2018:** Center for Microeconomic Data (November 2018). "Quarterly report on household debt and credit," www.newyorkfed.org/medialibrary/interactives/householdcredit /data/pdf/HHDC_2018Q3.pdf.

78   **At about the same time, Americans:** Ibid.

79   **Numbers released from the Federal Reserve:** ValuePenguin (March 2019). "Average credit card debt in America," www .valuepenguin.com/average-credit-card-debt.

80   **As Ariely explains, we give precedence:** For more from Ariely's interview, see www.nytimes.com/2016/04/13/technology /personaltech/googles-calendar-now-finds-spare-time-and-fills-it -up.html.

81   **But in his research:** Ariely, D., and Wertenbroch, K. (2002). "Procrastination, deadlines, and performance: Self-control by precommitment," *Psychological Science* 13, 219–24.

82   **In one study, amateur chefs:** Kruger, J., and Evans, M. (2004). "If you don't want to be late, enumerate: Unpacking reduces the planning fallacy," *Journal of Experimental Social Psychology* 40, 586–98.

82   **People who believed that:** Buehler, R., Griffin, D., and MacDonald, H. (1997). "The role of motivated reasoning in optimistic time predictions," *Personality and Social Psychology Bulletin* 23, 238–47.

83   **Scientists from the University of Waterloo:** Koehler, D. J., White, R. J., and John, L. K. (2011). "Good intentions, optimistic self-predictions, and missed opportunities," *Social Psychological and Personality Science* 2, 90–96.

5   In Sight, In Mind

87   **or their project *Dear Data*:** Lupi, G., and Posavec, S. (2016). *Dear Data*. New York: Princeton Architectural Press. To see Lupi and Posavec's postcards online, visit www.moma.org/artists/67122.

93   **Some choose based on snacks:** The Senate has archived records of the candy desk. Learn more here: www.senate.gov/artandhistory /art/special/Desks/hdetail.cfm?id=1.

93   **But more commonly, senators:** Roubein, R., and *National Journal* (June 1, 2015). "How senators pick their seats: Power, friends and proximity to chocolate," *The Atlantic*, www.theatlantic.com/politics /archive/2015/06/how-senators-pick-their-seats-power-friends-and -proximity-to-chocolate/456015.

95   **When we look at our electric bill:** Thaler, R. H. (2009). "Do you need a nudge?" *Yale Insights*, insights.com.yale.edu/insights/do-you -need-nudge.

96   **In 1909, a Hungarian physician:** Battaglia-Mayer, A., and Caminiti, R. (2002). "Optic ataxia as a result of the breakdown of the global tuning fields of parietal neurons," *Brain* 125, 225–37.

97   **This is called automaticity:** Wood, W., and Ruenger, D. (2016). "Psychology of habits," *Annual Review of Psychology* 37, 289–314.

98   **There was a brief period:** Clifford, S. (April 7, 2011). "Stuff piled in the aisle? It's there to get you to spend more," *The New York Times,* www.nytimes.com/2011/04/08/business/08clutter.html.

98   **Researchers went door-to-door:** Cohen, D. A., Collins, R., Hunter, G., Ghosh-Dastidar, B., and Dubowitz, T. (2015). "Store impulse marketing strategies and body mass index," *American Journal of Public Health* 105, 1446–52.

99   **This is why, in 2011:** *Federal Trade Commission Cigarette Report for 2017,* www.ftc.gov/system/files/documents/reports/federal-trade -commission-cigarette-report-2017-federal-trade-commission -smokeless-tobacco-report/ftc_cigarette_report_2017.pdf.

99   **In a one-year analysis:** Nakamura, R., Pechey, R., Suhrcke, M., Jebb, S. A., and Marteau, T. M. (2014). "Sales impact of displaying alcoholic and non-alcoholic beverages in end-of-aisle locations: An observational study," *Social Science & Medicine* 108, 68–73.

100   **Among Australian youths:** Dunlop, S., et al. (2015). "Out of sight and out of mind? Evaluating the impact of point-of-sale tobacco display bans on smoking-related beliefs and behaviors in a sample of Australian adolescents and young adults," *Nicotine and Tobacco Research* 761–68.

100   **In 2010, Anne Thorndike:** Thorndike, A. N., Riis, J., Sonnenberg, L. M., and Levy, D. E. (2014). "Traffic-light labels and choice architecture: Promoting healthy food choices," *American Journal of Preventive Medicine* 46, 143–49.

101   **The company has its own fleet:** Stone, M. (November 2, 2015). "Google's latest free lunch option is a fleet of 20 fancy food trucks—and the food looks incredible," *Business Insider,* www .businessinsider.com/googles-latest-free-lunch-option-is-a-fleet-of -20-fancy-food-trucks-and-the-food-looks-incredible-2015-10; Hartmans, A. (August 26, 2016). "21 photos of the most impressive free food at Google," *Business Insider,* www.businessinsider.com /photos-of-googles-free-food-2016-8.

101   **At the snack stations:** Kang, C. (September 1, 2013). "Google crunches data on munching in office," *Washington Post,* www .washingtonpost.com/business/technology/google-crunches-data -on-munching-in-office/2013/09/01/3902b444-0e83-11e3-85b6 -d27422650fd5_story.html. For more of Google's health nudges, see abcnews.go.com/Health/google-diet-search-giant-overhauled -eating-options-nudge/story?id=18241908.

102 **In Philadelphia and Wilmington, Delaware:** Davis, E. L., Wojtanowski, A. C., Weiss, S., Foster, G. D., Karpyn, A., and Glanz, K. (2016). "Employee and customer reactions to healthy in-store marketing interventions in supermarkets, *Journal of Food Research* 5, 107–113.

103 **Another study of supermarket produce:** Glanz, K., and Yaroch, A. L. (2004). "Strategies for increasing fruit and vegetable intake in grocery stores and communities: Policy, pricing, and environmental change," *Preventive Medicine* 39, 75–80.

104 **A survey of nearly three thousand smokers:** Wakefield, M., Germain, D., and Henriksen, L. (2008). "The effect of retail cigarette pack displays on impulse purchase," *Addiction* 103, 322–28.

105 **Psychologist Wendy Wood discovered:** Wood, W., Tam, L., and Witt, M. G. (2005). "Changing circumstances, disrupting habits," *Journal of Personality and Social Psychology* 88, 918–33.

105 **Researchers know that when monkeys:** Mirenowicz, J., and Schultz, W. (1996). "Preferential activation of midbrain dopamine neurons by appetitive rather than aversive stimuli," *Nature* 379, 449–51.

106 **A telecom company:** Holland, R. W., Aarts, H., and Langendam, D. (2006). "Breaking and creating habits on the working floor: A field-experiment on the power of implementation intentions," *Journal of Experimental Social Psychology* 42, 776–83.

6   Reading the Room Right

112 **Roy Baumeister, a psychologist:** Baumeister, R. F., Campbell, J. D., Krueger, J. I., and Vohs, K. D. (2003). "Does high self-esteem cause better performance, interpersonal success, happiness, or healthier lifestyles?" *Psychological Science in the Public Interest* 4, 1–44.

113 **The South Korean office:** Koo, M., and Fishbach, A. (2008). "Dynamics of self-regulation: How (un)accomplished goal actions affect motivation," *Journal of Personality and Social Psychology* 94, 183–95.

114 **Children as young as seven:** Wood, L. M., Parker, J. D., and Keefer, K. V. (2009). "Assessing emotional intelligence using the Emotional Quotient Inventory (EQ-i) and related instruments," in *Assessing Emotional Intelligence* (pp. 67–84). Boston: Springer. For

more on emotional intelligence, see Bradberry, T., and Greave, J. (2009). *Emotional Intelligence 2.0*. San Diego: TalentSmart; Salovey, P., and Mayer, J. D. (1990). "Emotional intelligence," *Imagination, Cognition, and Personality* 9, 185–211.

114 **Managers who can read emotions:** Wilderom, C. P. M., Hur, Y., Wiersma, U. J., Van Den Berg, P. T., and Lee, J. (2015). "From manager's emotional intelligence to objective store performance: Through store cohesiveness and sales-directed employee behavior," *Journal of Organizational Behavior,* onlinelibrary.wiley.com/doi/abs /10.1002/job.2006.

114 **Doctors who can gauge:** Shouhed, D., Beni, C., Manguso, N., IsHak, W. W., and Gewertz, B. L. (2019). "Association of emotional intelligence with malpractice claims: A review," *JAMA Surgery* 154 (3), 250–56.

114 **business students in Singapore:** Elfenbein. H. A., Foo, M. D., White, J., Tan, H. H., and Aik, V. C. (2007). "Reading your counterpart: The benefit of emotion recognition accuracy for effectiveness in negotiation," *Journal of Nonverbal Behavior* 31, 205–23.

116 **Results from the work of vision:** Du, S., and Martinez, A. M. (2011). "The resolution of facial expressions of emotion," *Journal of Vision* 11, 1–13.

117 **About thirty years ago:** Ekman, P., and O'Sullivan, M. (1991). "Who can catch a liar?" *American Psychologist* 46, 913.

118 **Our corrugator muscles:** For more on the muscles that differentiate one facial expression from another, see Ekman, P., Friesen, W. V., and Hager, J. C. (2002). *Facial Action Coding System: The Manual* on CD-ROM. Salt Lake City: A Human Face.

120 **In the same vein:** Beck, J. (February 4, 2014). "New research says there are only four emotions," www.theatlantic.com/health/archive /2014/02/new-research-says-there-are-only-four-emotions/283560.

121 **To prove the point:** Brady, W. J., and Balcetis, E. (2015). "Accuracy and bias in emotion perception predict affective response to relationship conflict," in *Advances in Visual Perception Research* (pp. 29–43). Hauppauge, NY: Nova Science Publishers.

123 **Billionaire investor Warren Buffett:** Gallo, C. (May 16, 2013). "How Warren Buffett and Joel Osteen conquered their terrifying fear of public speaking," *Forbes,* www.forbes.com/sites/carminegallo /2013/05/16/how-warren-buffett-and-joel-osteen-conquered-their -terrifying-fear-of-public-speaking/#667d5529704a.

125 **The work of a group:** Shasteen, J. R., Sasson, N. J., and Pinkham, A. E. (2014). "Eye tracking the face in the crowd task: Why are angry faces found more quickly?" *PLOS ONE* 9, 1–10.

126 **For older adults, this pattern of eye gaze:** Sanchez, A., and Vazquez, C. (2014). "Looking at the eyes of happiness: Positive emotions mediate the influence of life satisfaction on attention to happy faces," *Journal of Positive Psychology* 9, 435–48.

126 **Children who make this style:** Waters, A. M., Pittaway, M., Mogg, K., Bradley, B. P., and Pine, D. S. (2013). "Attention training towards positive stimuli in clinically anxious children," *Developmental Cognitive Neuroscience* 4, 77–84.

126 **college students who practiced:** Dandeneau, S., and Baker, J. (2007). "Cutting stress off at the pass: Reducing vigilance and responsiveness to social threat by manipulating attention," *Journal of Personality and Social Psychology* 93, 651–66.

126 **The same is true for salespeople:** Ibid.

127 **Carol Dweck is a psychologist:** Dweck, C. S. (2007). *Mindset: The New Psychology of Success.* New York: Ballantine Books.

128 **Psychologist Jason Moser:** Moser, J. S., Schroder, H. S., Heeter, C., Moran, T. P., and Lee, Y.-H. (2011). "Mind your errors: Evidence for a neural mechanism linking growth mind-set to adaptive posterror adjustments," *Psychological Science* 22, 1484–89.

129 **Researchers trained NCAA Division I:** Goodman, F. R., Kashdan, T. B., Mallard, T. T., and Schumann, M. (2014). "A brief mindfulness and yoga intervention with an entire NCAA Division I athletic team: An initial investigation," *Psychology of Consciousness: Theory, Research, and Practice* 1, 339–56.

130 **Bethany Hamilton is a professional surfer:** Lieber, A., director (2018). *Bethany Hamilton: Unstoppable.* Entertainment Studios Motion Pictures.

132 **At one point in Deci's career:** Deci, E. L., Connell, J. P., and Ryan, R. M. (1989). "Self-determination in a work organization," *Journal of Applied Psychology* 74, 580–90.

133 **Years later, Jacques Forest:** Forest, J., Gilbert, M.-H., Beaulieu, G., Le Brock, P., and Gagne, M. (2014). "Translating research results in economic terms: An application of economic utility analysis using SDT-based interventions," in M. Gagne, ed., *The Oxford Handbook of Work Engagement, Motivation, and Self-Determination Theory,* 335–46. New York: Oxford University Press.

7 Forgoing the Forbidden Fruit and Perceiving Patterns

137 **Researchers found more than two hundred:** Hofmann, W., Baumeister, R. F., Förster, G., and Vohs, K. D. (2012). "Every day temptations: An experience sampling study of desire, conflict, and self-control," *Journal of Personality and Social Psychology* 102, 1318–35.

138 **Remember the pantry attendants:** Baskin, E., Gorlin, M., Chance, Z., Novernsky, N., Dhar, R., Huskey, K., and Hatzis, M. (2016). "Proximity of snacks to beverages increases food consumption in the workplace: A field study," *Appetite* 103, 244–48.

139 **Along with Shana Cole:** Cole, S., Dominick. J. K., and Balcetis, E. (2019). "Out of reach and under control: Distancing as a self-control strategy," research presented at the Society for the Study of Motivation, 2015 Conference, New York.

144 **Employees work more efficiently:** The original studies were conducted at Western Electric's telephone manufacturing factory Hawthorne Works, near Chicago, between 1924 and 1933. The patterns are now referred to as the "Hawthorne effect." They are described here: Mayo, E. (1933), *The Human Problems of an Industrial Civilization.* New York: Macmillan; Roethlisberger, F. J., and Dickson, W. J. (1939). *Management and the Worker.* Cambridge, Mass: Harvard University Press; Gillespie, R. (1991). *Manufacturing Knowledge: A History of the Hawthorne Experiments.* Cambridge, Mass.: Harvard University Press.

144 **Kids as young as five:** Engelmann, J. M., and Rapp, D. J. (2018). "The influence of reputational concerns on children's prosociality," *Current Opinion on Psychology* 20, 92–95.

144 **Museum patrons move through:** Carbon, C.-C. (2017). "Art perception in the museum: How we spend time and space in art exhibitions," *I-Perception* 8, 1–15.

150 **Dutch students played:** Wiebenga, J., and Fennis, B. M. (2014). "The road traveled, the road ahead, or simply on the road? When progress framing affects motivation in goal pursuit," *Journal of Consumer Psychology* 24, 49–62.

152 **It was a cheeky test:** Fishbach, A., and Myrseth, K.O.R. (2010). "The dieter's dilemma: identifying when and how to control consumption," in Dubé, L., ed., *Obesity Prevention: The Role of Society and Brain on Individual Behavior* (pp. 353–63). Boston: Elsevier.

153   **Each dollar invested:** Allen, S. (2001). "Stocks, bonds, bills and inflation and gold," InvestorsFriend, www.investorsfriend.com /asset-performance.

154   **One reason analysts find:** Benartzi, S., and Thaler, R. H. (1993). "Myopic loss aversion and the equity premium puzzle," National Bureau of Economic Research, dx.doi.org/10.3386/w4369.

156   **Over thirty-five years ago:** Kirschenbaum, D. S., Malett, S. D., Humphrey, L. L., and Tomarken, A. J. (1982). "Specificity of planning and the maintenance of self-control: 1 Year follow-up of a study improvement program, *Behavior Therapy* 13, 232–40.

158   **Students trying to complete:** Buehler, R., Griffin, D., and Ross, M. (1994). "Exploring the 'planning fallacy': Why people underestimate their task completion times," *Journal of Personality and Social Psychology* 67, 366–81.

163   **For example, computer scientists:** Ferrara, E., and Yang, Z. (2015). "Quantifying the effect of sentiment on information diffusion in social media," *PeerJ Computer Science* 1, 1–15.

165   **They referred to him as simply K.C.:** Rosenbaum, R. S., et al. (2005). "The case of K.C.: Contributions of a memory-impaired person to memory theory," *Neuropsychologia* 43, 989–1021.

167   **Many neuropsychologists have studied:** Klein, S. B., Loftus, J. L., and Kihlstrom, J. F. (2002). "Memory and temporal experience: The effects of episodic memory loss on an amnesic patient's ability to remember the past and imagine the future," *Social Cognition* 20, 353–79; Tulving, E. (2005). "Episodic memory and autonoesis: Uniquely human?" in Terrace, H. S., and Metcalfe, J., eds., *The Missing Link in Cognition* (pp. 4–56). New York: Oxford University Press.

8   Getting Unstuck

175   **Researcher Carsten Wrosch:** Wrosch, C., and Heckhausen, J. (1999). "Control processes before and after passing a developmental deadline: Activation and deactivation of intimate relationship goals," *Journal of Personality and Social Psychology* 77, 415–27.

178   **In 2009, the New York Road Runners:** Parlaplano, A. (June 2, 2009). "Calling it quits," *The New York Times,* archive.nytimes.com /www.nytimes.com/imagepages/2009/06/02/sports/03marathon .grafic.html.

179 **Researchers from the University of Zurich:** Brandstätter, V., and Schüler, J. (2013). "Action crisis and cost-benefit thinking: A cognitive analysis of a goal-disengagement phase," *Journal of Experimental Social Psychology* 49, 543–53.

180 **Carsten Wrosch, studying the experience:** Wrosch, C., Miller, G. E., Scheier, M. F., and de Pontet, S. B. (2007). "Giving up on unattainable goals: Benefits for health?" *Personality and Social Psychology Bulletin* 33, 251–65.

183 **The economists wondered:** Camerer, C., Babcock, L., Loewenstein, G., and Thaler, R. (1997). "Labor supply of New York City cabdrivers: One day at a time," *Quarterly Journal of Economics* 407–41.

192 **I turned to the work:** Packer, D. J., Fujita, K., and Chasteen, A. L. (2014). "The motivational dynamics of dissent decisions: A goal-conflict approach," *Social Psychological and Personality Science* 5, 27–34.

193 **In fact, according to the Association:** Association of American Medical Colleges (November 9, 2018). "MCAT and GPAs for applicants and matriculants to U.S. medical schools by primary undergraduate major, 2018–2019," www.aamc.org/download /321496/data/factstablea17.pdf.

9 Doing More by Doing Less, and How to Think Beyond Today

196 **To get a baseline understanding:** Dabbish, L. A., Mark, G., and Gonzalez, V. M. (2011). "Why do I keep interrupting myself? Environment, habit and self-interruption," in *Proceedings of the International Conference on Human Factors in Computing Systems, CHI,* 3127–30.

197 **Andrew Ward and Traci Mann:** Ward, A., and Mann, T. (2000). "Don't mind if I do: Disinhibited eating under cognitive load," *Journal of Personality and Social Psychology* 78, 753–63.

198 **Researchers asked a group of volunteers:** Wang, Z., and Tchernev, J. M. (2012). "The 'myth' of media multitasking: Reciprocal dynamics of media multitasking, personal needs, and gratifications," *Journal of Communication* 62, 493–513.

199 **Clever developmental psychologists:** De Havia, M. D., Izard, V., Coubart, A., Spelke, E. S., and Streri, A. (2014). "Representations of space, time and number in neonates," *Proceedings of the National Academy of Sciences* 111, 4809–13.

202 **Adults showed brain activity:** Leroux, G., et al. (2009). "Adult brains don't fully overcome biases that lead to incorrect performance during cognitive development: An fMRI study in young adults completing a Piaget-like task," *Developmental Science* 12, 326–38.

203 **It was surprising, then:** Poirel, N., Borst, G., Simon, G., Rossi, S., Cassotti, M., Pineau, A., and Houdé, O. (2012). "Number conservation is related to children's prefrontal inhibitory control: An fMRI study of Piagetian task" *PLOS ONE* 7, 1–7.

203 **Researchers from Columbia Business School:** Meier, S., and Sprenger, C. (2010). "Present-biased preferences and credit card borrowing," *American Economic Journal: Applied Economics* 2, 193–210.

205 **Professors at the business schools:** Herschfield, H., and Roese, N. (2014). "Dual payoff scenario warnings on credit card statements elicit suboptimal payoff decisions," available at SSRN: papers.ssrn .com/sol3/papers.cfm?abstract_id=2460986.

207 **Diwas KC is a statistics guru:** KC, D. S. (2013). "Does multitasking improve performance? Evidence from the emergency department," *Manufacturing and Service Operations Management* 16, 167–327.

210 **The work of a team:** Naito, E., and Hirose, S. (2014). "Efficient foot motor control by Neymar's brain," *Frontiers in Human Neuroscience* 8, 1–7.

211 **Per week:** BBC Sport (August 29, 2017). "Footballers' wages: How long would it take you to earn a star player's salary?" www.bbc.com /sport/41037621.

212 **For example, when moving their fingers:** Jäncke, L., Shah, N. J., and Peters, M. (2000). "Cortical activations in primary and secondary motor areas for complex bimanual movements in professional pianists," *Cognitive Brain Research* 10, 177–83.

212 **Professional Formula One drivers:** Bernardi, G., et al. (2013). "How skill expertise shapes the brain functional architecture: An fMRI study of visuo-spatial and motor processing in professional racing-car and naïve drivers," *PLOS ONE* 8, 1–11.

212 **Expert air-pistol athletes:** Del Percio, C., et al. (2009). "Visuo-attentional and sensorimotor alpha rhythms are related to visuo-motor performance in athletes," *Human Brain Mapping* 30, 3527–40.

212 **Members of the Ladies Professional Golf Association:** Milton, J., Solodkin, A., Hluštik, P., and Small, S. L. (2007). "The mind of expert motor performance is cool and focused," *NeuroImage* 35, 804–13.

212 **And when envisioning:** Petrini, K., et al. (2011). "Action expertise reduces brain activity for audiovisual matching actions: An fMRI study with expert drummers," *NeuroImage* 56, 1480–92.

10 Showtime

219 **Researchers at Ghent University:** Feys, M., and Anseel, F. (2015). "When idols look into the future: Fair treatment modulates the affective forecasting error in talent show candidates," *British Journal of Social Psychology* 54, 19–36.

219 **You can find the same discrepancy:** Kopp, L., Atance, C. M., and Pearce, S. (2017). " 'Things aren't so bad!': Preschoolers overpredict the emotional intensity of negative outcomes," *British Journal of Developmental Psychology* 35, 623–27.

220 **I conducted a survey:** Balcetis, E., and Dunning, D. (2007). "A mile in moccasins: How situational experience diminishes dispositionism in social inference," *Personality and Social Psychology Bulletin* 34, 102–14.

222 **In just the same way:** Gilbert, D. (2007). *Stumbling on Happiness.* New York: Vintage Books.

Index

ABOUT THE AUTHOR

Emily Balcetis, PhD, is an associate professor of psychology at New York University. She received her PhD from Cornell University in 2006, and is the author of more than seventy scientific publications. Her work has been covered by *Forbes*, *Newsweek, Time*, Telemundo, National Public Radio, *Scientific American, The Atlantic, Cosmopolitan*, and *GQ*. She has received numerous awards for her work, including from the Federation of Associations in Behavior & Brain Sciences, the International Society for Self and Identity, the Foundation for Personality and Social Psychology, and the Society for Experimental Social Psychology. Balcetis has lectured at numerous institutions, including Harvard, Princeton, Yale, Stanford, Berkeley, and the University of Chicago. She lives in New York City with her husband and their toddler son.